INTERNATIONAL BARD COLLEGE ACADEMIC CONFERENCE EDITION

The Quest for Potential$^\infty$ theory

BOOK 2

Summa
Metaphysica II

D A V I D   B I R N B A U M

THE INFINITE DIVINE EXTRAORDINARIATION PARADIGM

HARVARD MATRIX™

A JEWISH CONTEXT

with commentary by

Daniel N. Khalil

New York

God and Good

A Unified Metaphysics/Theology/Philosophy

David Birnbaum

www.SummaM.org

MANHATTAN

WITH CREDIT TO
KTAV PUBLISHING

GOD AND GOOD

by DAVID BIRNBAUM

Summa Metaphysica proposes a comprehensive and integrated metaphysical structure – a new paradigm.

God and Evil (published 1988) and God and Good (first launched 2005 online) comprise Birnbaum's Summa Metaphysica series. The author has proposed that one fundamental concept – and one fundamental concept alone – Quest for Potential^{ffi} (recursive to the infinite power) – ignited – and drives – the cosmos – and the integral infinite divine.

Building upon his 1988 treatise, in God and Good (18 years later) the author lays out his overarching metaphysical structure in very significantly greater scope, depth, breadth and texture.

Birnbaum's paradigm is non-linear, as opposed to the linearity of the great bulk of Western philosophy. It is non-circular, as opposed to the circularity of much of Eastern philosophy. Rather, Birnbaum's paradigm is what the author refers to as a "spiral/reflexive" dynamic (elucidated in the text). The author proposes that this Quest for Potential$^{\infty}$ paradigm more elegantly explains the dynamics of the cosmos – and of life, in particular – than alternate propositions.

According to Birnbaum, only the full plethora of potentials – and the quest thereof – could have ignited the cosmos. The combined potentials for love, life, intellectuality, spirituality and, indeed, for an infinitely Perfect Divine, ignited, birthed, nurtured, and projected the cosmos onward on its quest towards infinity. 'Extraordinariation,' according to the author, is the overarching goal.

Thomas Aquinas wrote Summa Theologica c. 1273 within a Christian context. The Summa Metaphysica series, proposing an original, dynamic, overarching, and integrated metaphysics, is crafted within a Jewish context seven hundred years later.

www.Harvard1000.com

(master site)

---

www.Philosophy1000.com

www.History1000.com

www.Spinoffs1000.com

www.YouTubeX1000.com

www.AmazonX1000.com

www.eReader1000.com

About the Author

Private scholar David Birnbaum is known in academic circles primarily as the author of the *Summa Metaphysica* series: an overarching metaphysics. He is a graduate of Yeshiva Dov Revel, Yeshiva University High School, CCNY and Harvard.

God and Evil (1988), the first book in the landmark **Summa Metaphysica** series, has been assigned as a Required Text at universities around the world, and was a Book of the Month feature selection of the Jewish Book Club. The work has gone through Five Printings and eighteen thousand copies to date. The author is known as a leading conceptual theorist.

The two-volume *Summa Metaphysica* series was crafted over a twenty-six year span, 1982–1988 and then 2001–2008. It was the prime focus of a major international academic conference at Bard College (Annandale-on-Hudson, NY), April 2012. [see www.Bard1000.com].

Jews, Church & Civilization – Birnbaum's seven-volume integrated Jewish TimeLine work – was crafted in the 2002–2012 period.

David Birnbaum's works have been used as course texts at Brandeis, Hebrew University, Yeshiva University, Hebrew Union College, Tel Aviv University, Emory, JTS, Bar Ilan, and Union Theological Seminary, among others. His works have been reviewed by dozens of leading academic journals worldwide.

A long time ago, he taught "The Science of Strategy" at the New School in NY.

He lives and works in Manhattan.

***

published by: MILLENNIUM EDUCATION FOUNDATION, INC.

COPYRIGHT © 2005
DAVID BIRNBAUM

Library of Congress Cataloging-in-Publication Data

Birnbaum, David.

God and Good / David Birnbaum.

ISBN 978-0-9801710-1-3

1. Metaphysics.　　2. God and Good.　　I. Title.

MANHATTAN

WITH CREDIT TO
KTAV PUBLISHING

HarvardMatrix@gmail.com

www.HarvardMatrix.com

distributed by J Levine / MILLENNIUM

Danny Levine, Managing Director

(Harvard Matrix operates totally independently of Harvard University)

fax: (212) 398-9438

God and Good

MANHATTAN

Books by David Birnbaum

History–related

The Crucifixion
I and II

Jews, Church & Civilization
I, II, III, IV, V, VI & VII

Metaphysics–related

***

Summa Metaphysica series

God and Evil (1988)

God and Good (2005)

**spin–offs from
Summa Metaphysica:**

God's 120 Guardian Angels

The Lost Manual

Cosmic Womb of Potential

*

**"companion works" to
Summa Metaphysica
[artistic/graphic representations]**

Q4P I + II

Cosmic Womb of Potential I + II

Cosmic Tool Kit I + II

Cosmic Code I + II

Q4P∞™

COSMIC WOMB OF POTENTIAL PARADIGM•
SUMMA METAPHYSICA SERIES BY BIRNBAUM•

POSSIBILITY / POTENTIAL

AS CENTERPIECE

A central proposition of Summa:
'Possibility' is the sole "concept/dynamic" which can safely be posited as having been eternal.

By definition.

Meaning, by definition "Possibility" – and only 'Possibility' – can be conjectured to have been "eternal."

Upon careful reflection, the above is "self-evident."

Then, moving-right-along and hypothesizing that Quest for Potential∞ dynamically evolved from "Possibility" is, respectfully, not a major conceptual leap.

For "Possibility" vectored-in onto – and crystallized-into – its own maximal Potential.

"Possibility" thus achieved *traction* – and has never looked back.

– Birnbaum

Birnbaum's

Q4P∞™

Quest for Potential
(infinitely recursive)

Q4P (Q4P (Q4P ...

Quest for Potential

within

Quest for Potential

within

Quest for Potential

ad infinitum

GOD AND GOOD

"*A feast for the intellect, the senses, the higher consciousness*.....
Where spirituality and the divine –
blend with evolutionary dynamism and the calculus"

– Dalai Lama

Summa Metaphysica

"Since the nineteenth century the study of Metaphysics has typically been pursued within the history of philosophy. Advances in several disciplines, scientific and literary, as well as historical and philosophical, appeared to preclude Metaphysics as an analytic discipline.

Yet as the twentieth century progressed, science offered the uncertainty principle, literature discovered hermeneutics that explained how one horizon of discourse may merge into another, history changed its key from the study of atomistic data to the unfolding of meaning, and philosophy challenged empirical constructions of reality.

Works by David Birnbaum, chiefly his two volumes entitled Summa Metaphysica (1989 and 2008), suggest that Metaphysics may emerge as a critical field once again."

– Rev. Dr. Bruce Chilton

Professor of Religion
Chaplain of the College
Executive Director of the Institute of Advanced Theology
    Bernard Iddings Bell, **Bard College**
Founder
    Journal for the Study of the New Testament
Founder
    The Bulletin for Biblical Research
Executive Committee
    Christians for Fair Witness
Co-Chairman
    International Academic Conference
    on Summa Metaphysica
    April 2012 at Bard College

"A unifying concept of the Universe"

"David Birnbaum's *Summa Metaphysica* is a major philosophical contribution to the study of Being. According to *Summa*, Holy Potential is at the very epicenter of the Divine, and the quest for its fulfillment is the underlying core dynamic of the cosmic order.

Birnbaum considers Quest for Potential∞ to be ubiquitious and overarching holy cosmic dynamic. All of the countless components of the Universe, including humans, are striving towards the full realization of their particular potentialities.

Although centered on the problem of evil existing in the world created by benevolent and omnipotent God, *Summa* reaches far beyond theodicy. Deeply rooted in Biblical tradition, yet providing a modern and original approach to answering millennia-old questions, *Summa* represents a bold attempt to formulate a unifying concept of the Universe."

– Dr. Andrei Alyokhin
Associate Professor
School of Biology and Ecology
University of Maine
Orono, ME

"Is there a font/soul of the Universe?"

"Birnbaum stimulates, challenges and intrigues
across the spectrum
– simultaneously badgering, coaxing and challenging
the philosopher, the theist, and the physicist
to all consider unifying under his proposed
overarching conceptual umbrella.

Iconoclast Birnbaum makes a strong case
for his straightforward, original, dynamic,
and, arguably, unified and all-embracing metaphysics

His intriguing Q4P$^\infty$ metaphysical centerpiece is
simultaneously simple, yet intriguingly sophisticated and
powerful. Indeed, seductively powerful.

The potentially game-changing *Summa* thesis
has remained effectively *unchallenged*."

– Dr. Garry Hagberg
Chairman
Department of Philosophy
BARD College
Annandale-on-Hudson, NY

for 9-page recap, see
The Potential$^{\infty}$ Point:
Road Map
at end of book

Summa Metaphysica

- proposes an original metaphysics: **Quest for Potential**$^{\infty}$

The metaphysics is asserted to be:
    dynamic
    self-contained
    overarching / all-embracing
    elegant
    powerful
    seamless

The 2-volume series deals with all of these just-alleged fine attributes of Summa.

The objectives of the work include:

    # changing the way we view
        ourselves
        the cosmos
        our origins
        our purpose

    # uplifting the world

Modest objectives, for sure.

So, we shall all see what unfolds.....

Sincerely,

    THE AUTHOR

(And, yes, indeed, it can all be summed-up in one phrase –
Potential drives the cosmos.)

GOD AND GOOD

*"Birnbaum cuts a daring – sometimes breathtaking –
swath across philosophy, metaphysics and cosmology."*

– Prof. Emil Fackenheim,
Jerusalem

*"Iconoclast Birnbaum is one of the most daring
and dynamic intellects of the turn of the millennium..."*

– John Hospers
    Professor Emeritus of Philosophy
    University of Sourthern California

Author's fable

The Fisherman

….with the body of a "young" 90-year-old.

Weather-beaten face, slender but muscular body,
sinewy muscled…

The Fisherman had been *reeling in his line*
for several trillion millennia now…..

He would let out the line just a bit;
then *reel it in* 20–fold

Millennia after millennia now…

The Fisherman

[continued]

He had "the cosmos" *on his line*....

And he was a strong, disciplined angler –
and would not *let it (the cosmos) off*.....

Indeed, the cosmos had *"taken the bait"* –
of his "PERFECTION-lure"...

......a long, long time ago

Perfection / Potential / Eternity / Extraordinariation
...they were all embedded in the lure

cont'd

The Fisherman

[continued]

And He, the Fisherman, had been *reeling in the line* – ever since.

Hour after hour, day after day, year after year, century after century....

.....and on and on....

It was not easy *reeling in* an entire cosmos....

– even if you were the eternal metaphysical cosmic Fisherman....

The Fisherman

[continued]

And, of course….somehow He had to
"draw strength"….

For, this was eternal and arduous work…..

– no matter how lean and muscular He was…..

But, of course, He drew his strength
from the *"fish on his line"* –
that is, from the (struggling) Cosmos…
– questing for its manifold maximal potentialities

For He – the Fisherman – was, after all,
pure Potential, Himself….

"Remarkable and profound, God and Good rounds-out the author's powerful and original Cosmic Womb of Potential metaphysics."

        – Claude Levi-Strauss
           Paris

"Writing intuitively, Birnbaum nevertheless provokes...."

– Andrew E. Lange
Chairman Emeritus
Department of Physics,
Mathematics and Astronomy
CALTECH

"In all things of nature, there is something of the marvelous"

– Aristotle
(384 BCE – 322 BCE)

"For nature is pleased with *simplicity*,
and effects not
the pomp of superfluous causes."

              – Isaac Newton
              Principia Mathematica
              Book III
              c. 1683

"*Summa Metaphysica* is a profound and groundbreaking work which will impact the world – across and beyond the fields of Theology, Philosophy and Metaphysics. The original Birnbaum hypothesis elegantly and uniquely stiches-together Science and Spirituality."

> – Rev. Gheorghe Popa
> Vice Rector
> Cuza University
> Lasi, Romania

"Conceptual theorist David Birnbaum has proposed and elucidated an original, elegant and unifying concept – Quest for Potential$^\infty$/Extraordinariation. His work *Summa Metaphysica* – can and will serve as a crucial and uniquely powerful bridge between Science and Religion. This is a *sui generis* work, and is a conceptual breakthrough of the first order."

> – Gennady Shkliarevsky
> Professor of History
> Bard College
> Annandale-on-Hudson, NY

"It is early for me to say with certainty,
but I am inclined to think that *Summa Metaphysica*
represents the dawn of the period of metaphysical revision."

— Lawrence H. Schiffman
Vice Provost for Undergraduate Education
Yeshiva University
New York, NY

Note on the chronology of
Summa II: God & Good

2005: copyrighted & posted online

2008: first 'HardCover' printing

2011-12: addition of Z-exhibits

Note that in viewing *Summa Metaphysica*
through a Jewish philosophical prism,

Book I is tethered to
the Lurianic (*kabbalistic*) theme of *En Sof**

while

Book II is tethered to
the Ba'al Shem Tov's theme of *panentheism*.*

In both respective cases, *tethered*,
as opposed to *anchored*.

*These terms are explained and elaborated-on in the respective Summa books;
however, see (online) encyclopedia entries for these terms for quick-reference.

MANHATTAN

WITH CREDIT TO
KTAV PUBLISHING

Q4P∞™

Quest for Potential
(infinitely recursive)

ORGANIZATION OF BOOK

Introductory Section

Part I: The Cosmic Womb of Potential

Part II: God's 120 Guardian Angels

Part III: The Lost Manual

Appendix

Author's Finale Midrash

Competing Cosmological Theories

INDEX of Sculpted Terms

Road Map for Summa

Reprint of Summa Metaphysica - 18 Axioms

God and Good

TABLE OF CONTENTS

Introductory Section   **1**

Prelude   2

In Tribute   4

Dedication   5

extract from Book I Foreword   10

Clarification   13

Introduction: The Metaphysical Gates   16

Definitions   25

Theodicy re-visited   27

Author's First Midrash   29

    Genesis / "*Bereshith*"   31

    Midrash: God's 100 Archangels   32

The UNITY "POTENTIAL"   40

note: The Key Term   42

Encapsulization   44

Caution to dogmatists   49

Foreword by KHALIL   50

A "Subtle Dynamic"   59

Extension or Separate?   68

Overview   70

Author's Note   72

Part I: The Cosmic Womb of Potential 80

ALPHA: Lay-of-the-Land 82

BETA: Cosmic TOOL KIT- Shelf #1 85

GAMMA: Lead-in 100

DELTA: Embryonic Design 104

EPSILON: Notes & Observations 115

ZETA: "Principia Metaphysica" 118

ETA: Some reflections…insights 135

THETA: The two key (spiraling) SUPRA-DYNAMICS 142

IOTA: Reprise to the Cosmic Womb of Potential 150

KAPPA: The building blocks of the cosmos 153

LAMBDA: A fresh look at some of our concepts 155

MU: Cosmic TOOL KIT- Shelf #2 Extraordinariation 162

Part II: God's 120 Guardian Angels 179

Foreword by DROB 184

Preface 189

KEDUSHAH 192

from the Yom Kippur Machzor 196

Angels / Potentials 199

"Strength and Faithfulness" 203

Outline of 120 Angels 206

-Guardian Angels 1-20 215

-Guardian Angels 21-40 231

-Guardian Angels 41-60 258

-Guardian Angels 61-80 274

-Guardian Angels 81-100 292

-Guardian Angels 101-120 318

AFTERWORD to 120 Angels 351

INDEX (alphabetical) to 120 Guardian Angels 354

cont'd

God and Good

TABLE OF CONTENTS

[continued]

Part III: The Lost Manual   **357**

Appendix Section: **399**

Appendix A: Metaphysics Analysis   405

Appendix B: Schematically   409

Appendix C: Extraordinariation   414

Appendix D: Consciousness Connection?   417

Appendix E: Evolution from the Perspective   420
of Summa Metaphysica

Appendix F1: Hasidic v. Kabbalistic   422

Appendix F2: The Suffused Divine   426

Appendix G: Push v. Pull   427

Appendix H: "The Spiraling Collective"   428

Appendix I: Balance and Diversity   430

Appendix J: Convergence   431

Appendix K: Cracking the Cosmic Code   433

Appendix L: Life   437

Appendix M: Is Q4P Morally Neutral?   438

Appendix N: Extraordinariation juxtaposed v. *tohu va-vohu*   439

Appendix O: "Secular Divine" v. "Religious Divine"   440

Appendix P: Optimization   441

Appendix Q: Q4P juxtaposed v. Vicissitude   443

Appendix R: More Powerful v. Perfert   444

Appendix S: Boox #1 v. Book #2   445

Appendix T: Following the Analogy   448

Appendix U: By-definition *Telescoping Elasticity*   450

Appendix V: Hypothesizing about Cosmic Origins   451

Appendix W: Physics, Metaphysics & Poetry   452

Appendix X: Holographic Universe Theory,   454
    Information and SUMMA

Appendix Y: Counterposing *Summa Metaphysica*   456

Appendix Z1: Survival   458

Appendix Z2: Primordial Realm Hyphotesis   460

Appendix Z3: Launch   462

Appendix Z4: Where is Option B?   464

Appendix Z5: Cosmic Nesting (Iterativeness)   466

Appendix Z6: Modern Evolutionary Synthesis   468

Appendix Z7: *Anima mundi*   469

Appendix Z8: The Soul of the Universe   471

Appendix Z9: Possibility   472

Appendix Z10: "The Free Lunch?"   474

Appendix Z11: Birnbaumian Panentheism   475

Appendix Z12: Cosmic Level: Individual Level   477

Appendix Z13: Major Problems in Science   481

Appendix Z14: "Nothing" by David Birnbaum   483

Appendix Z15: Gnosticism   485

Appendix Z16: Atheist v. Potentialist   487

Appendix Z17: Particle Physics and Q4P$^\infty$ 488

Appendix Z18: A Fix-It "Conceptual Plug"?   491

Appendix Z19: Metaphysics and Physics   491

Appendix Z20: Take #2: Where Is The Competing Metaphysics   493

Appendix Z21: The Assertion/Claim   496

Appendix Z22: The Q4P$^\infty$ 'Package'   497

Appendix Z23: Explication   498

cont'd

God and Good

TABLE OF CONTENTS

[continued]

Appendix Z24: Context	500
Appendix Z25: Where is the Divine?	502
Appendix Z26: String Theory and 'Provability'	504
Appendix Z27: Multiverse Theory	505
Appendix Z28: Theory of Everything (in Physics)	506
Appendix Z29: Occam's Razor	508
Appendix Z30: Schopenhauer v. Birnbaum	509
Appendix Z31: Simple v. Simplistic	511
Appendix Z32: *Aesthetic Elegance*	512
Appendix Z33: The Red Queen Hypothesis	514
Appendix Z34: Punctuated Equilibrium	516
Appendix Z35: The Font/Soul of the Cosmos	519
Appendix Z36: Time	520
Appendix Z37: An Ultra- Dynamic Multi-Dimensional Organic Entity	522
AppendixZ38: "The Mind of God"	524
Appendix Z39: Metaphysical Assumptions	526
Appendix Z40: The "Double Play": Push-Pull	528
Appendix Z41: Framing Beliefs	530
Appendix Z42: New Paradigm Imminent	531
Appendix Z43: God	534
Appendix Z44: Man: Mortal or Divine	535

Appendix Z45: New Interpretations 537

Appendix Z46: Take #3: Physics & Metaphysics 538

Appendix Z47: "...*beyond science*..." 540

Appendix Z48: "The Same Recipe" 541

Appendix Z49 The Consciousness Continuum 542

Appendix Z50: "Backward Causation" 544

Appendix Z51: Galapagos 545

Appendix Z52: Ecology 546

Appendix Z53: A Compelling Case 548

Appendix Z54: *neo-Survival-of-the-Fittest* *551*
        or Q4P$^\infty$/Extraordinariation?

Appendix Z55: 1999: Cosmologist Martin Rees 555

Appendix Z56: 2000: Cosmologist Brian Greene 557

Appendix Z57: 2004: Cosmologists Tyson & Goldsmith 558

Appendix Z58: 2006: Cosmologist Leonard Susskind 559

Appendix Z59: 2006: Quantum Computation 560
        Theorist Seth Lloyd

Appendix Z60: 2008: Cosmologist Paul Davies 563

Appendix Z61: 2010: Cosmologists Hawking & Mlodinow 565

Appendix Z62: 2010: Cosmologist Haisch presents 566
        very similar to Summa

Appendix Z63: Quest for Possibility or Quest for Potential? 570

Author's Finale Midrash **577**

The Sixth Day of Creation 579

Competing Cosmological Theories **589**

INDEX of Sculpted Terms **597**

Road Map for Summa **601**

Reprint of Summa Metaphysica - 18 Axioms **614**

The first book of the series, God and Evil,
was heavily *intellectual* as the *major motif*
and heavily *intuitive* as the *minor motif*

The second book, God and Good,
is reversed in these regards

The presumptive power of the Summa series
lies in the compound power
of the two books – and of the two presentations –
in-tandem

───────────────────────────

Q4P = Quest for Potential$^\infty$

Q4F = Quest for Fulfillment

Introductory Section

Prelude

This is a highly intuitive work attempting to advance our speculative conjecture about the cosmos – but fully comporting to our knowledge of the spectrum of various realities, across the sciences, both physical and social.

Essentially, Summa "connects-the-dots" (all of them) – and sees both a pattern and a catalyst – *one-and-the-same.*

Summa then delineates this (sole) overarching and unifying universal theme/dynamic.

Respectfully, this has not been done successfully prior.

Whether one plugs-in 100 dots (facts) or 1,000,000, the theme/dynamic will hold*.

The theme/dynamic is Quest for Potential$^\infty$.

No facts lie outside its realm and dominion; no facts contradict it.

Respectfully, while my initial process was intuitive, the ultimate proposition is *empirical*. Indeed, a unifying theory does not get more empirical than the Summa proposition.

Now, "change" is difficult – and accepting that the "cosmic code" has indeed been cracked after 5,000+ years of sundry attempts – may be difficult. Especially if it was not cracked by an Oxford don. However, the Summa proposition is "bullet-proof." And elegant. And relatively simple.

The Summa proposition has intellectual integrity and elegance – and fire. I hope you will *enjoy the ride*.

The work is written within a Jewish context, but its motifs are universal.

If the construct proposed herein proves to "stand the test of time," science, philosophy and theology – as taught in their respective venues – will comport to its contours.

In due course... In due course...

* whether the fact is simple (like, say, 1+1=2) or whether the fact is an entire complex field (like, say Evolutionary Biology).

In Tribute

William Rice Kimball
(1919-2005)

President, Stanford Board of Trustees

Dedication

To My

"INNER CIRCLE"

*

HARVEY COHEN, Encino, CA.

STEVEN GROSS, Jerusalem *

GARY KAUFMAN, New York – Princeton

JOSHUA MILLER, Jerusalem **

SAMUEL WILCHFORT, Jerusalem ***

*   formerly of Manhattan
**   formerly of Great Neck, NY
***   formerly of Englewood, NJ

"A significant and possibly brand new way of seeing God and goodness as processes that can, in retrospect, be seen as embedded in the thrust of creation toward the (always still potential) fulfillment of potential..."

– Edward L. Greenstein
Professor of Bible
Tel Aviv University

"Birnbaum's *Summa Metaphysica* offers the possibility of a 21st Century metaphysics quite compatible with many important and historic belief systems, including but not limited to Judaism and Gnosticism. And not necessarily contradictory to other major systems."

– Dr. Bruce Chilton
Chairman, Theology Department
BARD college

GOD AND GOOD

Remember the former things of old:
That I am God, and there is none else;
I am God, and there is none like Me;
Declaring the end from the beginning,
And from ancient times things
that are not yet done.

– Isaiah 46:9-10

Radiant is the world soul,
Full of splendor and beauty,
Full of life,
Of souls hidden,
Of treasures of the holy spirit,
Of fountains of strength,
Of greatness and beauty.
Proudly I ascend
Toward the heights of the world soul
That gives life to the universe.

– A.I. Kook, *Lights of Penitence*, p. 376

He hangs the world upon nothingness.

– Job 26:7

[all cited, as well, in Book 1; Part Two, Section 100:04]

GOD AND GOOD

extract from

FOREWORD

God and Evil *

by

Dr. Sanford Drob **

* Book I (1988) of *Summa Metaphysica*

**Founding co-Editor, The NY Jewish Review

"Birnbaum's proposed solution to the question of divine origins, to the mystery of the kabbalists' *En Sof* (the infinite theistic principle giving rise to the God of Israel) is that "Holy Potential is at the epicenter of the Divine," that God is, by His very nature, *potential and possibility*, "transcending, space, time and cosmos," and ever-surging towards greater actuality. Birnbaum bases his thesis, in part, on the name by which God first became known to Moses and Israel: *Eheye Asher Eheyeh,* "I-will-be-that-which-I-will be" (Exodus 3:13-14) which he sees as a prooftext for his claim that *potential* is the holiest state of the Divine. Birnbaum sees the kabbalists' sefirot* as "primal quests for potentiality" which bridge the gap from "emptiness" to "somethingness," and thereby become the vehicles of creation."

* parallel to Plato's *Forms*

GOD AND GOOD

CLARIFICATION:

In the *physical realms* in which we deal, Quest for Potential$^\infty$ would be directly impacting **organisms**, and only indirectly impacting **inanimate** *entities*.

As regards *metaphysical realms*, clearly, according to the hypothesis herein, Q4P$^\infty$ would, at a minimum, be *operational*, and at a maximum, be *all-pervasive and encompassing*.

GOD AND GOOD

from Summa Metaphysica II - Beta: The Cosmic "Tool Kit"

Quest for Potential$^\infty$ is thus simultaneously –
• a FORCE
• a QUEST
• a POTENTIAL
• the ongoing open–ended COSMOS
• the Infinite Divine Extraordinariation
• the SPARK of LIFE
• the sum total of all eco–systems
• in other words, EVERYTHING as we know it

Not bad for a dynamic.

from *Moreh Nevuchim* chapter *72*

- *The Guide for the Perplexed*,
by The RAMBAM – Moses Maimonides]
Friedländer translation [1904]

lead sentence to Paragraph 1 of Chapter 72

> KNOW that this Universe, in its entirety,
> is nothing else but one organism

paragraph 15 (*en toto*)

"There also exists in the Universe a certain force which
controls the whole, which sets in motion the chief and
principal parts, and gives them the motive power for
governing the rest. Without that force, the existence of
this sphere, with its principal and secondary parts, would
be impossible. It is the source of the existence of the
Universe in all its parts. That force is God: blessed be
His name! It is on account of this force that man is called
microcosm: for he likewise possesses a certain principle
which governs all the forces of the body, and on account
of this comparison God is called 'the life of the Universe,'
compare 'and he swore by the life of the Universe' (Daniel
xii. 7)."

Introduction: The Metaphysical Gates of the Forest

by William Johnson,
Professor Emeritus of Philosophy
Brandeis University

"Why is Birnbaum's paradigm uniquely different from all pre-existing paradigms?"

Compare three and a half thousand year old Jewish philosophy to a majestic oak tree: roots, trunk, large branches, smaller branches and then leaves. Then figuratively, many of the daring medieval (Golden Age) Jewish philosophers often dealt with the trunk and the major branches, while many modern Jewish philosophers often deal with some of the branches, some larger, some smaller, and some of the interesting leaves. The Kabbalists often dealt with the roots, but generally from an acutely mystical, esoteric, and generally, obscure fashion.

Birnbaum maintains that the structural weaknesses in existing philosophical constructs, leave one no choice but to go after the major root. That if one gets a handle on the major root, one gets a handle not only on the major root system, and not only on the entire tree, but, indeed, on the entire forest. That is, one will have in-hand the hitherto elusive key to the gate of the mythical metaphysical forest.

Birnbaum, whose works are rooted partially in Lurianic Kabbalah, goes for the root of the roots, the tap root, and in a non–mystical fashion. As a Master Diamond Cleaver might attempt to cleave an extraordinary and large rough diamond with one deft tap, so too Birnbaum proposes to crack the cosmic code with one deft dynamic.

Birnbaum, the conceptual theorist, searched for a unique, transcendent dynamic which might, on the one hand, almost by definition, be Eternal, and which, on the other hand, could possibly be infinitely dynamic. He conceptualizes a candidate: Potential/Possibility. Then Birnbaum asks himself if that dynamic multiplied infinite-fold, could possibly achieve the necessary 'traction' to ignite and then propel a cosmos? He emerges with Quest for Potential$^\infty$ (recursive to the infinite power).

Birnbaum's approach and solution lies on the fault-line between Western and Eastern philosophy. Birnbaum avoids both classic Western linearity, as well as classic Eastern circularity in his formulation. However he will employ demanding Western Aristotelian deductive reasoning, as well as a plethora of Eastern concepts of complementarity.

Dealing in the realms of the infinite, Birnbaum in Book #1 brings to bear his original concepts of INFINITY-POTENTIAL, RECURSIVENESS-POTENTIAL and leveraged RETROACTIVITY-POTENTIAL, all in fashions certainly not employed previously in metaphysics or philosophy. He crafts his metaphysics methodically and very carefully anchored, while keeping a careful eye on the outer boundaries of Jewish theological tradition and doctrine.

In Book #2, Birnbaum labels the Genesis point as the *Potential$^\infty$ Point*. At the *Potential$^\infty$ Point*, potential Divine becomes the God of Potential. At the *Potential$^\infty$ Point*, potential energy becomes kinetic energy. At the *Potential$^\infty$ Point*, the Metaphysical becomes the Physical.

Moving to fill-out his overarching metaphysics, Birnbaum in Book #2 will daringly conceptualize and propose a series of sophisticated 'cosmic metaphysical tools'. The approach as well as the arsenal of 'tools' is original and powerful. In combination with Quest for Potential$^\infty$, these 'tools' drive the cosmic engine of Quest for Potential$^\infty$.

In Book #2, Birnbaum introduces the concept of *Infinite Divine Extraordinariation*. Coupled with his patented 'Quest for Potential$^\infty$' dynamic, his proposed 'Extraordinariation' concept will be employed by the author as a daring philosophical 1-2 punch.

The series of 'cosmic tools,' employed in combination with the above-noted three particular 'realm of the infinite concepts,' merged with yeshiva scholar Birnbaum's re-engineering of historical Lurianic and Hasidic concepts, net him his unified, overarching metaphysics. Deftly employing his key components, he sculpts his metaphysical diamond key, which he will use to "unlock the cosmic lock" to the metaphysical "Gates of the Forest".

Bringing to bear a repertoire of scholarship and a wide gamut of skills, conceptual theorist Birnbaum whose first Book,*God and Evil*, I have assigned to Masters Degree candidates at Brandeis in Advanced Religious Philosophy in the '90s methodically builds his carefully constructed case. Resolutely stalking-his-quarry, the author surrounds and entraps it in one conceptual net after another.

In Book #1, *God and Evil*, Birnbaum does so from a Theological-Academic Philosophical Metaphysical perspective (encapsulated in his section 99.00 Unified Formulation in that book; see "Reprint of Unified Formulation" in this book #2).

In Book #2 Birnbaum constructs his case first within a Metaphysical Philosophical construct ("The Cosmic Womb of Potential"). Moving into Section 2 of the second book, he builds his case within a Poetic-Mythical perspective ("God's 120 Guardian Angels") and then, finally, moving into the final section of the second book, ("The Lost Manual") Section 3 of *God and Good*, he builds his case within a Holistic – Self-Actualization Wisdom book construct.

Yeshiva Dov Revel's inquiring-mind student in the late '50s, Birnbaum in 2006 believes that the elusive quarry is now finally trapped and cornered. 'Forged in intellectual fire' under the multi-year tutelage of his rebbe and mentor, Yeshiva University's legendary Rav Shmuel Scheinberg, yeshiva-educated Birnbaum believes he has not only firmly anchored his work meticulously in the Torah itself, but has erected fairly impregnable theological shields via the works of Rashi, Ibn Daud, Luria and Abraham Isaac Kook, in particular, to protect his Right flanks. Simultaneously, Harvard grad Birnbaum believes he has the Aristotelian camp and St. Thomas Aquinas intellectually at-bay on his Left flanks. He anticipates, probably correctly, that the Eastern philosophical camps will grant him 'safe passage'. 18 years after the publication of *God and Evil* (1988) he is "good-to-go" for his long-awaited final assault on the 'throne room' of the Cosmic Code.

Birnbaum's works are dressed in establishment Aristotelian-style garb; but their soul is Lurianic. This unusual duality compounds the power of his works.

Modern-day Kabbalists are highly likely to be *simpatico* to his treatise: After 450 years on the very periphery of mainstream philosophy, Kabbalist Luria's ostensibly mystical 16th century *En Sof* is re-engineered by the author, and is now enshrined as a metaphysical centerpiece-anchor of Birnbaum's formidable 21st century major opus, *Summa Metaphysica.*

According to the Author, only 'possibility' or its first-cousin 'potentiality' could have existed eternally.

"BY DEFINITION", according to the Author.

This is key, because aside from the elegance and power of the SUMMA formulation, "BY DEFINITION" is what may very well render this construct quite uniquely "bullet-proof", and further secure its position in the pantheon of philosophy. By definition, according to the

Author, only *"Eheyeh"* 'possibility/potentiality' (*Eheyeh Asher Eheyeh* – I WILL BE THAT WHICH I WILL BE) Luria's *"En Sof"* can be eternal.

According to Birnbaum, METAPHYSICAL POTENTIALS – in parallel to Luria's *sefirot*, Rashi's angels, Plato's *Forms* – are the offspring. Our cosmos, in turn, is a latter-level reality–morphing of the same transcendent metaphysical dynamic. Philosophically and theologically elegant. As these esoteric matters go, Birnbaum's formulation "keeps it simple" and straightforward enough.

Birnbaum's Quest for Potential$^\infty$ (recursive to the infinite power), after Luria's *En Sof,* is the turbo-charged version of 'potential/possibility'. And everything according to the Author's hypothesis, is both part of – and driven by this one – overarching *sui generis* transcendent dynamic. (The Baal Shem Tov, founder of Hassidism, would certainly smile.)

Simply put, Birnbaum's Summa Metaphysica proposition attempts to totally overhaul the way the world – East and West – looks at absolutely everything.

His proposed paradigm endeavors to totally change the contours and boundaries of, among other fields, Philosophy, Metaphysics, Cosmology, Cosmogony, Physics and Biology, for starters.

As of this November, 2006, Birnbaum's key proposition of *"Eheyeh"* Holy Quest for Potential$^\infty$ (recursive to the Infinite power) and the Unified Formulation (see "Reprint of Unified Formulation" in this book) meticulously articulated therein, will have withstood 18 years of international scrutiny since the publication of *God and Evil* by KTAV in November 1988.

The Author posits: Discern and delineate the "highest common denominator" of the cosmos and that will lead you to the essence and core of Eternity, and, consequently, of the Infinite Divine Extraordinariation; Conceptualize/Discern an all-embracing unifying dynamic in the cosmos, and directly flowing from that dynamic, all major philosophical conundrums will melt before your eyes. Discern the dynamic and the key missing pieces in all the major sciences, including physics, anthropology and biology, let alone theology/philosophy/metaphysics, will inexorably fall into place, as well.

According to the Author, Quest for Potential$^\infty$ (to the infinite recursive power) is the Holy Qi that flows through Creation, through the smallest cell, through the oak tree, through Beethoven's symphonies, through the athlete, the hunter and the shop keeper, through the sunflower and butterfly, through the Biblical texts and through the far reaches of the Milky Way and the cosmos beyond. It flows through the lovers' twinkle, the baby's smile, and the intricate nine extraordinary months of fetal development.

However, a concept of the order of potential power noted above, is not proffered forth every day. It is challenging to "get one's arms around it". And, as noted above, the philosophical writer Birnbaum has employed two complete inter-related masterworks, conceptualized and crafted over multiple decades, to achieve that ambitious and formidable end.

Yeshiva Dov Revel's 1964 valedictorian has now completed his final homework assignment.

Summa Metaphysica will emerge as a pivotal landmark work in the history of ideas.

Professor William Johnson
Waltham, Mass.
Fall, 2005

(With credit for the idea for the title of this piece
to Elie Wiesel's *The Gates of the Forest*.)

GOD AND GOOD

Summa Metaphysica respectfully proposes an original[**]
and *simultaneous solution* to the key inter-related classic problems in philosophy/metaphysics/theology.

THEOGONY –
The "origins" of the Infinite Divine
or more broadly, of the Primal Force of the cosmos,
if such exists

COSMOLOGY –
The "origins," evolution, structure and prime dynamics
of the cosmos

THEODICY –
The classic *Problem of Evil*:
If there is a God who is all-powerful and all-merciful,
why is there (gross) evil

TELEOLOGY –
The purpose/end-goal of the universe and existence
(if indeed, there is *purpose*)

[**]note: The original God and Evil copyright by David Birnbaum was 1986.

GOD AND GOOD

Theodicy re-visited

Book #1 is primarily devoted to a solution of the age-old problem of the classic problem of Evil: *theodicy*.

THEODICY: If there is a God who is all-powerful and all-merciful, why is there gross evil?

The ultimate answer to the philosophical conundrum of *God and Evil*, however, may transcend neo-classical reasoned philosophical discourse. *En toto*, this work, *God and Good*, is *de facto* a philosophical response to *theodicy*, as well.

*

"What is it," French journalist Cheron asks the Jewish writer Wiesel, "that is most radically counter-poised to the mystery of death and the mystery of Evil?"

Replies Elie Wiesel: "The mystery of life and Good."

*

No question about it.

*

GOD AND GOOD

Author's First Midrash

GOD AND GOOD

Genesis / "*Bereshith*"

Midrash:
God's 100 Archangels

Before the beginning of form

Before the beginning of time

The God of Israel
Lord of Lords
King of Kings

gathered his 100 Archangels

from the far corners of the universe

They stood in a celestial phalanx
10 Archangels deep by 10 Archangels across
Each spanning a light year

Thus, by current measure, the celestial phalanx covered
100 square light years,
if such a comparison can even be made
facing the Divine

I have called you here, Archangels of the Universe

to advise me...
as to whether or not
to create
Heaven and Earth

Advise me, my celestial Archangels

Shall I proceed forward or not?

If I do not proceed, clearly you will never see realization
as more than Ideas
as more than Visions
as more than possibilities

interacting only with the Divine

But you must decide

I seek your celestial counsel.

One by one
the Archangels of the universe
stepped forth......

*

Do NOT create
admonished the Angel of LIGHT,
There will be too much suffering

Do NOT create

GOD AND GOOD

said the Angel of HOPE,
There will be too much suffering
Do NOT create
said the Angel of LOVE,
There will be too much suffering

Do NOT create
said the angel of BEAUTY,
There will be too much suffering

Do NOT create
said the Angel of VICTORY.
There will be too much suffering

Do NOT create
said the Angel of SPIRITUALITY,
There will be too much suffering

Do NOT create
said the Angel of POETRY,
There will be to much suffering

and so it went,
on and on

different Archangels
- but with the same utterance
Angel after Angel
quadrant after quadrant

with but one conclusion......

the Angel of the TIDES
the Angel of JOY
the Angel of CREATIVITY
the Angel of DREAMS
the Angel of ELEGANCE

...of EXPLORATION
...of FREEDOM
...of KINDNESS

...FULFILLMENT
...MERCY
...PASSION
...JUSTICE

one Archangel after another
stepped forward
to front–and–center
of the phalanx
faced the Divine

and said
each one almost verbatim

Do NOT create Heaven and Earth
There will be too much suffering

The 75th Angel, the 76th Angel, the 77th Angel...

the 85th, 86th, 87th...

moving towards unanimity...

GOD AND GOOD

...95th, 96th, 97th, 98th, 99th...
...up to the 100th Archangel

the one in the very back left quadrant/corner
of the celestial phalanx...

.....the Angel who BURIES the DEAD

and there was the slightest of pauses, almost
imperceptible
as the Archangel shuffled his way forward to the front...
in his patented trudge.......

stood before the Divine
stood silent for a few moments

then uttered very deliberately...

"UVACHARTA"

and thou shalt choose...

[the Angels of HOPE, LOVE and MERCY shifted slightly
and coiled...]

"BA-CHAYIM"

LIFE

and, simultaneous with the utterance...

The God of Israel
King of Kings
Lord of Hosts

arose in all glory from his celestial throne

[all 100 Archangels bowed down]

the Divine stretching forth his right arm

...and in one grand majestic sweep...

IGNITED THE COSMOS

CREATING THE HEAVENS AND THE EARTH

*

The UNITY "POTENTIAL"

יִגְדַּל

נִמְצָא וְאֵין עֵת אֶל מְצִיאוּתוֹ.*   יִגְדַּל אֱלֹקִים חַי* וְיִשְׁתַּבַּח,

גֶּעְלָם וְגַם אֵין סוֹף לְאַחְדוּתוֹ.   אֶחָד וְאֵין יָחִיד כְּיִחוּדוֹ,

לֹא נַעֲרוֹךְ אֵלָיו קְדֻשָּׁתוֹ.   אֵין לוֹ דְמוּת הַגּוּף וְאֵינוֹ גוּף,*

רִאשׁוֹן וְאֵין רֵאשִׁית לְרֵאשִׁיתוֹ.   קַדְמוֹן לְכָל דָּבָר אֲשֶׁר נִבְרָא,

יוֹרֶה גְדֻלָּתוֹ וּמַלְכוּתוֹ.   הִנּוֹ אֲדוֹן עוֹלָם* לְכָל נוֹצָר,

'YIGDAL'

יִגְדַּל *Exalted be the Living God* and praised,*
  *He exists — unbounded by time is His existence.**
He is One — and there is no unity like His Oneness.
  Inscrutable and infinite is His Oneness.
*He has no semblance of a body nor is He corporeal;**
  nor has His holiness any comparison.
He preceded every being that was created —
  the First, and nothing precedes His precedence.
Behold! He is Master of the universe to every creature,*
  He demonstrates His greatness and His sovereignty.

*A   יִגְדַּל אֱלֹקִים חַי — *Exalted be the Living God.*
This song of uncertain authorship summarizes
the 'Thirteen Principles of Faith' expounded by
Rambam [Maimonides] in his *Commentary to
Mishnah, Sanhedrin,* ch. 10, and stated
succinctly in the famous *Ani Maamin* prayer.
They comprise the basic principles that every
Jew is required to believe. In *Rambam's* view, to
deny any of them constitutes heresy.

[see "Yigdal" prayer (page prior) – in the original Hebrew plus English translation]

The UNITY "POTENTIAL" *[a]

SUMMA II will propose that this UNITY

– *encompasses all* – and always has

– is an integrated consciousness

– keeps evolving or generating additional layers, layers whose parameters are, perhaps, out of our ability to comprehend at all

– has at its core, Quest for Potential *[b]

– is an outwardly expanding spiraling vortex

– continuously *iterates* to keep re–optimizing and re–evolving and re–layering

– *mimics* on a grand level, that which we do on a human level (or *vice versa* perhaps being more accurate)

– *drives* the cosmic order *[c]

– is a penultimate '*COLLECTIVE*' of all

        – life–force
        – consciousness
        – spirit

*[a] see also **Appendix H**
*[b] à la the Kabbalistic *En Sof*
*[c] as per tradition

To give a very rough parallel:

a single individual red blood cell (in a single individual human) **IS**
to the *vast Milky Way Galaxy*

as

a *single individual human* **IS**
to the infinite *Quest for Potential*$^\infty$ *Unity*

note: The Key Term

Quest for Potential∞
should always be understood as
Quest for Potential∞ (recursive to the infinite power)
meaning
Quest for Potential∞ (within Potential (within potential...
...*ad infinitum*

Quest for Potential∞

is infinitely recursive;

an infinitely recursive, unique supra-dynamic:

Quest for Potential∞

within Quest for Potential∞

within Quest for Potential∞ (.......*ad infinitum*)

hence, the INFINITY symbol

Another way of looking at this schematically would be

Q4P (Q4P (Q4P ....

Yes, like those wooden Chinese/Russian

dolls-within-a-doll, within-a-doll, etc.,

usually, ~6 – 10 dolls

But in our case, it is a

dynamic-within-a-dynamic, within-a-dynamic, etc.

ad infinitum

(to the power of INFINITY)

– and *ad infinitum* means an awful lot of
'coiled potential'

===

Q4P = Quest for Potential$^\infty$

Q4F = Quest for Fulfillment

Encapsulization

Quest for Potential∞ is at the core of the Divine

Quest for Potential∞
(to the Infinite Divine Extraordinariation power)
drives the cosmic order
– Book #1

Quest for Potential∞ –

the embryonic Divine

...an infinitely expanding,

fully integrated METAPHYSICAL WOMB –

encompassing all in its wake –
from the beginning

through the forward reaches of TIME

energizing
life-actualizing
optimizing
nourishing
and
potentializing
our cosmos –

.....and all cosmos

– as it actually IS the cosmos –

...striving for complete fulfillment

and striving to attain Infinite Divine Extraordinariation

*

Quest for Potential[∞]
is at the core of the infinitely questing Divine

They are essentially one-and-the-same

* * *

Quest for Potential[∞]
IS the cosmic order

*

The dynamic IS the cosmos

*

The cosmos IS the dynamic

***

Quest for Potential[∞]
gobbles-up 'nothingness'

"We hope to explain the entire universe in a simple formula you can put on your T-shirt"

– Leon Lederman (Nobel Prize in Physics) c. 2004

Q4P∞™

Quest for Potential
(infinitely recursive)

Wheeler

pre-Summa II

> *"To my mind, there must be at the bottom of it all, not an utterly simple equation, but an utterly simple IDEA. And to me that idea, when we finally discover it, will be so compelling, and so inevitable, so beautiful, we will all say to each other, 'How could it have ever been otherwise?'"*

– Professor John Wheeler, former Chair of the
  Physics Department at the University of Texas at Austin,
  (from the PBS science documentary,
  "The Creation of The Universe" **2004**)

post-Summa II

> *"Birnbaum's God and Good
>   is a major intellectual triumph and
>   potential conceptual breakthrough"*

– Professor John Wheeler
  Professor Emeritus of Physics
  Princeton University, **2008**

"All revolutions take time to settle in"

– Lanza del Vasto (1901-1981)

"All that was new in the work, was false,
and all that was true, was old"

> – May 1859
> sample / negative initial academic reaction
> by Professor Samuel Haughton
> of Dublin, Ireland
> to Charles Darwin's newly-published
> *Origin of Specie*

Caution to dogmatists:

This book supplants centuries–old perspectives.

This book peels away layers of the cosmic code.

This book attempts to "cut-to-the-core".

Parental guidance suggested.

FOREWORD

by Daniel N. Khalil

*

   Jewish philosophy is often resigned to the assumption that fundamental descriptions of God and the universe are beyond the grasp of the human intellect. Questions of Jewish philosophy are generally posed in the context of a mysterious framework that is rarely examined *per se*. Such a mindset is often more concerned with man's place, role, and duties in the world, than it is with the contours of the universe and the latter's relationship to the Eternal:

   "[The reason of Jewish philosophy] is the reason that we find in chess...Chess offers the greatest possible scope for calculation...But all this takes place in accordance with a set of rules that determine which moves are permitted and which are not and how the pieces are set up. The rules themselves are the limits of reason in chess. They are not questioned nor need they be justified because the rationality of chess begins after the rules have been set down...This is Jewish intelligence...[it] has a sense of limit, of the *vanity* involved in *hurling* questions at the limits..."

– Michael Wyschogrod, *The Body of Faith* I, 3.
[italics mine]

Of course, there have been noteworthy attempts to defy this generalization. Maimonides is perhaps the most prominent example of a Jewish philosopher who would analyze – if not challenge – Judaism's fundamental suppositions. In his *Guide of the Perplexed,* Maimonides describes a Judaism that dovetails seamlessly with an understanding of the universe as established primarily by Aristotle. As Maimonides holds Judaism to the light of Aristotle's logic, he finds concordance on all topics, with merely one exception: the question of eternalism.

Aristotle is the 'eternalist,' believing that the universe is eternal and that God comes into existence at some point in time. Maimonides asserts the converse: that God is eternal and that the universe is actively brought into being. It is striking that Maimonides, who accepts Aristotle's position on an array of topics, including the essence of both God and man, cannot find agreement with Aristotle on the relationship between God and the cosmos. It is even more astounding that neither Maimonides nor Aristotle claim to prove their respective positions *vis-à-vis* God's relation to the cosmos. It is as if both men probe to the depths of metaphysics together in complete accord, only to resign, quite openly, to their respective presuppositions at the end of the journey.

Both sides appear to be missing tools that are essential to complete this journey. And both sides admit their respective unpreparedness by abandoning the very thought-process that brought them to this point:

"As for the matters concerning which we have no argument or that are too great in our opinion, it is difficult for us to say: why is this so? For instance, when we say: Is the world eternal or not?"
  – Aristotle, *Topica* I, 11

"The eternity of the world or its creation in time becomes an open question, it should in my opinion be accepted without proof... it is not in the power of speculation to accede."

  – Moses Maimonides, *Guide of the Perplexed*, II, 16

It is at this juncture that David Birnbaum enters the forum. He does so by delineating the relationship between God and eternity in the context of a unified metaphysics that concurrently addresses the relationship of God to the cosmos and the cosmos to eternity.

Such is the philosophy expounded in his first work, *God and Evil*. It is this simultaneous solution that lays the foundation for the work's understanding of the existence of gross evil in the world. Birnbaum's is a solution that has been left almost entirely unchallenged in the eighteen years since its publication in 1988. In the current work, *God and Good*, Birnbaum has looked further into the implications of this metaphysics and found the individual to be central. Here *the individual is revealed as the engine of cosmic evolution*. The relationship of man to God, man to the cosmos, and man to eternity thus become the focus of this work.

Birnbaum feels no compulsion to obey the rules that his intellectual predecessors followed. Building on the foundation of ancient Jewish principles, particularly Kabbalistic ones, he is not afraid to draw on Eastern principles of temporal circularity, concepts from biology and physics that have yet to be applied to metaphysical issues, or insights from other scientific and humanistic disciplines that have been left untapped in philosophy.

Asserting that previous attempts to characterize the essence of the cosmos have fallen short for their lack of an adequate conceptual arsenal, as exemplified by Maimonides' and Aristotle's impasse, he consolidates these eclectic influences into a defined set of metaphysical 'tools.' Birnbaum presents these tools at the outset of *God and Good*. He then uses them to build a model that is applicable to all the arenas from which its influences were initially derived.

The implications of Birnbaum's original – markedly straightforward – doctrine therefore, range from the most general to the most specific. The doctrine is unified by the central thesis that unbounded potentiality pulls both the individual and the cosmos towards a Divine ideal. Potential is universal. Potential is the nexus:

"One of the great afflictions of man's spiritual world is that every discipline of knowledge, every feeling, impedes the emergence of the other...This defect cannot continue permanently. Man's nobler future is destined to come, when he will develop to a sound spiritual state so that instead of each discipline negating the other, all knowledge, all feeling will be envisioned from any branch of it...No spiritual phenomenon can stand independently. Each is interpenetrated by all."

– Abraham Isaac Kook, *Lights of Holiness*, I, p. 22

Interestingly, in spite of its novelty, the paradigm elaborated by Birnbaum is no less firmly anchored in Biblical and Talmudic concepts than the previous Jewish perspectives that were restrained by these same influences. For instance, God's self-identification as "I will be that which I will be" (Exodus 3:14) is perhaps the single best articulation of *God and Good*'s description of potentiality's association with God.

In his first work, Birnbaum meticulously dissects Adam's Garden of Eden dilemma (Genesis 2:17), understanding it as humankind's choice between potential/infinite growth and bliss/limited growth. Birnbaum then goes on, throughout *God and Evil* and now *God and Good*, to reveal the theme of potential in traditional Jewish narratives and even Judaism's specific commandments.

At the outset of *God and Evil* Birnbaum boldly asserts that he aims to provide an integrated and novel solution to the problem of (1) the origins of the cosmos, (2) the nature, as it were, of God, and (3) the presence of gross evil in a world governed by an omnipotent God. At this point, the expectation, at least for this reader, is for a complex, convoluted theory too abstract to be considered objectively. The result, however, a "potentiality model," is just the opposite: profoundly discrete, yet overarching enough to satisfy the three initial aims.

With the presentation of the second book, this model now has four distinct dimensions. First, in *God and Evil*, it is thoroughly rooted in Biblical and academic theology. Second, in part one of *God and Good*, the metaphysical implications of the model are described. Third, in part two of *God and Good*, the model is presented in the form of 120 mythical Angels, adding texture to the metaphysics and drawing it into the realm of daily human reality. And finally, in the third section of *God and Good*, the 'potentiality model' is translated into a practical template for self-actualization.

It is difficult to recall a metaphysics as unified, yet as widely applicable, as the one presented here. The model's foundation is concrete, while its implications are personal and thus varied. Each reader, therefore, will glean that which augments his or her own spiritual sensibility. As an Orthodox Jew, I find much in Birnbaum's two works that bolsters my understanding of traditional Judaism.

No less *sui generis* than the scope of Birnbaum's work, is its relentless appeal to profound innate human understandings that cannot be adequately explicated in standard prose. Birnbaum employs a linguistic ensemble that at times resembles the water-tight, nitty-gritty reasoning of *God and Evil*, while at other times feels like terse jolts to the psyche. The author has turned away from the prevalent style of philosophy that so fervently analyzes metaphysical mysteries only to expose its own limitations. In breaking from convention, Birnbaum has taken a risk. He has gambled acceptance by refusing to succumb to a more traditional framework that would inevitably fail to fully represent the depth of ideas presented here.

The test lies in the heart of the reader. For all of its details and implications, the core of this work is unabashedly simple: potential drives existence. Does this concept seem foreign? or does it feel natural? If Birnbaum is successful, the reader will detect that the idea has an inherent organic power. This power can be explained in certain general contexts using standard language, but in others – particularly in the context of the individual – traditional explanations do not suffice.

Birnbaum posits that the force driving the cosmos pulsates within the soul of each individual, and so only a visceral response from the reader can fully reflect its impact. Is this achieved? Do the grand, general, cosmic principles yield to an understanding of the self? Does this awareness, in and of itself, have meaningful and practical implications for daily life? If it does, then Birnbaum has achieved something utterly unique.

He has raised a preciously simple metaphysical centerpiece and enshrined it through its intrinsic affinity for the mind and the heart of the reader.

"I will cause a new utterance to be heard in the land:
Peace peace to the far and near, said the Lord."
Isaiah 57:19

Daniel Khalil
Cold Spring Harbor
New York

Dr. Daniel Khalil is a scientist with the National Institute of Health.

He teaches Jewish Philosophy at Long Island University.

GOD AND GOOD

A "Subtle Dynamic"

When I was ~11 years old, (in the early 1960s), I was a sixth grade student at (scholastically demanding Modern Orthodox) Yeshiva Dov Revel in Forest Hills, (in Queens, NY of tennis championship fame). About a third of my fellow students were children of Holocaust survivors, or of 1930s *emigrés* from Europe. The evils of the Holocaust were raw – and it was not at all clear that the theology could handle it.

The philosophical situation was not much better for more general philosophical or general inter-related scientific questions, like: How did this universe come to be? If God existed, where did this all-powerful God come from? If God did not exist, what drove the universe? Why was there anything at all?

Thus, we were in sixth grade in a top Jewish Day School, and the fundamental and core philosophical, theological, and scientific questions remained thoroughly unanswered – at home, at *shul* (synagogue), and at school.

I intuitively felt that out there, there was one elegant yet subtle dynamic – a potentially relatively simple idea –

which everyone was just missing – which, if uncovered, would, indeed, "crack-the-cosmic-code," and perhaps the bulk of these issues simultaneously. I felt that it was at the very edge of human awareness. Waiting to be discerned. However, it was clear that discerning it might take years...

At the same time, I was frankly not all-that-sure that Orthodox Judaism or Judaism or monotheism would survive the "code breaking." My gut-feeling was that it would be a close-call.

I determined to learn what I could learn about the world – and observe what I could observe – and, as an aside to my life, try to uncover that elusive 'code-cracking' dynamic. I embarked on an informal odyssey seeking this philosophical and theological "Holy Grail": the "highest common denominator".

In January 1982, ~two decades later – on the beach in the Barbados of all places, "matters crystallized." The elusive "simultaneous solution." The precise moment is ingrained in my psyche, of course, freeze-framed.

The dynamic which I discerned may have been "subtle," but it was certainly not without power. I was now more than quite fully "psyched-up."

First, I had to get back to NY, to a library, a big library. This was pre-GOOGLE, and then we really needed big libraries for potentially "original concepts."

I did two reality-checks, the first with my Yeshiva University High School comrade, intellectual *consigliere*, and close friend-to-this-day Steven Gross (of NY and Jerusalem) 30 days into the project. He was a GO.

The second reality-check was at the ~6 month mark, with my Great Neck neighbor (who I had never actually met prior) and soon-to-be quite world-renowned, Lawrence Schiffman, Professor of Jewish History at NYU, and budding Dead Sea Scrolls expert's expert. He too was a GO – and admonished me to maintain total secrecy until the book was actually out. He would, in due course, unilaterally volunteer to personally Copy Edit the manuscript start-to-finish – TWICE – Draft #1 (in 1985) and Draft #2 (in 1986) – to maintain its total confidentiality, and prep-it for submission to the putative publisher in due course. Schiffman valiantly moved to vigilantly protect and advance the project and insure the manuscript's power and viability. Once-in-a-while in life, one encounters a truly extraordinary individual, dedicated to his craft and to the pursuit of knowledge and truth. The Dead Sea Scrolls – and the Discovery Channel – would have to wait just a touch more....

A solitary five years of work after that epiphanous 'moment' on the beach in the Barbados, the manuscript for *God and Evil* was completed in time for the birth of my first child, Rafaella, January 1986. The editors at KTAV Publishing, who accepted the book for publication later in 1986, cautioned me that if one comma was out-of-place on my erstwhile revolutionary thesis, I would be crucified – by the Jews. And they did not want to be party to a crucifixion. I frankly thought they were a little overwrought, but in any event, the book was micro-edited over the course of 1987, and then published and released in November 1988.

At first there were "sounds of silence." But then matters began to roll. The work would go through Five Printings between 1988 and 2000.

The primary editor, scholar-*extraordinaire* Yaacov Elman of Yeshiva University did a fastidious job with his plodding hyper-perfectionism. Word by word of the text, then the 600+ footnotes, footnote by footnote. No word of the text or related has been changed in any of the printings, including the printing incorporated now into the 2-book Summa Metaphysica series.

Before the Jewish journals got around to reviewing the book, in their own good time, to our astonishment the major Jesuit publications around the world, in-short-order – reviewed it – in-depth and enthusiastically. Theological Studies Journal (then at Georgetown University) *led the charge* – juxtaposing the concepts of the work against those of Aquinas very specifically. Sounded good to me...

Simultaneously, Brandeis University started assigning the work as a Required Text – Masters Degree graduate Term Papers and all – in Advanced Religious Philosophy. In the early 1990s, Hebrew University

(Jerusalem), Yeshiva University, Jewish Theological Seminary, Union Theological Seminary (Christian) and, later, Emory, started assigning the work in Philosophy and/or Jewish Thought. Other universities in the USA and around-the-world would follow.

It sounds like a simple enough journey. But it was a very, very solitary and hi-risk endeavor.

I believe the hypothesis is on-the-mark. Its core inherent power gave me the motivation to embark on the project.

D.B.

To the reader -

My (previously) agnostic SOHO WebSite designer,
after reading the text said I should add the following
alert at the very beginning of the book,
so here-it-goes…

*"Hey you – potential Reader – THIS, all this, applies to
YOU, don't go away, read this! It isn't over your head;
it IS your head… This book about GOD is a
transcendent work… Read this work and enter an
extraordinary realm"*

From   Dena Crowder
       Silicon Valley, CA
       Conceptual Solutions for Fortune 500 companies

"Birnbaum is asking people to dream/vision/think beyond the metaphysical "box" they've been trapped in for centuries.

Birnbaum's paradigm has the "think different" flavor of the Apple campaign of a couple of years ago.

Summa's system is as much a solution, as it is an opening to a new conversation, and an invitation to an entirely new discourse."

*"God is, as well, both in the nucleus of the cell
and in the stardust of the distant nebula"*

– Rabbi Allen Schwartz
rabbi, Congregation Ohab Zedek

New York, NY

Shabbat sermon

November 5, 2005
Parshat Noach

also see sub-section
Extension or Separate ?
in the introduction to this book

"Adoshem Echad, u-Shemo Echad" *

– Zechariah 14:10

at the finalé of the iconic liturgical prayer *Aleinu*,

which itself is generally at the service finalé

*

possible translation #1:
    "God is One, and His name is One"

possible translation #2:
    "God is a Singularity, and His name is a Singularity"

possible translation #3
    "God is One Dynamic, and His name is One Dynamic"

Extension or Separate ?

Is the universe an *extension* of God

- or *separate* from God ?

"If you don't see God everywhere,

you don't see him anywhere"

– the Kotzke Rebbe
(1787 - 1859)

Jewish Encyclopedia Online, http://www.jewishencyclopedia.com/
view.jsp?artid=18&letter=B (accessed October 5, 2009)

BAAL SHEM TOV
("The Besht")

"The foundation-stone of Hasidism as laid by Besht is a strongly marked pantheistic conception of God. He declared the whole universe, mind and matter, to be a manifestation of the Divine Being; that this manifestation is not an emanation from God, as is the conception of the Kabbalah, for nothing can be separated from God: all things are rather forms in which He reveals Himself…"

As noted in Encyclopaedia Judaica on *Baal Shem Tov* {1997} [CD-ROM]

BASIC IDEAS OF HASIDISM
Creator and Universe

"'The hasidic leader R. Menahem Mendel of Lubavich observes (*Derekh Mitzvotekha* (1911), 123) that the disciples of the Ba'al Shem Tov gave the "very profound" turn to the doctrine of the oneness of God so that it means not alone that He is unique, as the medieval thinkers said, but that He is all that is:…there is no other existence whatsoever apart from His existence, blessed be He. This is true unification…just as there was no existence apart from Him before the world was created so it is even now." …as a corollary of hasidic pantheism (more correctly, panentheism)…'"

(author's note: there are no extant writings of the Besht)

(see also Appendix F1: Hasidic v. Kabbalistic)

Overview

God and Good, this companion–work and sequel to
God and Evil (1988)

is composed of
3 inter–related works:

Part I: The Cosmic Womb of Potential

An original proposed metaphysics.

It dovetails with the metaphysics explicated in the first
book of the series, *God and Evil*

Part II: God's 120 Guardian Angels

A quasi–mythical work of quasi–poetry which
is used as a vehicle to explicate and flesh-out
"Quest for Potential∞" from a different angle.

Part III: The Lost Manual

This work plays with applicability of the metaphysics
noted in the prior sections, but on an INDIVIDUAL level.

The work maintains that Quest for Potential$^\infty$ drives not only the COSMOS as well as the DIVINE but also, the INDIVIDUAL, all in 1:1 parallel to one another.

.....and that "enlightened Self-Actualization" is front–and–center in human development.

The Lost Manual is a self–actualization guide as well as a 21st century (alleged) "Wisdom Book" along with several other treats.

═══════════════════════════════════════

Q4P = Quest for Potential$^\infty$

Q4F = Quest for Fulfillment

Author's note

Metaphysics is ultimately about the questions that 5-year-olds ask.

for example,

Why is there anything ?

Where is everything headed ?

Where is God ?

Therefore, to write Metaphysics one must be at least as smart – and as 'open' as – a 5-year-old

That is not necessarily as easy as it sounds

*

This work attempts to advance our understanding of the cosmos.

This work attempts to get us where others have not… into the very "throne room" of metaphysics…

But, the infinitely evolving, morphing and expanding cosmos does not yield its secrets easily

We will need to peel-it-away layer-by-layer

Approach by approach. Theme by theme.
Conjecture by conjecture. Hypothesis by hypothesis.

With no significant mistakes at any level

– as that would throw-off the expeditionary journey

Please note that, respectfully, I only write one treatise /
lifetime – and this is it. There are no philosophy books
before – or after.

Be assured that I have endeavored to be very, very
careful with what I commit to paper.

* * *

Oh, one last thing......

To understand the infinite cosmos, one truly need not
spend-a-life-time peering through large telescopes or
fathoming hyper-complex physics equations or wading-
through dozens of esoteric writings.....Indeed,
respectfully, they will not advance you beyond, say,
"second base." One needs, however, to attempt to
listen very carefully to the very core of one's soul.*

Sincerely,
David Birnbaum

*a little *poetic license* taken here

GOD AND GOOD

All notes and footnotes in Book #1 (*God and Evil*)
are crafted by BIRNBAUM.

All NOTES in this volume, Book #2 (*God and Good*),
are by KHALIL.

note that KHALIL re-starts his NOTES numbering
(starting again from 1)
in each sub-section in which he has commentary.

Q4P∞™

Quest for Potential
(infinitely recursive)

Part I:
The Cosmic Womb
of Potential

GOD AND GOOD

Part I: The Cosmic Womb of Potential
TABLE OF CONTENTS

Part I: The Cosmic Womb of Potential   **80**

ALPHA: Lay-of-the-Land   82

BETA: Cosmic TOOL KIT- Shelf #1   85

GAMMA: Lead-in   100

DELTA: Embryonic Design   104

EPSILON: Notes & Observations   115

ZETA: "Principia Metaphysica"   118

ETA: Some reflections…insights   135

THETA: The two key (spiraling) SUPRA-DYNAMICS   142

IOTA: Reprise to the Cosmic Womb of Potential   150

KAPPA: The building blocks of the cosmos   153

LAMBDA: A fresh look at some of our concepts   155

MU: Cosmic TOOL KIT- Shelf #2 Extraordinariation   162

Part I: The Cosmic Womb of Potential

(the first of the three major parts of *God and Good*)

The "Cosmic Womb of Potential" nourishes, enhances, and sustains the potentializing of all aspects of the Cosmic order – including itself. Nourished, enhanced and sustained within this womb, and, indeed, integral to it, we live and attempt to thrive and advance.

The infinitely expanding and traversing aspect stretches forward through time…from the very origin of origins to the forward reaches of time.

It is this time–spanning infinitude which renders all of us an integral neo–infinite part of this infinite dynamic/entity.

This infinitely expanding dynamic/entity strives after its own maximal potential, relentlessly advancing and expanding, again, recursively, a womb woven within a womb within a womb.

Potential is the amniotic fluid of the infinitely expanding Cosmic Womb.

*

[Parallel to a womb, the temperature of the universe is actually a Constant. Throughout its vast expanse. Of course, the temperature of the universe is a slightly colder at 2.73 degrees above Absolute Zero. (Absolute Zero is -459.67 degrees Farenheit, or -273.15 degrees Celsius). But it is a Constant.]

[Some formations found towards one end of the Universe appear as almost **twins** on the other side of the Universe. Contemporary scientific theory is at-a-loss to explain...]

"U–vacharta ba–chayim"

(And thou shalt choose Life – Deuteronomy)

Q4P = Quest for Potential$^\infty$

Q4F = Quest for Fulfillment

ALPHA: Lay–of–the–Land

Where did it all come from? (question of 5 year–old)

Why is there anything at all? (5 year-old in Private School kindergarten...future Talmud scholar)

What are the origins of the cosmos? (Cosmogony)

[inter-related with...]

What triggered the "Big Bang"? (Physics question)

What drives the cosmos? (Cosmology)

If there is a God, what are the origins of god? (Theogony)

If there is a classic God, why is there gross Evil?
(Theodicy)
Why is there "REALITY" at all?
(enlightened college student)
[similar to question above of 5 year-old in private kindergarten]

Is there REALITY at all?
(college student taking too many philosophy courses)

What is "CONSCIOUSNESS"?
(enlightened layman)

Wherefore "CONSCIOUSNESS"?
(putative best-selling biology writer)

What is the purpose of man?
("Purpose of Man" question)

What is the purpose of the cosmos?
(uncategorized)

If DARWIN was right,

Wherefore, for instance, the extraordinary intricacies of 9 month fetal development – in the greater context of interdependent life? (Darwinian Theory challenge)

If mainstream (linear) INTELLIGENT DESIGN is right, who or what – is the DESIGNER? – and who designed the DESIGNER?
(classic conundrum faced by classical Intelligent Design proponents...very imminently to be answered)

To the Reader: As promised, this Summa Metaphysica SERIES will present an original – and presumably compelling – approach, answer and solution. Relax, sip a low calorie drink, and enjoy the ride... As prior, we do value your time, and fully intend to "deliver the goods." Note that while there is some 'fancy footwork' along the way, the core theme, which you are aware of, remains intact – and flows through the core of the work consistently. So, follow the flow of the book. Don't get stuck on any one sentence or paragraph or page.

If ~stuck on a sentence, re-read it once, perhaps, then roll forward regardless. No one sentence or paragraph makes-or-breaks Book #2. The concepts are all attaching to the core 'spinal column' of POTENTIAL.......Extraordinariation. Your subconscious will connect-the-various dots. Matters will crystallize further.

Then, as appropriate, consider looping-around for a second run at the entire book. It should have a different texture in subsequent run-throughs. We are endeavoring to "get-our-arms around" the Cosmic Code, and, indeed, around the INFINITE. If this were so simple, it would have been done previously.

At this point, I am going to rapidly introduce the first series of hypothesized "Cosmic Tools." Each is actually inter-related with the others. Note that the explanations for each are perhaps less intimidating than the individual 'tool names.'

– Birnbaum

BETA: The Cosmic "Tool Kit"

COSMIC TOOL KIT
Shelf #1

[COSMIC TOOL KIT- Shelf #2 is to be found at the end of Cosmic Womb of Potential]

tools:
* DIVISION INTO POLARITIES & DUALITIES *
* SIMULTANEOUS PUSH / PULL TENSION *
* INFINITELY-COILED SPIRALITY *
* COSMIC 'LEVERAGED BUYOUT' ("BOOTSTRAPPING") *
* (INFINITE) RECURSIVENESS & (INFINITE)
  LOOP-ABILITY *
* 1:1 METAPHYSICAL CORRESPONDENCE *
* MITOSIS OF "0" *
* INEXORABLE LIFE-QUESTING *
* VACUUM-BUSTING *
* INEXORABLE & INFINITE ASCENTS *
* MULTI-DIMENSIONAL MORPHING *
* OPTIMIZATION *
* COSMIC-TAPESTRY-WEAVING *
* QUEST FOR INFINITE DIVINE EXTRAORDINARIATION *
* INTERLOCKING DIVINE INFINITUDE QUEST *
* HYPER-COSMIC RESOURCEFULNESS *

note:
Starting with this sub-section, there are NOTES by KHALIL;
There are approximately three dozen NOTES total by KHALIL – all in this Part I of the book – "THE COSMIC WOMB of POTENTIAL".

*

"A carpenter needs good tools"

– Carpenter's union

Hypothesis:
We propose and hypothesize the following Cosmic "Tool Kit"

[This "Tool Kit" is key and integral to our proposed metaphysics]

This "Tool Kit" might seem to be a 'light' section, but essentially provides the "SET of KEYS" necessary to open the vault containing the elusive 'Cosmic Code' …once you examine the Tool Kit, the Holy Grail of metaphysics is laid bare… discern the Tool Kit – and the construction of the Metaphysics of the Cosmos falls *readily into place*[1,2]

(sounds presumptuous enough)

(all "TOOLS" are direct sub-components of the overarching Quest for Potential∞)

••• TOOL:
* DIVISION into POLARITIES & DUALITIES *

Polarities and Dualities
as well as assorted complementary
Positives / Negatives,
are the BUILDING BLOCKS
and counter-point balancers
of the cosmic order
(Articulation of this concept – whose core is not original
– commenced in *God and Evil*…. The 'spin' may be
original, but there is, indeed, voluminous literature
on the subject in many cultures and many languages
stretching back thousands of years)

NOTES by KHALIL

---

[1] "readily into place" A: In his preamble to *Derech Hashem* Moshe
Chaim Luzatto writes that before a subject such as this can be
mastered it must be understood in a most general way first.
General principles and overarching themes are to be understood
before details are probed. Once the framework of the subject
is made clear, one will then be able to place each detail into its
proper context automatically, and he will "delight" in understanding
new facts that add texture to the framework. This work – *God and
Good* – is written with this concept in mind.

[2] "readily into place" B: The Cosmic Womb of Potential, and
particularly the Tool Kit, will elucidate the general principles that are
central to the paradigm presented here. The "Master Craftsman" of
the cosmos employs a cosmic tool kit. Extraordinary tools open–
the–way for a potentially extraordinary construct. Examine the Tool
Kit, and you will grasp the dimensions of the cosmic construct.

••• TOOL:
* SIMULTANEOUS PUSH / PULL TENSION *
(my term)

Masculine / Feminine
Components of the cosmos are in
DYNAMIC TENSION and/or ENGAGEMENT
Some components simultaneously
PUSH from one dimension, and PULL from another realm
For example: a component may PUSH from a
metaphysical level,
while it PULLS from a REALITY realm – or from a still
further-out POTENTIAL realm.

••• TOOL:
* INFINITELY-COILED SPIRALITY *
(my term)

INFINITELY-COILED SPIRALITY is the favorite infinity-tool
in the Tool Kit.

One can conjecture that the specific 'spirality' parallels a
double-helix.

Meaning, COILED SPIRALITY is the "cosmic highway".

Encapsulization: The cosmos is more like an infinitely
coiled – and expanding – and regenerating – spiral spring.

SPIRALITY is closely inter-linked with…
"BOOTSTRAPPING" (another cosmic tool, next)

••• TOOL:
* COSMIC 'LEVERAGED BUYOUT' ("BOOTSTRAPPING") *
(my term)

Leveraging (infinite) POTENTIALS down–the–road[3, 4, 5]

(forward towards infinity) to energize the 'present'

A key concept positioned centrally in the predecessor
work *God and Evil*, but using more prosaic terminology
here. This above–proposed "TOOL" alone could keep
metaphysics – and physics – busy for a thousand
years or so.

Encapsulization: Potentials down-the-road energize the
PRESENT (and initially ignited CREATION itself).

••• TOOL:
* (INFINITE) RECURSIVENESS & (INFINITE) LOOP–ABILITY *
(my term)

An entity or theme repeating within itself.....indefinitely...
is a key cosmic theme. For instance POTENTIAL, as we
define it, is recursive... i.e.

Potential within Potential within Potential ad infinitum

Recursiveness of Quest for Potential∞:

   The power of Q4P (Quest for Potential∞) hinges on its
   (infinite) recursiveness. Like an infinitely coiled spring.
   To the extent that it keeps iterating infinitely outward and

onward, it self–charges and perpetuates its power. Another way of looking at this is always assuming Q4P to mean – Q4P to the power–of–infinity.

NOTES by KHALIL

[3] Leverage A: "Leveraged Buyout" is a term from finance. It refers to a case in which a financier buys a company using future earnings as the collateral. For instance, a financier might offer to pay $1 million dollars a year for ten years to buy a company. And where, does he plan to get the million dollars per year? From the future projected earnings of the company – of $1.5 million dollars a year. The financier essentially buys the company using the company's own future earnings (i.e. He buys the company with the company's own potential). Birnbaum is positing throughout Summa Metaphysica that the original "leveraged buyout" concept was cosmic. The cosmos was created, he hypothesizes, out of the cosmos' own potential.

[4] Leverage B: Plato had infused in Western philosophy that "God" created the universe out of 'primal matter' even though Plato never articulates just where this primal matter came from – just as he never explicates where "God" came from. Platonic thought – and, indeed, most Western philosophical thought – including classic Jewish philosophy – is linear, i.e. A created B created C, etc.

Birnbaum's paradigm, on the other hand, is 'bootstrap', i.e. the potential of A ignites A retroactively. The Torah Itself has a one – phrase all–encompassing treatise on Jewish philosophy: *"Eheyeh Asher Eheyeh"*. This is Potential within Potential within Potential, which Birnbaum seizes upon as the crux of Summa Metaphysica.

[5] Leverage C: A classic theme in Jewish thought is "yesh mai–ayen," the creation of somethingness, from nothingness. This 'magic trick' receives an elegant 'makeover' in Birnbaum's "leveraged buyout" theme, namely that potentials down–the–road ignited the cosmos. Now, finance is not cosmology – and cosmology is not finance, but the "leveraged buyout" theme can indeed be applied to both. Indeed, there is a 1:1 parallel between the two.

But what does that mean?

It really means infinite recursiveness,
tracking forward to the "end of time"

~Example 1: like those painted doll–within–a–doll
Russian or Chinese dolls, where there is always yet
ANOTHER (smaller) doll within

~Example 2: an ONION… where there is inevitably yet
another (smaller) layer
[carrying within itself still other smaller layers]

Note that there is actually a 'double power' to this:
First, is its infinite ~spring effect.

Second is the nature of the proposed dynamic –
whereby infinitely compelling potentialities 'down-the-
road', "ignite" the present.

••• TOOL:
* 1:1 METAPHYSICAL CORRESPONDENCE *
(my term)

1:1:1:1:1:1 Multi–directional infinite
CORRESPONDENCE

* * * metaphysical: cosmic: human * * *

1:1:1:1:1 (to the infinite level) correspondence exists
between what occurs on

metaphysical
cosmic
human
molecular
sub–molecular
      levels

●●● TOOL:
* MITOSIS OF "0" *
(my term)

We do not know what existed pre–*Big Bang.*
Let us call it "0"

We can make assumptions about "voids" of various
flavors, but we certainly do not know

Best to just call it "0"

Now, moving forward…

At CREATION, "0" is presumably divided in multiple
ways, many beyond our capability of even beginning to
fathom at this point…
counter–balancing Negatives and Positives…

0 divides into
+1, -1……….+2, -2 etc.,

Positives and Negatives;
Polar and anti-Polar,
Male and Female; * * * (see Book #1)

Split the atom and create an atomic bomb;
Split "0" and ignite a cosmos (a powerful concept,
even by the standards of this volume)
Hypothetically, split "0" into Emerging Potential...and a
Cosmic Vacuum
and you will have a rapidly and dynamically expanding
Potential

So, we see that both
examining "0"
and/or
examining the possible   >>> splitting of "0" <<<
are both very rich mines to plumb.

••• TOOL:
* INEXORABLE LIFE-QUESTING *
(my term)

UNQUENCHABLE / INSATIABLE / INEXORABLE
THIRST / THRUST for (diversity of) LIFE[6]

an INEXORABLE craving/drive to bring forth LIFE
(and diversity thereof)
is a primary cosmic thrust
The nuance just depends on which prism you look
through…

cont'd

NOTES by KHALIL

---

[6] Thirst for Life: Life – seeking to bring forth life – seeking to bring
forth life… is a quintessential example of recursive potentialities.

Quest for Potential$^\infty$ is thus simultaneously –
• a FORCE
• a QUEST
• a POTENTIAL
• the ongoing open–ended COSMOS
• the Infinite Divine Extraordinariation
• the SPARK of LIFE
• the sum total of all eco–systems
• in other words, EVERYTHING as we know it

Not bad for a dynamic.

••• TOOL:
* VACUUM–BUSTING *
(my term)

Abhorrence of vacuums on all different levels
(metaphysical, reality and other levels)

Vacuums – metaphysical or otherwise – are abhorred[7]
Nature abhors a vacuum. And it presumably abhors a
'vacuum of principles,' as well.

So, 'initially,' if 'initially' can be said to exist, we are
faced with a potential 'vacuum' situation.

NOTES by KHALIL

---

[7] The Physical Vacuum: This 'abhorrence,' as it were, can be
allegorized as 'negative pressure.' A vacuum exerts a 'pull' on
adjacent matter and thereby seeks its own obliteration. The greater
the relative vacuum, the greater the negative pressure, the greater
the 'abhorrence,' and the more likely the vacuum is to obliterate
itself.

The vacuum–breaker principle was quest for a possibility of a principle – or embryonic Quest for Potential$^\infty$.

And perhaps, reacting to a potential VACUUM situation, Q4P then ultimately achieves a 'life of its own,' feeding upon itself, looping around itself billions upon billions of times, seeking to achieve critical mass... and eventually apparently doing so, first metaphysically, and then in full–blown reality.

●●● TOOL:
* INEXORABLE & INFINITE ASCENTS *

ASCENDING LEVELS
of REALITY & ACTUALIZATION & FULLNESS &
CONSCIOUSNESS
        – are ongoing cosmic imperatives

●●● TOOL:
* MULTI-DIMENSIONAL MORPHING *
(my term)

Metaphysical Realms are not static; they are dynamically morphing.

The Emotional Richness of the Cosmic Order is not static; it is dynamically morphing.

The Intellectual Richness of the Cosmic Order is not static; it is dynamically morphing.

The Consciousness Level of the Cosmic Order is not static; it is dynamically morphing.

The Reality Richness of the Cosmic Order has not been static; it has morphed to this point.

Combine all-of-the-above dynamics, and you have a *symphony* of ongoing morphing and ever-increasing richness and advance.

Creation / "Big Bang" [the *Potential$^\infty$ Point*] was possibly at the boundary where metaphysics "morphed" into physics, and thus both fields (metaphysics and physics) are fully engaged.

We, in contemporary times, for example, intersect with this extraordinary pulsating, morphing advancing Cosmic Order at-one-specific particular-point-in-time. But understand that between the time you started this sentence and the time you finish it, the entire Cosmic order will have incrementally morphed.

••• TOOL:
* OPTIMIZATION *

On every level, the cosmos and its components, have an uncanny instinctive ability to OPTIMIZE[8]

[simple and elegant enough]

NOTES by KHALIL

---

[8] Optimize: The individual must have the patience and decisiveness to act at precisely the opportune time. This ability to 'seize the moment' was harnessed at the Genesis Point to create the universe.

••• TOOL:
* COSMIC–TAPESTRY–WEAVING *
(my term)

Quest for Potential$^\infty$ weaves an ever-expanding, ever-richer, ever-more-sophisticated, wondrous, multi–dimensional multi–thread cosmic tapestry encompassing and integrating ***
ALL fields…(cosmic threads) metaphysics, philosophy, theology, physics, astrophysics, chemistry, biology, medicine, mathematics, astronomy, psychology, architecture, art, music *et al*.

in ONE inter–connected cosmic tapestry

You know the favorite refrain here.....

"Adoshem Echad, u-Shemo Echad"

"God is ONE and his NAME is ONE"

All part of the ongoing cosmic Infinite Divine Extraordinariation

*** see ••• TOOL: OPTIMIZING COMPLEXIFICATION / CONTOURIZATION * below in section MU [Shelf #2]

[not COMPLEXIFICATION for complexity's sake (as is often viewed in the Physical Sciences as a universal imperative); rather, 'complexification' when it advances the key thrusts of multi-dimensional POTENTIAL and OPTIMIZATION]

[Interesting how a religious service in an extraordinary cathedral, for instance, might bring together so many of these themes, e.g. spiritual as well as the extraordinary aesthetic (art, choir music, organ music, architecture) simultaneously at one time, in one place, all under a majestic roof with spires directed heavenwards]

••• MASTER TOOL:
* QUEST FOR INFINITE DIVINE EXTRAORDINARIATION[9, 10] *
(my term)

---

* * * Quest for INFINITE DIVINE EXTRAORDINARIATION:

Fullness/Richness/Beauty/Diversity/Meaning/Fulfillment/Potential *et al.* is the key "tool" and metaphysical theme we will posit (to 'crack–the–cosmic–code')
This particular hypothesized "tool" will finally unlock the final locked door in METAPHYSICS

key note: this Quest is anti-polar to:
"aimless nothingness"

NOTES by KHALIL

---

[9] Infinite Divine Extraordinariation A: With this concept, the author presents a concrete endpoint towards which the path of both human and cosmic potential is directed. It represents the completion of a metaphysical framework introduced in *God and Evil* and described more fully here.

[10] Infinite Divine Extraordinariation B: The quest for one's potential need not be a spiritual experience, particularly if the endpoint is left undefined. Here the author takes a clear stand as to the endpoint, describing it as necessarily spiritual and indeed Divine. The concept of the *Potential$^{\infty}$ Point* still allows for a multiplicity of goals (as will be exemplified in the 120 Angels) but it ties these goals together in the singular aim of reaching the state of Infinite Divine.

••• TOOL:
* INTERLOCKING DIVINE INFINITUDE QUEST *
(my term)

The Quest (the journey) is at least as important as the denouement.

The ongoing QUEST is itself / ITSELF integral to the Infinite Divine Extraordinariation.

One cannot separate the Divine from the ongoing Divine Quest.

••• TOOL:
* HYPER-COSMIC RESOURCEFULNESS *
(my term)

Q4P will tap-into the full panoply of cosmic assets (meaning, of its own assets), in its (ongoing) development of new species and organisms.

GAMMA: Lead-in

from Book 1 (*God and Evil*)

Quest for Potential[∞]
drives the cosmos

All advance, life, reality, creativity, texture, progress
flows from this one Singularity

Quest for Potential[∞] is at the epicenter of the Divine

Now, Book #2 (*God and Good*) can be encapsulated
in one phrase...

At the end–of–the–rainbow,
the Infinite Divine Extraordinariation[1, 2, 3]
retroactively ignites Creation.

The most awesome potential of all might be... after all,
...Potential Divinity...
meaning... at the "end–of–the–rainbow"... at the end
of hopefully many millennium of human advance
in consciousness... almost as an INFINITY to be
approached, but not quite realized, is "INFINITE
DIVINE EXTRAORDINARIATION"...and it is this
awesome POTENTIAL at the very end-of-the-rainbow
which IGNITED Creation.

Meaning, YES, via its awesome POTENTIAL
"the DIVINE" at Infinity–forward, retroactively ignites
Creation at Infinity–backwards...

* * * for, only this INFINITE DIVINE EXTRAORDINARIATION
would have the POTENTIAL–power to suck LIFE &
CREATION from out of the VOID * * *

So, is the Divine
  - *at the beginning,* or
  - *ongoing,* or
  - *at the end?*

NOTES by KHALIL

---

[1] Infinite Divine Extraordinariation A: With this, "Divine Perfection"
which was left somewhat dangling metaphysically in *God and Evil*, is
hereby made crucial for the creation and sustenance of the cosmos.
Divine Perfection is rescued, as it were.

[2] Infinite Divine Extraordinariation B: In *God and Evil* the prime role of
the Divine was as igniter of the cosmos. In *God and Evil* the Divine
was seemingly detached from the maintenance of the universe. Now it
is clear, the Divine has a direct role in the perpetual progression of the
cosmos, as Quest for Potential$^\infty$ pierces through time and space to
continually energize life and existence.

[3] Infinite Divine Extraordinariation C: As in Book #1 (*God and Evil*)
the reader is essentially given the implicit option of jettisoning the
"religious" Divine, for a "secular" Divine of pure potential. The author
tilts in the "religious" direction, and writes his works in that context,
but both works can be read either way – and the author is meticulous
in leaving both options implicitly open. Essentially the author, while
writing within the Jewish context he works within, is saying (at not
inconsiderable theological peril) that philosophically the cosmos can
be viewed – and approached – either way.

GOD AND GOOD

Infinite Divine Extraordinariation is consequently FULLY
MANIFEST only at the hypothetical "END", at the
"end–of–the–rainbow" (but the DIVINE POTENTIAL
also "ignites" the 'BEGINNING') the (embryonic) DIVINE
courses right through all, through all humanity and life,
and is inextricably part–and–parcel of all the Cosmos
and all of its life-components through all eternity.

Thus, Divine POTENTIAL
is not only at the beginning,
it actually ignites the BEGINNING…
and IGNITES the Cosmos.

DIVINE POTENTIAL ignites the "journey" from
"POSSIBILITY"
through
"the METAPHYSICAL"
onward through
"REALITY"
and onward through ever–ascending levels of
"CONSCIOUSNESS"
and presumably towards
INFINITE DIVINE EXTRAORDINARIATION.

In my first opus (G & E),
I posit that
Quest for Potential$^\infty$
drives the cosmos.

This has the advantages of being
ELEGANT, SIMPLE, POWERFUL.

I posit that POTENTIAL
is at the epicenter of the Divine.

But the still–open–question here is:
What POTENTIAL – or bundle–of–potentials –
was powerful enough to IGNITE the cosmos?

Is man's potential, and the 'cosmic potential' a powerful–
enough "MATCH" to light–up the cosmos?
The most awesome potential of all might be… after all,
Infinite Divine Extraordinariation…

*

To our Readers -

By now you "have-the-drift" regarding the core concept
of Quest for Potential$^\infty$,

but "having-the-drift" is not sufficient for a major
metaphysics presentation,

– so we will proceed forward in more formal fashion….

DELTA: Embryonic Design

"The Embryonic Divine Design" Formulation

Quest for Potential$^\infty$ is an overarching and all –
encompassing
Near–Infinite Entity/Dynamic transcending TIME and
SPACE
seeking to evolve fully into Infinite Divine
Extraordinariation.

"Viruach Elohim mirachefet al p'nei hamayim,[1]"

["And the breath/spirit of God was hovering upon the
surface of the waters"]

(Genesis / *Bereshith* 1:1,2)

NOTES by KHALIL

---

[1] Torah use A: There are two ways to quote a biblical passage.
One might either reference a detail from the Torah and use it
merely to introduce a concept that is otherwise unrelated to
biblical principles. Or, one might take a hold of – and embrace –
central biblical principles, and use them as the foundation for
developing a thought. The former approach uses the Bible
artificially as a veneer to make foreign concepts palatable. The
latter, clearly the method of this author, reflects a natural comfort
with the Torah. This author does not employ the Torah as an
afterthought to build an argument; rather, to him the Torah is
a primary source for this novel metaphysics. He discerns key
metaphysical themes permeating the Torah.

Everything – Past, Present and Future – is integral to this ONE entity/dynamic, of which we are an organic part.

Again,

> *"Adoshem Echad, u-Shemo Echad"*

> "God is ONE and his NAME is ONE"

> Deuteronomy 6:4

It is this ONE singular dynamic which both encompasses all, and which drives – and indeed, IS, the entire cosmos. It is, as well, simultaneously the embryonic Divine, seeking to become Infinite Divine Extraordinariation. Q4P chases after it's own tail. Meaning, Quest for Potential$^\infty$ seeks it's infinite perfect potential.

Q4P has always pervaded the abstract and physical dimensions of the cosmos

Q4P seeks after its full Divine and truly Infinite manifestation

> *"Eheyeh Asher Eheyeh"*

> "I WILL BE THAT WHICH I WILL BE"

The metaphysical currents – and the equations – and the metaphysical manifestations of the Divine Potential – explored the different options for the planned *Big Bang [Potential$^\infty$ Point]*, ...intended to transform POSSIBILITY into REALITY... from thence

onto LIFE itself... and from thence onward towards the Infinitely Infinite Divine Extraordinariation...
Too much intensity in the initial ACTUALIZATION spark (the intended "Big Bang" *[Potential$^\infty$ Point]*), and the newly actualized cosmos would spin out of control into cosmic debris; Too little intensity, and the cosmos–creation–attempt would fold back into itself and implode.[2]

The odds of just the INTENSITY alone
(let alone the COMPOSITION)
being just right are in the realm of longer than
1 in 10 to the trillionth power... very very remote for hitting something perfectly by random chance.
But the calibration for the attempt was set[3] .
The cosmic fuse was lit.
The billions of POTENTIALITIES were now all lined up... as if a billion gates were aligned perfectly... finally, finally... *enfin*
And at the very, very end of the matrix was the Infinite and, Infinite Divine Extraordinariation.

Everything was set.

The ultimate "high drama."

Untold billions of eons in the making.

NOTES by KHALIL

---

[2] Balance: Do we not face the same caveats regularly in our lives? Such considerations are important in our relationships, our spirituality, our careers, etc. This is merely one example of how humanity's dilemmas are reflected in the cosmos. To put it concisely: Not too much; not too little.

[3] The calibration: The description of this ultra–precise calibration necessitates a timeless calibration.

Billions of variable potentialities now, indeed at this very particular point in cosmic time, in Optimal Cosmic Metaphysical Alignment...

The Divine clarion rang forth!

שְׂאוּ שְׁעָרִים ׀ רָאשֵׁיכֶם
וְהִנָּשְׂאוּ פִּתְחֵי עוֹלָם
וְיָבוֹא מֶלֶךְ הַכָּבוֹד׃

(Psalms / *Tehillim* 24:7)

Open Up Yea Cosmic Gates!

And escort through the Majesty of the Infinite!

[author's spin]

"Ye–hi Or!"

"Let there be Light!"

(Genesis 1:3)

[the Potential[∞] Point]

and the *Big Bang* was, indeed, Q4P "making–its–move"...

Thunderation! The *Big Bang [the Potential[∞] Point]*

And, 13.2 billion years later, the emergence onto Land

* *Nous avons arrivé* *

* We have arrived *

Q4P pervades love, passion, emotion

Q4P pervades – and is integral to – Humanity in full intensity

Q4P pervades – and is integral to – all life and all inert substance,
all humanity and absolutely all components of the cosmic order – for absolutely everything is part of this one dynamic
Individually, we are both autonomous, and, as well, one of many "Human Heads"

Collectively, we are "embryonic Divine"

We are all, indeed, Quest for Potential$^\infty$.

"Let us make man in our image[4], after our likeness…" [b'zalmeinu[4]]

וַיֹּאמֶר אֱלֹקִים נַעֲשֶׂה אָדָם
בְּצַלְמֵנוּ כִּדְמוּתֵנוּ…

And God created man in His image, in the image[5] of God He created him;… [betzelem[5]]

וַיִּבְרָא אֱלֹקִים אֶת־הָאָדָם
בְּצַלְמוֹ בְּצֶלֶם
אֱלֹקִים בָּרָא אֹתוֹ…

(Genesis / *Bereshith* 1:26, 27)

NOTES by KHALIL

[4] b'zalmeinu: The classic question is: why the plural? Perhaps it is potentiality, the Cosmo's timeless force [and it's inter–related cumulative cosmic consciousness] that is God's metaphysical interlocutor.

[5] betzelem: In Chapter One of his *Guide of the Perplexed* Maimonides draws on Platonic concepts and explains: "The term image [tzelem]… is applied to the natural form, I mean to the notion in virtue of which a thing is constituted as a substance and becomes what it is." Incredibly, this concept –
developed in the very beginning of Maimonides' treatise –
fits perfectly with this author's novel concept of *Potential$^\infty$ Point*.
Indeed by declaring that man is created "in our image" the Torah indicates that humankind will "become what it is." Embryonic Divine will become the *Potential$^\infty$ Point*.

The dynamic which MORPHED from "OUT–OF–TIME" into TIME, from the POSSIBILITY mode to the EQUATION mode,[6] from the EQUATION MODE to the METAPHYSICAL mode to the REALITY mode as we know it today[7, 8, 9]

We (and we are all Q4P) are ONE, inter–connected Supra–Entity+

cont'd

NOTES by KHALIL

[6] Equation mode: The equation mode is a world well known in science: a world of positives and negatives. Our lives exist on this continuum and our decisions determine our position. Neutrality is elusive, and human action will generally influence the direction in which we move.

[7] Modes (A): The author uses these four modes as an explanatory vehicle. There have been a spectrum of 'modes' in the 'run–up' to today's reality.

[8] Modes (B): Modes are not replaced by subsequent modes. All exist today. One mode will simply overlay the preceding one, as the universe is made more textured and nuanced. The individual whose perception allows him to penetrate that which is immediately apparent on the surface, will discern inter–related universal constructs unifying all. The penetrating mind will thus find some level of universality behind the world's complexity.

[9] Modes (C): Under Birnbaum's schema, the divine achieves "full flower" at the infinite 'end' of the process – as opposed to the 'beginning' of the process. Again, Humanity is not separate from the Divine, but rather, it is intertwined with the Divine, in its work–in–progress capacity as ever–ascending embryonic Divine.

GOD AND GOOD

– an infinite entity transcending time, space
and the cosmos

We are all essentially ONE

"We break beyond our own limitations and connect
in unity with God..."

– Rabbi Noah Weinberg
"Five Levels"
AISH.com 10/06/06

Clearly, we are closest to our nuclear family, our
children and Significant Others, and not particularly
close to the Hamas terrorist in Gaza... and even a
touch further from a random amoeba.

...but, yes, we are all integrally interconnected
in one Whole

We are AUTONOMOUS, but we are also simultaneously
a COLLECTIVE

(No, I don't know how the voting goes)

Not only are we all, indeed, connected;
we are, on some level, at least intermittently
COMMUNICATIVE,[10,11] as well

We are all connected, not just on the *molecular*
level, not just on the *atomic* level, and not just on
the *biological* level, but, as well, somehow on the
consciousness level.

We individually and cumulatively aim and advance
towards an "Infinite Divine Extraordinariation."

NOTES by KHALIL

[10] Communicative (A): In *Orot Teshuva*, Rav Kook writes that with
sin man experienced detachment from fellow creatures. Man
becomes isolated and alone until he repents. Rav Kook reasonably
points to a familiar emotional response – the 'outsiderness'
associated with sin or failure. With regard to this he writes: "It is
impossible to express this vastly profound concept." The author's
principle that all creation is communicative, provides insight into
how such feelings arise.

[11] Communicative (B): Considering Rav Kook's spiritual
observation in light of the author's framework, it can be concluded
that when an individual sins – failing to advance towards his
potential – the collective cosmos objects to this action, and the
individual senses this dissatisfaction. In the fourth chapter of his
Orot Teshuva Rav Kook writes: "The individual and the collective
soul, the world soul, the soul of all realms of being cries out like
a fierce lioness in anguish for total perfection, for an ideal form of
existence, and we feel the pain, and it purges us... And the soul
grows toward perfection." Thus, Rav Kook (a man of astonishing
spiritual sensitivity) detected a sort of global inter–communication
that was driving man towards his potential and spiritual perfection.
[Birnbaum's themes dovetail with Kook's from the very beginning
of the Summa Metaphysica series.]

GOD AND GOOD

It is this Infinite Potential Perfection which pulls all
forwards (and, indeed, into existence itself) ...just as
it is this inexorable Drive for Potential which drives
the 'advance,' because Q4P is SPIRAL with elements
of circularity ...and therefore both "pulling" as well as
"pushing" simultaneously.

And when we do have something to say to our
'cousins' concerning potentially optimizing this
'advance,' however infinitely removed these 'cousins'
are, we will, indeed communicate on some level, for,
we are all "Forward Scouts" in the vast cosmic army of
POTENTIAL...

probing for potential ADVANCE

probing for an OPENING

probing for a Line–of–Attack

but we are also each individually partner-Generals
in this Collective / Array–on–the–March
cumulatively assessing and analyzing any genetic
mutation which presents itself...one infinite organic
system of pure and "unbridled potentiality" arching
through – and encompassing all – Time and Space and
Physical and Non–physicality... stretching throughout
TIME and pre–TIME...

We are ONE timeless organic entity... as discomforting
as that might seem, and we are inexorable in
our collaborative quest for INFINITE DIVINE
EXTRAORDINARIATION:

infinite consciousness, infinite actualization, infinite
beauty, infinite spirituality, infinite creativity and infinite
emotional, sensual and other fulfillment... a relentless
cosmic Conquistador

forever on–the–march

seeking – and indeed often fashioning – the next
advance

manipulating and fashioning and crafting

genes, organisms, and indeed even equations

The Infinite Divine Extraordinariation: this Infinite multi–
faceted GOAL is the Divine perfection we seek;

but simultaneously we all ARE embryonic Divine
and this Infinite Perfection Divine is a GOAL, a
hypothetical end–point, to be approached,
but never actually reached...

Thus, while we are "embryonic Divine[12]" we will always inevitably still be embryonic Divine, just at a "later-stage embryonic"... for the Infinite Divine Extraordinariation is a GOAL... like Infinity... to be approached, but never quite, quite realized.

We are all, cumulatively, therefore, eternally "embryonic Divine"

...seeking inexorably to become more fully "Divine"

Holy Crusaders, for sure

enroute to Jerusalem

end / beginning

[12] Embryonic Divine: The embryo is representative of the period, subsequent to conception, of rapid physical development. Humankind is in a comparable period of phenomenal growth in which we evolve tools – as the embryo would develop organs – that potentiate our ultimate ascent.

EPSILON: Notes & Observations

Note:

If there is a mutation or natural selection which Quest for Potential$^\infty$ assesses will optimize further the course towards this "Divine," we re–orient, and 'morph' the entire species in that direction; Else, if perceived to offer no particular advantage, it is Thank You, but No Thank You. Evolution is driven primarily by the overarching imperative of Potential. Ditto for natural selection.

Q4P$^\infty$ as related to Evolution/Natural Selection is hypothesized here to have at least six core inter-related key levels:

I list them in ascending levels, with the foundation level listed first:

      initial viability potential

      survivability potential

      diversity potential

holistic potential (to enhance the potential of the greater environment of organisms)

potential to potentially 'father' more advanced potentials
    (medium-long term)

extraordinariation potential
    (long term)

So, the process may be more profound than the raw data may reveal.

Regarding those who argued for the "Intelligent Design" theory and those who argued for "Evolution," both were partially correct. However, remember, it was the Evolutionists who attempted (pretty successfully) to thoroughly invalidate the champions of ID (Intelligent Design) – not the other way around.

But the author of Intelligent Design is, ultimately, actually, ourselves, the transcendent Embryonic Infinite Divine Extraordinariation.

> "When we study the world, it shows us that it is entirely the plan of a Designer, the work of a single Creator..." *Rabbi Bachya ibn Pakuda, Chovot Ha-Levavot, Shaar* (c.1161-80)

PUSH from the *Genesis* point, forward.

PULL from the Infinity–point, backwards.

And, while evolution does occur, and is employed by Quest for Potential$^\infty$ when advantageous, it is but a subcomponent of the grander saga.

So, on some dramatic level, the Potential Divine-reality actually is 're-inventing' itself…over-and-over the span of many billions of eons of the cosmic drama.

Traversing from the metaphysical…presumably then through a 'bridge state' of some sort…traversing onward into reality (at the *Potential$^\infty$ Point**) and then onto ever-higher and higher ultimate Infinite Divine Extraordinariation…

"This then is the meaning of the expression *from the eternity to eternity you are God* (Psalm 90), literally 'from world to world,' for the divine spark enters into world after world, in ever-ascending order of perfection." *Rabbi Israel Lipschitz, Drush Or Ha-Chayim* (c.1820)

---

* *Big Bang* point…*Genesis* point…*Bereshith* point

ZETA: "Principia Metaphysica"

SUMMA METAPHYSICA is articulated via two
formulations – and their incorporated EIGHTEEN
groups of propositions
(9 + 9 respectively).

* * * Summa Metaphysica * * *

an overarching and unified metaphysics

UNIFIED FORMULATION	**PRINCIPIA METAPHYSICA**
[in Book #1]	[in Book #2]
9 propositions	9 propositions
proposition groups: (100–900)	proposition groups: (1100–1900)
Philosophical/Metaphysical	Metaphysical

The UNIFIED FORMULATION in Book #1:

(see "Reprint of Unified Formulation" in Book #2)

with nine Proposition Groups numbered 100-900:

and PRINCIPIA METAPHYSICA to be presented here
– with nine Proposition Groups numbered 1100–1900

So, in this sub-section (Zeta), I present PRINCIPIA
METAPHYSICA – the second group of PROPOSITIONS
of the overarching metaphysical construct – SUMMA
METAPHYSICA.

*

So, the Overview would be as follows:

In Book #1 (*God and Evil*),
the Outline Summary of the (first) nine GROUPS OF
PROPOSITIONS
– The UNIFIED FORMULATION: Proposition Groups
100–900
is introduced in section 99.00. One would most easily
categorize this first batch
as-a-whole as: *Philosophical / Metaphysical*
propositions.

In Book #2 (*God and Good*) here,
the Outline Summary of the next nine GROUPS OF
PROPOSITIONS
– PRINCIPIA METAPHYSICA: Proposition Groups
1100–1900
are summarized here in ZETA. One would most easily
categorize this second batch
as-a-whole as: *Metaphysical propositions*.

*

In the first book, the fleshed-out version of The Unified Formulation spans the entire PART TWO of the book.

In this second book, the fleshed-out version of PRINCIPIA METAPHYSICA spans the entire PART I of the book – The Cosmic Womb of Potential. Meaning, in this second book, the fleshed-out version wraps around the SUMMARY section ZETA (here).

Note that the two Cosmic Tool Kit sections (Shelf #1 and Shelf #2) – both in this Part I: Cosmic Womb part – deliberately – one BEFORE Principia Metaphysica – and one AFTER – are integral and key sub-axioms to Principia Metaphysica.

The orientations of The Unified Formulation v. Principia Metaphysica are slightly different – but obviously dovetail and have overlap.

The two formulations should 'stitch together' seamlessly.

(You will note that Group 1000 seems to be missing; The reason is that we employed the 1000 number for the APPENDICES in Book #1 [in 1988], following upon-the-heels of the Unified Formulation, for ease-of-reference for our readers. In retrospect, the APPENDICES should not have been assigned the 1000 number.)

*

Now, as we know, my key concept is Quest for Potential$^\infty$ [to the infinite power]. But the work also posits that polarities and inverses drive the cosmic order.

Furthermore, Quest for Potential$^\infty$ alone may be "curiouser" than it appears at first look. Indeed, I would conjecture that, going-forward, beyond the scope of this two-volume series, and beyond the 'tenure' of this author, it will prove ever richer-and-richer.

In dealing with Quest for Potential$^\infty$, we are dealing with a dynamic of transcendent and *approaching-Infinite* power.

*

Now, there are powerful complementary sub-dynamics which ensemble constitute Quest for Potential$^\infty$

As articulated clearly in this Book #2, I posit that REALITY parallels METAPHYSICAL REALMS. I propose that one can extrapolate missing components in metaphysics from dynamics in reality – and vice versa. This powerful concept may ultimately morph the field of metaphysics into a highly stylized and more formal field.

In any event, at the risk of 'shocking the innocent', (and with precedent in both Kabbalah and Eastern religions) I do believe that very direct 1:1 parallels exist between 'intimacy' and the primal drives of the cosmos.

In Principia Metaphysica espoused here, I articulate how TWO complementary sub-dynamics (of Quest for Potential$^\infty$): Quest-for-ADVANCEMENT/fulfillment – with a strong neo-masculine AGGRESSIVE component,

– and

Quest-for-FULFILLMENT/advancement – with a strong neo-female EMOTIONAL component,

– are interlocked in an intricate double-helix cosmic dance.....and generate "creation of the cosmos" ...and continue their nuanced double-helix *cosmic Tango* propelling the dynamic cosmos onward and upwards

– and propelled forward and outwards

*

SUMMA METAPHYSICA
– via the inter-related
Unified Formulation (presented in Book # 1)
and
Principia Metaphysica (to be presented at this point)
'covers the key bases'

– and offers an integrated and overarching unified
metaphysics.

We now present Principia Metaphysica –

Principia Metaphysica Outline:

1100 Series

Possibility.
(by definition)

Then,

Embryonic Quest for a POTENTIAL

1200 Series

1225

"Quest for Quest for INFINITE DIVINE
EXTRAORDINARIATION"
emerges as the primary engine of the cosmos

1250

The principles of the hard and soft sciences
sought their full potentials of ACTUALIZATION,
FULL EXPRESSION, LIFE, LOVE, CONSCIOUSNESS
and ultimately, of INFINITY

1300 Series

"Quest for INFINITE DIVINE EXTRAORDINARIATION"
emerges as the evolved overarching drive
of the cosmos

1400 Series

1405

The Infinite Divine Extraordinariation...
at the end-of-the-rainbow – as first, IGNITION,
and then, as GOAL

1410

Quest for Potential$^\infty$ pervades the cosmos

The cosmos IS integrated into Quest for Potential$^\infty$;

1414

This **core** cosmic dynamic is ETERNAL, ENDURING
and TRANSCENDING

1416

Q4P$^\infty$ feeds upon Itself

1417

It unites – and, indeed, is comprised of – all life:
past, present and future

1418

At the vanguard, possibly, is a Godhead

1419

Our individual, extraordinary core Potential
flows within this Eternal and Infinite stream

1420

The Infinite Divine Extraordinariation...
at the end-of-the-rainbow – as first, IGNITION, and
then,
as GOAL – exerted PULL, while full-spectrum
Quest for Potential$^\infty$ exerts DRIVE – and PUSH
(note parallel to CHILDBIRTH)

1500 Series

1505

Quest for Potential$^\infty$ is, in turn,
composed of two Supra–Dynamics:
Quest-for-ADVANCEMENT/fulfillment and
Quest-for-FULFILLMENT/advancement

1507

These Supra-Dynamics are intertwined with each other
in an Eternal cosmic (double-helix) dance,
and in-tandem cascadingly advance,
playing-out their potential Infinitude

1510

The complementary Supra–Dynamics –
are juxtaposed against each other

in a dynamic and eternal hi-tension
cosmic "tango"

1515

Juxtaposed centrifugal[1] – centripetal[2] forces
perpetually replenishing and stimulating each other...
producing, in turn,
Quest for Additional Possibilities

1520

The panoply of ACTION & ADVANCE
is complemented by the complementary spectrum of
EMOTION & FULFILLMENT & CONSCIOUSNESS

1530

Quest for ADVANCEMENT probes outward
Quest for FULFILLMENT vortexes inward

NOTES by KHALIL

---

[1] Centrifugal: The personal quest for potential$^\infty$ is centrifugal in that it releases energy outwardly. Energy is projected into the cosmic collective and all existence is energized and thus propelled forward.

[2] Centripetal: The personal quest for fulfillment is centripetal in that it releases energy inwardly. Quest for fulfillment relates to constant personal needs and desires. It thus provides an ongoing reflective motivation that is readily translated into the grander quest for potential$^\infty$.

1540

Quest for Potential∞
finds its ultimate CATALYST – and MOTIVATOR…
in its contending sub-strands
Quest-for-ADVANCEMENT and
Quest-for-FULFILLMENT

1550

Quest-for-ADVANCEMENT
and Quest-for-FULFILLMENT
are drawn inexorably towards each other,
…"as the moth to the flame"
– while they simultaneously seek to play-out their
autonomous potential

1560

Through an Asian prism,

Quest-for-ADVANCEMENT is *Yang*
Quest-for-FULFILLMENT is *Ying*

balancing out the cosmos

complementary
opposite
countervailing
~opposing, but mutually enriching

*

Through a Jewish prism,

"ezer k'negdo"
(Genesis / Bereshith 2:18)

~complementary, juxtaposed
and counterbalanced sexes

1570

Through a KABBALISTIC prism,

Quest-for-ADVANCEMENT/fulfillment
is majority MASCULINE energy,
minority FEMININE energy

Quest-for-FULFILLMENT/advancement
is majority FEMININE energy,
minority MASCULINE energy

Both are inextricably intertwined,
inextricably interchanging

Cosmic lovers
in an eternal dynamic tension

1580

The dynamic tension between
Quest-for-ADVANCEMENT and Quest-for-
FULFILLMENT
can be presumed to have escalated
for infinite eons pre–reality
to that famous explosive point
which actualized the COSMOS

1590

The reality–void hitherto had not found
either ACTUALIZATION or a mode of expression of
FULFILLMENT, EMOTION, CONSCIOUSNESS

1600 Series

1610

"The void could not 'take it' anymore"
–Solomon Birnbaum 2004

1615

"Voids abhor voids"
–D. Birnbaum

1620

The reality–void sought
EMOTIONAL RELEASE and REALIZATION,
SPIRITUAL FULFILLMENT,
INTELLECTUAL ATTAINMENT,
HIGHER LEVEL (actually INFINITE) CONSCIOUSNESS,
PURE GOOD-ness / GIVING-ness,
and full–spectrum ACTUALIZATION

1640

at "Creation,"

NOTHING

separates (MITOSIS of "0") into
(steadily expanding)

"actualized POTENTIAL"
and its complement,
(a steadily diminishing)
"VOID"

1645

POTENTIAL energy
>
KINETIC energy

1650

"actualized POTENTIAL"
(an ever–expanding–cosmos...
expanding on multiple levels)
increasingly gobbles–up
physical and emotional
and intellectual and spiritual, etc.
TURF
formerly occupied by VOID

<u>1700 Series</u>

1725

At the end–of–the–rainbow,
Infinite Divine Extraordinariation
(perhaps most importantly - the infinitude of
Consciousness and Givingness)

[this is the spiritual SINGULARITY]

retroactively ignites the
Emptiness
["*tohu va-vohu*"]
at the Creation-point

1750

ONLY infinite and unbounded POTENTIAL
as a goal, as a theoretical 'end–point,'
could and would have the power to ignite a Cosmos

<u>1800 Series</u>

1825

and what actualizes the putative Divine?

The DIVINE is–in–the–process of infinite
SELF–EVOLVEMENT
ongoing for billions of eons
...traversing from metaphysical realms
to ever–fuller and richer
PHYSICAL ACTUALIZATION
...as it courses towards
the "very–end–of–the–rainbow"

*

almost 'by definition' POTENTIAL always existed

*

It is merely potential, possibility

initially

*

By definition, It (potential possibility) is the ONLY
dynamic which can possibly be eternal.

*

We are all part of the Embryonic Divine

"Science cannot solve the ultimate mystery of nature. And that is because, in the last analysis, we ourselves are part of nature and therefore part of the mystery that we are trying to solve." *Max Planck* (c.1932)

1835

Thus, if Possibility/Potential is infinite,
and Possibility/Potential is the core of the Divine,
the Divine is Infinite +

1850

Potential/Possibility may have more facets and
dimensions to it
– Divine or otherwise – than we were alerted to in
contemporary culture,
but by definition only potential/possibility is eternal.

1900 Series

The DIVINE – as opposed to the Embryonic Divine –
is simultaneously EVERYTHING + A GOAL
to be approached in ever–greater–and–greater
fullness and richness and consciousness

* * *

end of Principia Metaphysica

* * * * * * * * *

[Don't get hyper over the male-female orientations. As in
down-to-earth reality, both 'components' certainly have all the
elements of potential, including Quest for Advancement and
Quest for Fulfillment. It is a question of the slightest degree of
tilt in internal general orientation and priorities.]

*

Now, *sof kol sof*, (after all-is-said-and-done) as
KOHELETH (*l'havdil**) might have said, once the core
dynamic – Quest for Potential$^\infty$ – is discerned/

conceptualized – as it has been over the span of
Book #1 – Book #2 – as

being a Singularity
being Infinite
Questing after Its Own Potential
being 'at the core of the Divine'
being infinitely ITERATIVE & RECURSIVE
being eternal – initially at least in metaphysical realms
being 'REFLEXIVE,' and 'RETROACTIVE,'
   i.e. infinite potentiality ' down-the-road' ignites
   Creation retroactively**
being simultaneously 'the embryonic Divine' –
   while simultaneously being 'infinite'
encompassing the eternal cumulative consciousness
   and LifeForce, as well

then,

all the other propositions inevitably flow from this one
AXIOM.

(deep breath)

---

 * the term *l'havdil* is a rabbinic expression generally meaning –
   that the two (works) are not truly on the same spiritual level
** this is the core thread of the core idea]

ETA: Some reflections...insights

Summa Metaphysica's "String Theory"[1, 2, 3]

The Infinite Divine Extraordinariation at the end-of-the-rainbow...

draws a string from the precursor milieu to Creation... through Creation (at the dawn of time)... through the eons...to Itself – showing the line of optimal Potential

* * *

SECULARISTS can call this proposed dynamic –

Infinite Consciousness and Givingness and Will and LifeForce

(no intervention; no Godhead)

RELIGIOUS traditionalists can call Infinite Divine Extraordinariation, the God of Abraham

KABBALISTS can very readily embrace this proposal

HASIDIC purists can savor the Bal Shem Tov's prescience

SPIRITUALISTS can ride somewhere in the middle

BUDDHISTS can call this Divine...
Ultimate Perfection and Harmony

PHYSICISTS can put down their electron microscopes
for a few minutes...and savor the non-quantifiable
wonders of the cosmic order

– because, to "solve" the elusive missing pieces of
physics, physicists must take the leap into metaphysics
(meaning, this particular work, boys)

NOTES by KHALIL

---

[1] Summa Metaphysica's "String Theory": With this the author
makes clear that cosmic evolution is not defined solely by a start–
point and an end–point. There is something connecting these
points, which is with us today – a "road" [string] connecting origin
to destination.

[2] Summa Metaphysica's "String Theory"– and the Torah: The Torah
is the thread that directs humankind towards Divine Perfection,
providing continual guidance. This effect is powerful enough to
drive all of creation, yet subtle enough to only be detected by the
most spiritually perceptive souls. As he approached his final hours,
Jacob – whose life was particularly difficult and arduous, would
bless Joseph in the name of God "who was my shepherd from my
inception until this day" (Genesis 48:15).

[3] Summa Metaphysica's "String Theory"– and Biology: One of
the presuppositions of Darwinism is that evolution cannot be
teleological (i.e., evolution cannot plan for the future; it can only
favor traits that support survival in the current environment). Thus
a species can only acquire traits that suit its environment at the
specific time. The author's string theory model, in contradistinction
to Darwin's model, and in one of Birnbaum's crucial pivots, asserts
that evolution is, indeed, most definitely goal-directed, as well.

DARWINISTS can be reconciled that they were partially correct...as evolution is clearly a part of the process.

The "INTELLIGENT DESIGN" camp can readily adopt this (Summa Metaphysica) thesis as core doctrine. It has the not inconsiderable advantage of being more precisely 'on-the-money' and fully compatible with the general thrust of their approach, although the *avant garde* 'identity' of the Intelligent Designer may take some time getting-used-to.

All roads, in any event, will inevitably, in any event, lead to this ineffable Infinitude.

"When all is said and done, what we each seek is to reach out of this finite world and connect with the Infinite. To become one with God."

– Rabbi Noah Weinberg
"Five Levels"
AISH.com 10/6/06

The ramifications are abundant...We are all one[4]

We are all united

We are all very integral parts of this
cosmic symphonic projectory

* * *

The one is inextricably part of the Whole
The Whole is ever-evolving embryonic Divine

* * *

Thus, there is a sort-of triple-paradox at-play:

On the one hand we are AUTONOMOUS –
and wish to be AUTONOMOUS.

cont'd

NOTES by KHALIL

---

[4] "We are one": Quest for Fulfillment is a force originating from the individual that is directed right back at the individual's CORE – a force directed back towards its center (centripetal). quest for potential$^\infty$ as a quest also originating from the individual but pushing infinitely outwards, unleashing its energy into a cosmic collective that energizes time and space – making it more of an outward driving (or centrifugal) force.

Without Quest for Fulfillment constantly re–energizing the individual, quest for potential$^\infty$ might be unsustainable. And without Quest for Potential$^\infty$ there would be insufficient collective energy to ignite the cosmos and drive forward and onward, and thereby create the framework in which quest for fulfillment can thrive as well.

On the second hand, we want to become ONE
with the Divine.

On the third hand, we already are INTEGRAL
to the Divine.

* * *

All three dynamics would seem to be operating
in-tandem.

Three cardinal tenets of Advanced Metaphysics are
in perpetual tension*.

Seque'-ing from one modality to another
energizes the very core of our being – and presses
the forward wave of the cosmos, ever-forward still...

* * *

Ascents in human consciousness are a key goal.
Ascents in human goodness and givingness, probably
are, as well

HUMANITY's evolvement was to be the route to the
realization to these primal cosmic thrusts. Through
HUMANS, Q4P potentially has its OPTIMAL route

---

* the Religious add yet a fourth – SUBLIMATING oneself to the divine

Through HUMANS, Q4F potentially (and the gamut of EMOTION) plays out MAXIMALLY

It is not that HUMANS happen to have evolved INTELLECTUALLY and in CONSIOUSNESS; Rather that potential/future evolvement is one of their key *raisons d'etre*[5, 6]

cont'd

NOTES by KHALIL

[5] *Raisons d'etre* (A): Philosophers from Aristotle to Descartes have asserted the centrality of human intellect. By designating intellectual development as the essence of humanity, the path, – if not the destination – was made clear. This concept augmented human potential markedly by making humankind aware that its loftiest pursuit is the quest for elevated consciousness, yet the ultimate benefit of this journey had remained undefined until now.

[6] *Raisons d'etre* (B): In *Nicomachean Ethics*, Aristotle concludes that it is the "role" of the human to cultivate that faculty which is uniquely human, namely the intellect. He does not, however, explain how or why this would be beneficial either for the individual or more generally. Others (including Maimonides) have reached the same conclusion about the centrality of the intellect but have struggled (or not attempted) to elucidate its personal or global benefits. The author's conclusions are apparently the first to do so in the context of universal metaphysical principles. Others have neglected to put the refinement of human intellect into a framework, arguing that it is an ends unto itself. Here the author finally puts this lauded act into a structured metaphor.

It is not that EMOTION happens to be the byproduct of human interaction; Rather, part of the *raison d'etre* of humans' ever-ascending complexity and sophistication, albeit continuing primitive brutality, is to develop and play out the panoply of EMOTION in ever-increasing range and nuance.

"Human aggressiveness" plays into both key themes:

The cosmos itself is hyper-aggressive; Only a hyper-aggressive dynamic could have burst forth into REALITY from the VOID. As hypothesized, human dynamics parallel cosmic dynamics; In addition, aggressiveness is a key to reaching various potentialities.

The by-products of aggressiveness… even the very severe 'bad' ones, e.g. victimization, murder, destruction, enslavement, torture, betrayal, humiliation… play out the dark-side gamut of emotion. This "dark side" gamut of emotion is presumably symmetric to the "light side" gamut (e.g. joy, happiness, exhilaration, love, etc.). It is conjectured here that one could not have the "light side" of the gamut, without its symmetric "dark side".

A diabolical spin on the above would conjecture that the cosmos indeed wanted to play-out BOTH sides of the emotional spectrum.

I would hope that such is not the case.

THETA: The two key (spiraling) SUPRA-DYNAMICS

The two key sub-components of Quest for Potential$^\infty$:

Note that both
Quest-for-ADVANCEMENT/fulfillment
and
Quest-for-FULFILLMENT/advancement
are *sui generis*,
each thoroughly unique in its own way

Both are SUPRA-Dynamics

...in a plane – and class – by themselves

Interlinked in a cosmic double-helix;

rocketing-forward *ensemble* to Infinity

pulsating with infinite energy and dynamism and
internal tension

independent and inter-dependent alternatingly

feeding-off of each other's Infinitude and
un-quenchable cosmic appetites

locked in eternal embrace and stylized pulsating dance

the ultimate Cosmic Tango (as noted prior)

– seeking consummate POTENTIAL

*

BOTH are infinitely recursive tracking forward to the
end of time… and indeed, maybe looping around
infinity right back through Creation… and then back
upon itself

Quest-for-Advancement is infinitely OUTWARD-bound

Quest-for-Fulfillment, is infinitely CORE–bound
all–embracing…embracing all the dynamism and
emotion of the cosmos and attempting deep, deep
multi–leveled fulfillment.

On a human level, which we POSIT parallels the
cosmic dynamic, Quest-for-Fulfillment simultaneously
EMBRACES emotion / spirituality / creativity /
relationships / sensuality / hopes & dreams / among
other components, while buffering DRIVE and
AGGRESSION.

*

GOD AND GOOD

The implications of all-of-the-above are, of course, stunning.

*

As but one example, albeit a powerful one – the wondrous and bountiful beauties and variety of the planet, and, indeed, of the cosmos, serve, as well, both as potential fulfillment for the senses and as potential objects, in one area or another, for advancement.

Thus I started out the Treatise in Book #1 with ONE PRIMARY dynamic,

On closer examination, this one dynamic is comprised of first, two primary interwoven spiraling threads, (themselves each comprised of.....)

which, as a shorthand, for the various respective 'packages' of potentiality they embrace, we're calling, respectively –

Quest-for-ADVANCEMENT

and

Quest-for-FULFILLMENT

co-equal, but with 2 different tilts

Independent, but co-dependent simultaneously.
Both equally extraordinary.

*

Quest-for-ADVANCEMENT was originally "just"
metaphysical proto-MALE

Quest-for-FULFILLMENT was originally "just"
metaphysical proto-FEMALE

*

Over the eons, a trajectory from the metaphysical
realm morphs....

They ultimately have a physical embodiment in our
cosmos as
MALE v. FEMALE
- as they seek a modality (autonomous but paired)
to reach for ULTIMATE REALIZATION of POTENTIAL (the
"mother ship")

and the realization of the extraordinary
('Extraordinariation' – to be amplified upon below)

In our cosmos, in our dimension,

Quest-for-ADVANCEMENT/fulfillment morphs to
(and embodied by) Male

Quest-for-FULFILLMENT/advancement morphs to
(and embodied by) Female

GOD AND GOOD

"Va-yomer Elokim: 'Na-ase adam b'tzalmeinu, k'dmusaynu...

...Zachar u-Nekeyvah barah otam"

[*Bereshith* 1:26-28]

"And Elokim said: 'Let us make Man in Our image, as Our likeness'

...Male and Female, He created them"

[Genesis 1:26-28]

So, respectfully, while our proposal may be revolutionary,

it does happen to fit elegantly with the Biblical text -

and certainly perfectly with Rashi's Commentary:

i.e., Rashi says to read the text as:

"God says to his ANGELS
(read: Metaphysical Potentials – author):
'Let Us make Man in Our Image'"

*

So, indeed, one can make the case that Rashi's Commentary actually IS our formulation.

(and it may be somewhat challenging to excommunicate Rashi)

*

As with the Exodus prooftext: *"Eheyeh Asher Eheyeh"*
"I WILL BE THAT WHICH I WILL BE"
for the core proposal of
God as the God of Potential, the prooftext here is, as
well, eerily on-the-mark.
Once you discern it, it sort of 'jumps-out-at-you'.

*

Now, the dominant potentiality thread in MALE may be
(51 % Quest-for-Advancement; 49% Quest-for-
Fulfillment – as overarching, but certainly not exclusive,
dynamics)

and

the dominant potentiality thread in FEMALE may be the
obverse side of coin
(51% Quest-for-FULFILLMENT; 49% Quest-for-
ADVANCEMENT – as overarching, but certainly not
exclusive, dynamics)

– but that tiny percentage swing in orientation
somewhere along the trajectory is what ultimately
makes all-the-difference
(This one last sentence should keep psychologists
busy for a 1,000 years or so...)

*

But why enter this terrain at all?
Why not just let matters rest with the original
Quest for Potential∞?

Why enter this MALE-FEMALE zone, which, like
a mythical siren, always seems to pull sundry
metaphysics over-the-millennia out into some sort of
philosophical 'la-la land'?

We only go here because we are inexorably led here by
the logical imperatives of our schema.

Quest for Potential∞ cannot forever stand alone as a
UNITARY DYNAMIC – while "everything else under-the-
sun" has polarities and dualities.

Aside from that, male-female, across the stratum of
species, pervades our planet.

Beyond that, once we operate under the self-articulated
premise that there are direct parallels between
METAPHYSICAL realms and REALITY realms, and
once we see a tantalizing parallel, we are motivated
to articulate it.

However, overriding all-of-the-above is the fascinating
proposition that GENDERS are the embodiment of
>> morphed-METAPHYSICAL POTENTIALS <<
- or, as RASHI might say, the embodiment of
>> morphed ANGELS <<

The implications – stretching eternally in both directions in time – give one pause for awe.

It turns out that possibly the most daring components of our multi-layered hypothesis, i.e. the core proposition of Potential with the follow-through hypothesis of its two key sub-Potentials – are the components most directly tethered in the Torah.

Tethering the most daring parts, on some level anchors the entire metaphysics.

IOTA: Reprise to The Cosmic Womb of Potential

"Eheyeh Asher Eheyeh"

"I WILL BE THAT WHICH I WILL BE[1]"
calls the voice from the Burning Bush[2]

THE NAME OF GOD
Is Potential – and retroactive – and recursive

NOTES by KHALIL

[1] I WILL BE: God is only asked directly to identify Himself by name one time in the Tanach. And He answers twice. In Exodus 3:14 God identifies Himself as both "I will be that which I will be" and then, in the same verse, more concisely as "I will be." The importance of this revelation is clear from the Biblical context, but what does it mean?

[2] Burning Bush: The context of the dialogue between *Hashem* [God] and Moses is almost as important as the dialogue itself. Moses poses his question to God on behalf of the Jewish slaves (he will ask to know God for his own sake while atop Mt. Sinai, Exodus 33:13). According to the Midrash, the Jews at this point were at a historically low spiritual level. And liberation is imminent. It is therefore clear that the potential of the Jews (a spiritually impoverished [deprived] people on the verge of redemption) at this moment was maximal, and it is not a coincidence that God identifies Himself to the Jewish slaves via Moses at this moment, as "I–will–be."

I AM: QUEST FOR INFINITUDE

I AM: QUEST FOR ALL-ETERNITY

I AM: QUEST FOR FULFILLMENT

I AM: QUEST FOR POTENTIAL$^{\infty}$

* * *

Nature abhors a vacuum
  – axiom from physics (~*noted prior*)

Q4F sets up a proto-vacuum[3] in the reality-void

And, reality-voids abhor a vacuum

NOTES by KHALIL

[3] Proto–vacuum: Just as the individual seeks elevation in the framework of Quest for Fulfillment, so does the cosmos. It was therefore the initial absence of fulfillment sensed by the pre–cosmos that was so inherently, viscerally abhorrent – just as an absence of love, for example, is abhorrent to an individual. The result was a resolute "escape–release" in the form of creation, a' la Solomon Birnbaum's formulation, noted in the text, that "the void could not 'take it' anymore."

"V'r'uach Adoshem mirachefet[4] al p'nei ha–maim"
"And the Spirit of God Flows over the Face of the Waters"
    – Genesis 1:2

"Flowing from the Essence of the Divine, the infinite holy potential of the Divine demanded more expression. Among these elements were the potentials for creation of the universe, and within the latter, the potentials for man to quest for his spiritual potential, as well as others, including mercy, love, truth, justice, beauty and harmony..."

    From the book *God and Evil*
    PART TWO, Section 100.02

Life

Life was necessary
Because only through life could the gamut of emotions find expression
And only through life could Quest for Potential$^\infty$ optimize its nascent potentialities

---

NOTES by KHALIL

---

[4] Mirachefet: This term implies unsettled motion. This manifestation of God was explicitly restless, as it were. Something was unbearable, something needed to happen.

KAPPA: The building blocks of the cosmos

QUEST FOR POTENTIAL$^\infty$
(the core dynamic)

CUMULATIVE CONSCIOUSNESS & WILL
(the godhead of the cosmic dynamic)

INFINITE RECURSIVENESS
(from the tool kit of the cosmic dynamic)

My dear friends,
We are all integral parts of an ever–unfolding cosmic dynamic of almost indescribable extraordinariness.

We are, each of us, microcosm cosmos

Paralleling in our own lives and aspirations, cosmic aspirations

Quest for Potential$^\infty$ drives the cosmos, drives humanity and humans, and, is, indeed, our eternal essence

For, humans, are, indeed,
Not so human after all

GOD AND GOOD

It is far from clear how many levels there are to
Quest for Potential∞
For, indeed, our cosmos, may be part of a
still–larger entity,
Indeed, and that one, part of a still larger one

Even, *ad infinitum*
All questing for – and driven by – that one inexorable
(proposed) dynamic

*

Man quests for the infinite – and, indeed for God
And it must be presumed that the cosmos itself quests
for the same

for the infinite – and for God

It so happens that the entire cosmos happens to be
embryonic Divine,

And that schematically, it is the embryonic Infinite
Divine Extraordinariation, which seeks after its
own potential

*

Eheyeh

I motivate the baby trying to walk
I motivate the 10 year–old boy shooting hoops
I motivate the couple falling–in–love
And I motivate the wage–earner trying to get ahead
But my scope is far, far vaster than any of the above

LAMBDA: A fresh look at some of our concepts

1:1 CORRESPONDENCE

There is a 1:1 correspondence between what is true on an individual human level, and what is true on a cosmic level.

Man seeks life.
The cosmos seeks life.

Man seeks his potential.
The cosmos seeks its potentiality.

Man seeks ascendance in knowledge.
The cosmos seeks ascendance in consciousness.

Man seeks immortality.
The cosmos seeks immortality.

Man seeks beauty.
The cosmos seeks beauty.

Man seeks love.
The cosmos seeks love.

Man seeks fulfillment.
The cosmos seeks fulfillment.

Man seeks full actualization.
The cosmos seeks full actualization.

Man seeks fulfilling relationship(s)
The cosmos seeks fulfilling relationship(s)

Man seeks The Infinite.
The cosmos seeks The Infinite[1].

NOTES by KHALIL

[1] The Infinite and the Cosmos: In passages such as this one it is clear
that the author rejects Aristotle's concept of "eternalism", a model
in which the cosmos is eternal and The Infinite is an actor within the
cosmos. This same rejection of eternalism was defended in the *Guide
of the Perplexed*, in Maimonides' key divergence from Aristotelian
principles. The rejection of eternalism remains a key metaphysical
distinction between traditional Jewish thought and classical Aristotelian
thought. The author basically dismisses classic Aristotelian thought as
fatally linear and simplistic.

Spiral

Western philosophy is essentially linear.
"A" created "B" and then "B" created "C."
Plato: God took Primal Matter and created the Earth, etc.
Biblical literal: God created heaven and earth.
Then, God took a rib of Adam and created Eve.
Oriental philosophy is essentially circular,
Or Ying/Yang complementary within a circularity.

Our own Q4P philosophy is essentially spiral.
Mimicking somewhat the shape of galaxies… or,
interestingly enough, the shape of DNA double–helix,
the blueprints for "life."
It is a Reverse Vortex.
With Infinitude emerging from the Void.

Einstein astutely postulated an Atomic Bomb
encapsulated within an atom.

Split the atom – and unleash atomic power.
We postulate Infinity as encapsulated within the Void.

Split the Void – and… "*voila*"… create the cosmos…
and actualize Infinity,
(Some 1:1 correspondences are more intriguing
than others.)
Infinity… and within which, babies smiling, young girls
giggling, lovers caressing, monks pietizing, poets
poetizing, astronauts astronautizing, etc.

Creation and Closures

At the Creation–point... 0 divides into negatives and positives... male and female... and a key part of the cosmic *symphony* is male and female trying to find their soulmates to reconnect and co–join and then procreate the next level of Creation...

...to advance the cosmic drama. The ultimate, sanctified union of unions might, hypothetically be two lovers uniting for the first time on their wedding night in rapture and bliss and love and explosive union to create offspring... combining so many powerful cosmic themes simultaneously... Return, Closure, Potential, Spirituality, Romance, Advance, Creation... a little grander than just the "honeymoon suite at the Grand Hotel" might suggest.

Closure with a Quest for Potential$^\infty$ lift–off

The symbolic 1:1 parallels are bemusing
Metaphysical Lift–off and launch

With a little luck, re–creating and re–enacting
the *Big Bang* [*Potential$^\infty$ Point*] of Creation

[I will, of course, categorically deny any association with the above.]

Tikkun Olam

CHI meridians course through the human body;
And we must presume that parallel meridians course
through the cosmos.

We can open up *CHI* channels in the human body via
SHIATSU or other modes;
But how can we repair the cosmos?

Perhaps by following a life of giving and spirituality,
we open up cosmic channels and meridians,
we "repair the cosmos"… We effect *"Tikkun Olam"*

(Do not assume, however, that I personally am a nice
guy) :)

The *Big Bang* [the *Potential*$^\infty$ *Point*] – the CREATION point -

The cosmic void–womb stirred. A metaphysical friction
stirred it. An ascending yearning for fulfillment. The
VOID simply "could not take–it any more". Thousands
of POTENTIAL Themes… billions of potential Life
Forms stimulate its sensitive metaphysical touch–
points…

…The yearning for fulfillment grew stronger and
stronger…

…All the billions of eons of loneliness waiting for *just–*

the–right–combination of potentials lined–up… could the leap be effected… for + and - : plus (+) and minus (-)? It had tried so many, many times before? Only to be betrayed or let down by one potentiality or another? But this time seemed different… everything seemed lined–up… there was an exciting stir deep, deep within the void… and the potentials of Truth, Mercy, and Spirituality were nicely lined up with the potentials of Freedom and Glory and Love…

Abstract Dynamic / ENTIRE Dynamic

Retired Israeli Supreme Court Justice Haim Cohen, in my discussions with him at his Jerusalem (Rehavia) apartment in 1989… described my "Quest for Potential$^\infty$" as an "abstract dynamic". And the Second Printing of *God and Evil* was adjusted to include this observation.

The advantage of postulating an eternal Abstract Dynamic, as Cohen agreed, is that it is conceptually easier to conceptualize an Abstract Dynamic as having preceded everything, than to posit the conscious, intervening God of Israel as having preceded everything.

Within a religious Orthodox framework, one could say that Q4P is the embryonic Divine and at the core of the infinite Divine Extraordinariation.

Within a more secularized framework, one could simply
take Q4P "the distance"… all the way through infinity.

But, actually Q4P is not forever just an Abstract
Dynamic; Rather it emerges as the ENTIRE dynamic.

We are all integral parts of it. It permeates the sub–
macro–cosmic level and the molecular level.

CHI is the blood stream of it.
SPIRIT is the oxygen energizing it.
INFINITE DIVINE EXTRAORDINARIATION is
intertwined with it.

MU: Cosmic "Tool Kit" Extraordinariation

COSMIC TOOL KIT
Shelf #2

The second set of cosmic tools is elucidated in this section:

[The first set was elucidated in BETA (above)]

tools:
*   SUBJECTIVITY OF "INFINITE DIVINE" *
*   HYPER-ITERATION *
*   SIMULTANEOUS OPERATION LEVELS *
*   ONE ORGANIC SUPER-EQUATION *
*   INSTINCT-DNA *
*   RECURSIVITY IS REGNANT (RECURSIVITY REIGNS) *
*   EXTRAORDINARIATION *
*   EMOTION-EXPRESSION-DRAMA *
*   OPTIMIZING COMPLEXIFICATION/CONTOURIZATION *
*   MACRO-HOLISTIC-OPTIMIZATION *
*   CHERRY-PICKED EVOLUTION *
*   TEMPLATE FIDELITY *
*   METAPHYSICAL > PHYSICAL LEVERAGED BUYOUT *
*   CUMULATIVE / MASSED-ARRAY DESIGN *

●●● TOOL:
* SUBJECTIVITY OF "INFINITE DIVINE
EXTRAORDINARIATION" *

"INFINITE DIVINE EXTRAORDINARIATION " may be
used as
"religious DIVINE"
or
as a spiritual-perfection DIVINE;
or
as an INFINITE DIVINE EXTRAORDINARIATION with a
RELIGIOUS DIVINE "GODHEAD"

(but one can make a strong case for a spectrum of
possibilities)

There are, of course, infinite striations of this.

Addition to Cosmic Tool Kit:
(although alluded-to in the text multiple times,
but less formally)

●●● TOOL:
* HYPER–ITERATION *
(my term)

On multiple levels, MACRO, and MICRO,
the cosmos continuously hyper-iterates, i.e.
All organic entities ask and re-assess:
Given my current assets, and given the multiple layers

of contexts,
what is my best next move (evolvement)
– to advance both my individual Q4P
and the overall cosmic Q4P?
[How often? Unclear]

••• TOOL:
* SIMULTANEOUS OPERATION LEVELS *

The cosmos may very well be operating on multiple
levels simultaneously, all INTERACTIVE with each other.

a) Potentiality-level
b) Equation-level
c) Proto-Metaphysical-level
d) Metaphysical-level
e) Reality-level
f) Infinite Divine Extraordinariation-level

Broadly speaking, presumably we are in (e)
flanked by (d) and (f).

Would need a separate book just to more fully elaborate
on the above "quick snapshot."

God and Good deals with these issues in this part,
Cosmic Womb.

••• SUPER-TOOL:
* ONE ORGANIC SUPER-EQUATION *
(my term)

All subjects and fields and emotions, and, indeed, all

history past and future, are all part of our one supra–
equation – Q4P$^\infty$
All fields and subjects ultimately dovetail into the supra–
equation.
We see distinct snippets, like, say, Biology, Chemistry.
Anthropology.
But at some point Biology connects to the Calculus, etc.
The interaction of Quest for Potential$^\infty$ – at the
Genesis / Big Bang / Potential$^\infty$ point – with, what I have
called the "Mitosis of "0", adds major, major complexity
into an already complex proposition.

Nevertheless, we can only take matters as far as is
appropriate to hypothesize at this point.

••• TOOL:
* INSTINCT-DNA *
(my term)

Complex instinct mechanisms, whether for SURVIVAL,
food-HUNTING, SEXUAL–hunting, MATING,
PARENTING, INTER–PERSONAL BEHAVIOR and others,
are potentially transmittable genetically via (hypothesized
here / what I call) INSTINCT–DNA

••• TOOL:
* RECURSIVITY IS REGNANT (RECURSIVITY REIGNS) *
(my term)

Potential within potential within potential.
Schematically:

potential (potential (potential..........
grandfather (father (son (grandson ....

possibility (metaphysical realms (primitive reality realms
(modern reality realms (post-modern reality realms

Torah (Mishnah (Gemorah (Commentary
(Commentary on Commentary.............

cosmic drama (cosmic drama (cosmic drama.............

(complex (extraordinary (more extraordinary (even
more extraordinary (...............

layer (layer (layer
[see following section .... EXTRAORDINARIATION........]

••• TOOL:
* EXTRAORDINARIATION *
(my term)

The Cosmic Order endeavors to become ever-more
extraordinary and wondrous.

EXTRAORDINARIATION is both the work-in-progress
and ultimate goal.

Complexification and Variation have as their end-goals,
EXTRAORDINARIATION.

The 'cosmic trajectory' is from the bottomless VOID to
the limitless EXTRAORDINARY.

This is the "cosmic bootstrapping" I have hypothesized since Book #1. The potential of mega-EXTRAORDINARY enroute towards the end–of–the–rainbow is the "force-multiplier" – the ultimate *sui generis* 'metaphysical magnet' – which propels the cosmos forward.

Only this potential EXTRAORDINARY could have the power to divide the initial timeless void into 'positives' and 'negatives,' thereby igniting and creating the cosmos.

As extraordinary as one may think matters get, and they are indeed quite extraordinary already in-front-of-our-eyes, one must hypothesize that ultimate matters are quite 'unbounded.'

(Others may categorize or hypothesize this as Messianic Era, Perfection, Redemption;
But, according to our hypothesis, "supra-EXTRAORDINARIATION" – on-all-fronts – encompassing all secular and spiritual – is the target.)

Extraordinariation helps explain, among other things, the flourishing of –

literature, poetry, art, music

the thousands of species of dainty butterflies, for example

the beauty of thousands of varieties of flowers

Magnificent sunsets

Talmudists

GOD AND GOOD

Violin virtuosos

the beauty of the heavens

art in all its variations

the 'pull' of spirituality

and, last but not least,

HUMANS – individually and collectively

– with all their wondrous complexity and drives

– and their emergence as the dominant players
  on the planet

Like the trek towards INFINITY in math,
EXTRAORDINARIATION is, according to this thesis,
more of a PROCESS, an ongoing endeavor, an ongoing
work-in-progress. The PROCESS is the deal, not
necessarily the ultimate ATTAINMENT of a specific
discrete goal, which is by definition unbounded,
in-any-event.

The unboundedness of the 'goal' ...with the infinite
richness inherent, retroactively empowers the 'leap
from the void' questing with unquenchable thirst for
this (unbounded) infinite attainment.

This work proposes that EXTRAORDINARIATION –
in concert with the bootstrapping quest thereof –
QUEST for POTENTIAL$^\infty$ – is the hitherto elusive
couplet "holy grail" of metaphysics.

Like two complementary overarching super-dynamic tornadoes, hypothetically linked at their epicenters, these two intertwined dynamics propel the cosmos forward.

Connect-all-the-dots and you will sense better what I am articulating.

We are in the midst of the cosmic "Potential Storm"; Consequently we see "individual trees", as opposed to the forest (Quest for Potential$^\infty$) as-a-whole.

All the billions of components and themes dovetail into these intertwined super-dynamics (Quest for Potential$^\infty$/Extraordinariation). We prefer to maintain them as a couplet, as opposed to merging them into one concept – Quest for Extraordinariation, as that would not truly be *on-the-mark*.

On an individual level, we quest for potential$^\infty$, and, in rare cases, for potential which is extraordinary. On an ongoing cumulative level, the quest is ultimately for the extraordinary.

EXTRAORDINARIATION – and its inexorable voracious hunger for variety and drama, as well – "casts a wide net" – including Predator / Prey ..... with all the unending brutality entailed, as well. This is philosophically difficult to deal with. Drama in all its permutations, may be cosmically desired. *Sof-kol-sof (after all has been reviewed and weighed)*, it would seem that DRAMA has its place in the pantheon of cosmic imperatives.

(Maybe Khalil can get me out of this one ;)

All roads lead to EXTRAORDINARIATION.

[EXTRAORDINARIATION[1] is inter-related with......]

••• TOOL:
* EMOTION-EXPRESSION-DRAMA *
(my term)

EMOTION seeks ACTUALIZATION, plus the fullest possible EXPRESSION.

Emotion, hard to clinically measure or analyze or photograph,
seeks the fullest possible realization and drama.

Emotion's actualization-imperative, may play a far greater role in the cosmic odyssey, than hitherto discerned.

••• TOOL:
* OPTIMIZING COMPLEXIFICATION /
CONTOURIZATION *
(my term)

---

an inexorable evolvement to ever–more
COMPLEX & SOPHISTICATED & MULTI–FACETED & WONDROUS & OPTIMIZED EFFICIENT life forms,

NOTES by KHALIL

---

[1] Extraordinariation: At very end of book, see Appendix C by Khalil on this theme.

fitting in as optimally as possible into the evolving
contours of the local and cosmic ECOSYSTEMS,
as the cosmos orients towards the richest possible
optimally inter–dependent efficient bio–diversification.

The above is an ongoing thrust of the cosmos,
on both a physical level, and on a metaphysical level

– all geared towards the goal
of INFINITE DIVINE EXTRAORDINARIATION
within the objectives of optimizing
diversity / beauty / reproductiveness / survivability /
viability / efficiency *et al.* within the contours of the eco–
system and within the evolving realities of the broader
environment

Optimizing COMPLEXIFICATION / CONTOURIZATION
is closely inter–linked with overarching tool.........

●●● TOOL:
* MACRO-HOLISTIC OPTIMIZATION *
(my term)

The cosmos OPTIMIZES and EVOLVES & MORPHS –
as it seeks OPTIMIZATION, an iterative macro–holistic–
optimization of eco–systems towards the ultimate goal
of INFINITE DIVINE EXTRAORDINARIATION presumably
incorporating vanguard species.

The cosmos both PUSHES and PULLS towards the goal
of potentially advancing the WHOLE equation and cosmic

thrust, factoring–in ALL of its (Quest for Potential∞) goals in the context of the current base–line.

For instance: the sudden introduction of a billion species of EAGLES might not qualify for macro–holistic–optimization, as it would both throw-off the various natural balances and inter-dependencies, while crowding–out other species and, last, but not least, the dominance of eagles might not be the optimal ROUTE towards INFINITE DIVINE EXTRAORDINARIATION.

The cosmos does this on an ITERATIVE basis – meaning it is constantly re-assessing its optimal route.

It does this on a MACRO (cosmic) basis all the way down through the MICRO (sub-cellular level). It is difficult for me to fine-tune the lexicon on this.

••• TOOL:
* CHERRY-PICKED EVOLUTION *
(my term)

Evolutionary paths are not determined by "survival of the fittest" (as per the *conventional wisdom*); Rather, evolutionary paths are determined by Quest for Potential∞ 'cherry-picking' among various path-options ("survivability" is just one component thereof).

The CUMULATIVE CONSCIOUSNESS, in concert with Quest for Potential∞/Extraordinariation directs evolution.

Please see Appendix E: Evolution from Perspective of Summa Metaphysica

••• TOOL:
* TEMPLATE FIDELITY *
(my term)

Once the cosmos commits to a particular template, it will tend to play-out very extensive permutations and extensions of the template[1]. What is truly happening in the picture, however, is that the particular template was perceived by the cosmos from the *get-go* as potentially an optimal/efficient/versatile building-block for *"Q4P-projection"* (my term). The template consequently will often be found in many applications and permutations.

••• TOOL:
* METAPHYSICAL > PHYSICAL LEVERAGED BUYOUT *
(my term)

Extraordinary potentials *down-the-road* are leveraged in metaphysical realms retroactively at the *Genesis* point into the ignition of REALITY and the Cosmic Order, as we know it.

This is a key motif of this two-book treatise.
The theme is developed somewhat in Book #1.

NOTES by KHALIL

[1] Template Fidelity: This template is particularly conserved between species at the genetic level. Extensive similarity can be found in the genomic sequence of any two organisms, regardless of how different they seem.

There is a limit to how far I can take it because of its
all-enveloping power.
On some level, this one 'tool' defines the 'revolution'
proposed by Summa Metaphysica[2].

••• TOOL:
* CUMULATIVE / MASSED-ARRAY DESIGN *
(my term)

The cumulative array – physical (organisms) and
metaphysical (entities) – interacting and integrated
with permeating Quest for Potential∞,
and factoring-in the current landscape,
and most certainly in conjunction with the *Mother Lode*
Life Force (Godhead?) cumulatively design the next
level organism.

NOTES by KHALIL

---

[2] Leveraged Buyout (in the Torah): The Torah calls for that which
God and Good describes as Leveraged Buyout on both the
personal as well as the national level.

In the fourth chapter of Exodus a frightened Moses is commanded
by God to approach the King of Egypt not as the refugee-
shepherd that he now is, but as the formidable leader and
revolutionary into which God would soon transform him. Later, the
national disheartening of the Israelites subsequent to the negative
report of their spies (Numbers 14:1) is criticized as a fatal error
(ibid., 14:11,12). It seems from this episode that the Israelites'
mistake was to regard themselves as a vulnerable coalition of freed
slaves, instead of a nation that would, in the future, conquer a land
promised to them.

These two narratives are examples, among others throughout
the Tanach, of the requirement to rely now on the success of the
future. It is a powerful tool, based in an otherwise irrational faith,
which allows one to overcome impossible odds in the here-and-
now.

(*deep breath* after the above paragraph)

This is an ongoing iterative process. Daily.

At some point the Cumulative / Massed-Array achieves radar-lock on the DESIGN for other or higher-level organisms – which will optimize the potential and fullness/diversity of the cosmos.

* * *

With two "shelves" of cosmic tools – all with different levels of originality – we now have-at-our-disposal many of the necessary – and previously lacking – "TOOLS" for a powerful – and viable – Metaphysics.

Essentially, we must 'think' in totally different terms than hitherto in contemplating the dynamics of the cosmic order.

We cannot think "linear Western" or "circular Eastern."

We must think in terms of, for want of a better term, "Spiral/Potential/Birnbaumian"
– complete with the two-shelf cosmic tool kit.

*

Only then, do the hitherto elusive key building blocks of the cosmic code start *falling-into-place.*

Birnbaum's

Q4P∞™

Quest for Potential
(infinitely recursive)

Q4P (Q4P (Q4P ...

Quest for Potential

within

Quest for Potential

within

Quest for Potential

ad infinitum

GOD AND GOOD

Part II:
God's 120
Guardian Angels

GOD AND GOOD

"Potential is the holiest state of the Divine. Q4P is the key to understanding the Divine, Creation and theodicy. Indeed, 'I-will-be-that-which-I-will be' is the name by which God first became known to Moses.

It is perhaps trite, but it is true,
At Creation, the Cosmos had HOPE that FULFILLMENT
was at the end of the journey...
Not only does 'hope spring eternity,'
From hope sprang ETERNITY
          (from Birnbaum's Guardian Angel of Hope)

Summa Metaphysica II then reminds us that each of us is at the center of this cosmic drama of Q4P while presenting 'God's 120 Guardian Angels.' Those 120 Angels represent 120 quests for potential in a beautiful and heart-felt poetic form and diction (sometimes even humorously).

I would read one poem a day for the next 120 days and then reread them again."

- Prof. Masako Nakagawa
Philosophy Department
Villanova University

GOD AND GOOD

Part II: God's 120 Guardian Angels
TABLE OF CONTENTS

Foreword by DROB	188
Preface	193
KEDUSHAH	196
from the Yom Kippur Machzor	200
Angels / Potentials	203
"Strength and Faithfulness"	207
Outline of 120 Angels	211
-Guardian Angels 1-20	219
-Guardian Angels 21-40	235
-Guardian Angels 41-60	262
-Guardian Angels 61-80	278
-Guardian Angels 81-100	296
-Guardian Angels 101-120	322
AFTERWORD to 120 Angels	351
INDEX (alphabetical) to 120 Guardian Angels	354

Foreword by Sanford Drob

"God's 120 Guardian Angels"

Eighteen years in the making, David Birnbaum's "120 Guardian Angels", the poetic portion of his new book *God and Good*, is a beautiful and fitting complement to his 1988 masterpiece, *God and Evil*. Nearly everything about this new work, with the exception of its genuine excellence, contrasts markedly with Birnbaum's earlier book.

Whereas *God and Evil* was discursive, closely argued and philosophical, "120 Guardian Angels" is poetic, highly personal, and mythological. Whereas *God and Evil* was profoundly serious, "120 Guardian Angels" is often light and humorous.

Whereas *God and Evil* spoke with the highest imaginable degree of generality (declaring, for example, that "Holy Potential is at the epicenter of the Divine") "120 Guardian Angels" can be extraordinarily particular (Guardian Angel #62 is "Snowstorms on School Days, and #88 is "Playing Chess with Your Son"). However, while Birnbaum's new work is "particular" in the Aristotelian sense that knowledge of the particular brings clarity to the universal, it is hardly particular in the sense of "particularistic" or "parochial". Indeed, Birnbaum's angels, while they do seem to have a fondness for Jewish ideas and activities (Guardian Angel #25 is "Lighting *Shabbos* Candles" and #75 is "Gemorrah *Chavrusahs*"), are ecumenical enough to include in amongst them #71 "*Ju Jitsu*" and #89 "Catholic School Marching Bands."

Birnbaum, in *God and Evil*, argued that "Holy Potential" is the "primal thrust of the cosmos" and that man, created in the divine image, has as his purpose the actualization and fulfillment of that potential. In this new book, Birnbaum's angels speak to us directly and inform us precisely how this potential can be attained. Many of the angels, of course, reflect universally acknowledged ideas and values (Guardian Angel #4 is "Freedom" and #5 is "Mercy"), but it is in the more idiosyncratic amongst them (e.g. #44 "Five-Year Old Girls Giggling", #50 "Putting-the-Kids-to-Bed", and #58 "Iron Mill Workers") that we get the sense that the factory of Holy (and human) Potential is really working.

Reading Birnbaum's book, I cannot help but also view it as a complement to Lin Yutang's 1937 Confucian classic *The Importance of Living*, in which the author speaks so eloquently and so spiritually of life's simple pleasures, like "lying in bed" and "sitting in chairs". Lin tells us "If you can spend a perfectly useless afternoon in a perfectly useless manner, you have learned how to live." Birnbaum, in *God and Evil*, espoused a much more active, and hence Jewish/Western, view of life's meaning, but here in "120 Guardian Angels" he makes room for such dalliances as "Bubbles" (angel #13), "Kite Flying" (#54) and "Catching the Moment" (#40). There appears to be an appreciation that in matters of actualizing Holy Potential there is, indeed, as Lin Yutang articulated, both "the noble art of getting things done [and] the noble art of [sometimes] leaving things undone.

The Kabbalists, in whom much of Birnbaum's thinking is rooted (angel #109 is "Lurianic Kabbalah"), held that there is a coincidence of opposites governing both God and humanity; Birnbaum's latest effort, especially when placed in the context of his earlier one, (with the complementary book titles explicitly forewarning us) most certainly seems to embody this dialectical spirit.

Chayyim Vital, whose great work *Sefer Etz Chayyim*, is the classic exposition of Lurianic Kabbalah, once acknowledged that the world is for the most part evil, with only the slightest bit of good mixed in. Adin Steinsaltz, the contemporary rabbinic sage and Kabbalist, has said that the full meaning of Vital's seemingly pessimistic dictum is that "ours is the worst of all possible worlds in which there is yet hope, and that this is paradoxically the 'best of all possible worlds.'" The reason for this, Rabbi Steinsaltz tells us, is that only in such a world of extreme adversity, a world "on the brink" of total disaster, can humankind be motivated to realize the emotional, spiritual, aesthetic and intellectual possibilities that have been bequeathed to it by our creator.

David Birnbaum's mythic 120 Guardian Angels are a celestial chorus imploring us to do just that, to realize our full cosmic potential as human beings and thereby act as partners with the divine in actualizing the potential of our world.

Dr. Sanford Drob
May 19, 2006
Founding co-Editor, The NY Jewish Review
www.NewKabbalah.com

GOD AND GOOD

Preface

God and Evil is, of necessity,
written in neo-academic style.

God and Good looks at the obverse side of the coin:
Good.

And what we discover of the cosmic order is quite
majestic and elegant, and, indeed, beyond incredible.

"God's 120 Guardian Angels", is my very carefully
chosen vehicle to flesh–out further my core proposition
of Quest for Potential∞. The book is a very deliberate
and calibrated attempt to deal with an infinite and
profound concept – through finite means: literary
devices (120 Angels), gentle poetic prose, and mythical
constructs.

Ultimately, the final leap – in accepting or rejecting an
overarching metaphysics – must be to feel it in your
gut – as no one has been at the Cosmic Center – or
at the Creation point - or 'far enough out' to have a
perspective encompassing all. Indeed, to-the-end-of-
time the full and complete truth will never be proved
conclusively. Indeed, in any event, it might take until the
end of time to relate and explicate the full truth.

GOD AND GOOD

Cosmic Drama Focus:

The Mode of Metaphysical presentation

Now, the mode of presenting my solution is not so simple. At the one extreme is the one sentence proposition:
"Quest for Potential∞" drives the cosmos. Take it or leave it.

At another extreme is to attempt to delineate tens of thousands of nuanced potentialities.

"God's 120 Guardian Angels" tries to flesh-out the core proposition by playing with 120 potentialities or concepts related to Quest for Potential∞. This is my chosen vehicle.

Cracking cosmic codes and articulating the infinite is not that simple.

We are, each of us, at the very center of – and integral to – the cosmic drama.

The dimensions of the drama are, indeed, infinite. Each of us...each and every one of us...is an entire cosmos–in–microcosm.

And each of us is part-and-parcel of this "divine unfolding."

So here we go, my friends... Open your souls and hearts...

The next phase of this journey commences...

"And one [angel] will call another and say:"

KEDUSHAH *1

נַעֲרִיצָךְ *(We will revere You and sanctify You* according to the counsel of the holy Seraphim, who sanctify Your Name in the Sanctuary) as it is written by Your prophet: "And one [angel] will call another and say:*

All — 'Holy, holy, holy is HASHEM, Master of Legions, the whole world is filled with His glory.' "¹ ❖ His glory fills the world.* His ministering angels ask one another, 'Where°° is the place of His glory?' Those facing them say 'Blessed':

All — 'Blessed is the glory of HASHEM from His place.'² ❖ From His place may He turn with compassion* and be gracious to the people who declare the Oneness of His Name; evening and morning, every day constantly, twice, with love, they proclaim 'Shema.'*

---

*1 The **Kedushah** ("the Sanctification") is the holiest portion of the holiest prayer (the *Amidah* – the "18 Benedictions") in most key prayer Services. It is recited only when a formal quorum is present.

„וְקָרָא זֶה אֶל זֶה וְאָמַר: "

קדושה

(**נַעֲרִיצְךָ** וְנַקְדִּישְׁךָ* בְּסוֹד שִׂיחַ שַׂרְפֵי קֹדֶשׁ, הַמַּקְדִּישִׁים שִׁמְךָ בַּקֹדֶשׁ) כַּכָּתוּב עַל יַד נְבִיאֶךָ, וְקָרָא זֶה אֶל זֶה וְאָמַר:

All—קָדוֹשׁ קָדוֹשׁ קָדוֹשׁ ה' צְבָאוֹת, מְלֹא כָל הָאָרֶץ כְּבוֹדוֹ.[1]
❖ כְּבוֹדוֹ מָלֵא עוֹלָם,* מְשָׁרְתָיו שׁוֹאֲלִים זֶה לָזֶה, אַיֵּה°° מְקוֹם כְּבוֹדוֹ, לְעֻמָּתָם בָּרוּךְ יֹאמֵרוּ:

All—בָּרוּךְ כְּבוֹד ה', מִמְּקוֹמוֹ.[2] ❖ מִמְּקוֹמוֹ הוּא יִפֶן בְּרַחֲמִים,* וְיָחֹן עַם הַמְיַחֲדִים שְׁמוֹ, עֶרֶב וָבֹקֶר בְּכָל יוֹם תָּמִיד, פַּעֲמַיִם בְּאַהֲבָה שְׁמַע אוֹמְרִים.A*

A* עַם הַמְיַחֲדִים שְׁמוֹ ... שְׁמַע אוֹמְרִים — The people who declare the Oneness of His Name … they proclaim 'Shema', Israel joins in the sacred chorus of the angels.

A* source: Scherman, *The Complete Artscroll Machzor Yom Kippur*, p. 406-407.

GOD AND GOOD

angels...

GOD AND GOOD

SHACHARIS (MORNING SERVICE) FOR YOM KIPPUR

And so, to Him Who is awesome over them, they fearfully express reverence. *(1)

The force of Your praise is rendered
   א *by heavenly angels,*
   ב *by beings that glow like lightning,*
   ג *by lofty bands,*
   ד *with a still, thin sound** — (2)   *and Your holiness is in their mouths!*...

· · ·

The force of Your praise is rendered
   ט *by pure heavenly nobles,*
   י *by hastily fleeing angels,** (3)
   כ *by Cherubim of glory,*
   ל *by flaming legions* —   *and Your holiness is in their mouths!*...

· · ·

The force of Your praise is rendered
   פ *by those whose names are unknowable,** (4)
   צ *by legions of wakeful ones,** (5)
   ק *by ancient holy ones,*
   ר *myriads of chariots** — (6)   *and Your holiness is in their mouths!*...

---

(3)   יְדֹּדּוּן יְדֹּדּוּן — *By hastily fleeing angels.* The angels hurry to carry out the tasks God assigns them.

(4)   בְּפִלְיאֵי שֵׁמוֹת — *Whose names are unknowable.* As the angel told Manoach, an angel is identified only according to the nature of his mission, so no one can know from moment to moment what its name will be *(Rashi, Judges 13:18).*

(5)   עִירִין — *Wakeful ones,* i.e., the angels who are always alert, ready for their next mission.

(6)   רֶכֶב רִבֹּתַיִם — *Myriads of chariots.* When God appeared at Mount Sinai, He was escorted, as it were, by tens of thousands of angelic chariots *(Rashi, Psalms 68:18).*

source: Scherman, *The Complete Artscroll Machzor Yom Kippur*, p. 398-399.

from the Yom Kippur Machzor (prayer book)

וּבְכֵן, לְנוֹרָא עֲלֵיהֶם

(1) וּבְכֵן, לְנוֹרָא עֲלֵיהֶם, בְּאֵימָה יַעֲרִיצוּ.*

אֲשֶׁר אֹמֶץ תְּהִלָּתֶךָ, בְּאֵילֵי שַׁחַק, בְּבִרְקֵי נֹגַהּ,
בִּגְדוּדֵי גֹבַהּ, בְּדִמְמָה דַקָּה,* (2) וּקְדֻשָּׁתְךָ בְּפִיהֶם. ...

· · ·

(3) אֲשֶׁר אֹמֶץ תְּהִלָּתֶךָ, בְּטַפְסְרֵי טֹהַר, בְּיִדֹּדוּן יִדֹּדוּן,*
בִּכְרוּבֵי כָבוֹד, בִּלְגִיוֹנֵי לַהַב, וּקְדֻשָּׁתְךָ בְּפִיהֶם. ...

· · ·

(5) אֲשֶׁר אֹמֶץ תְּהִלָּתֶךָ, בְּפִלְיאֵי שֵׁמוֹת,* (4) בְּצִבְאוֹת עִירִין,*
בִּקְדוֹשֵׁי קֶדֶם, בְּרֶכֶב רִבֹּתַיִם,* (6) וּקְדֻשָּׁתְךָ בְּפִיהֶם. ...

· · ·

___

(1) וּבְכֵן ... בְּאֵימָה יַעֲרִיצוּ — *And so ... they fearfully express reverence.* Filled with awe and fear, the angels express their reverent praise of God. Nevertheless — even though God has at His disposal the lofty songs of heavenly beings, it is the praise of mortal human beings that He desires. The *piyut* alternates between these two themes: four lines extolling the angels and then four lines describing the frailty of human beings, whose praise God prefers. The reason for this preference is that man must struggle against his animal instincts and passions to achieve a recognition of God's greatness, while the angels are created with a proximity to God and without an evil inclination.

(2) בְּדִמְמָה דַקָּה — *With a still, thin sound.* God's greatness is not accompanied by pomp and crescendo but a hushed sound (*I Kings* 19:12).

GOD AND GOOD

Angels / Potentials

(5,000 or 5 BILLION years later)

> *To Life, To Life, L'chayim*
> *L'chayim, L'chayim To Life*
> —Fiddler on the Roof

* * * "The Metaphysical Plan" * * *

God's 120 Guardian Angels is my mode of explicating the abstract dynamic – Holy Quest for Potential$^\infty$ – which I proposed in my first book *God and Evil* (in 1988), and which I posit as being the core and underlying dynamic of the cosmos.

Using the construct of 120 "guardian angels," I focus on slices of the richness of the universe and on some important metaphysical themes which directly relate to the metaphysics, which I propose.

Some of these themes are relationship-oriented, some are metaphysical, self-actualization-oriented, some hybrid, but all track back to the core dynamic. I chose

120 specific ("guardian angels") potentialities, but please note that each individual – including this author – views the richness of the universe through his/her own subjective lens at any given point in time.

Please note that the Guardian Angels of the universe, represent, as well, and most importantly,

POTENTIALITIES.

According to *God and Evil:* A Unified Theodicy / Theology / Philosophy

these infinite potentialities are at the crux of the cosmic order.
– at the core of the Divine.

And according to God and Evil, these infinite potentialities demanded to be more than just Potentialities –

They demanded EXPRESSION.

They demanded REALITY.

They did not want to infinitely be only ideas or potentiality.

"Na-ase adam b'tzalmenu"
– Bereshit 1:26

"Let us make Man in Our image"
– Genesis 1:26

***

Lead-in to 120 Guardian Angels…

the composite…

an excerpt from the *Yom Kippur* service follows >

GOD AND GOOD

facets of Divine potential

"And so, let us declare Your Strength, You Who lives eternally"

"Strength and Faithfulness"

THE ARK IS OPENED.

Congregation and chazzan:

And so, let us declare Your strength, You Who lives eternally.

הָאַדֶּרֶת	Strength and faithfulness	are His Who lives eternally; *
ב	Discernment and blessing*	are His Who lives eternally;
ג	Grandeur and greatness	are His Who lives eternally;
ד	Wisdom and speech	are His Who lives eternally;
ה	Glory and majesty	are His Who lives eternally;
ו	Convocation and authority*	are His Who lives eternally;
ז	Refinement and radiance	are His Who lives eternally;
ח	Accomplishment and power	are His Who lives eternally;
ט	Adornment and purity	are His Who lives eternally;
י	Oneness and reverence	are His Who lives eternally;
כ	Crown and honor	are His Who lives eternally;
ל	Study and insight*	are His Who lives eternally;
מ	Kingship and dominion*	are His Who lives eternally;
נ	Beauty and triumph	are His Who lives eternally;
ס	Eminence and supremacy	are His Who lives eternally;
ע	Might and modesty	are His Who lives eternally;
פ	Redemption and splendor	are His Who lives eternally;
צ	Desire and righteousness*	are His Who lives eternally;
ק	Summons and sanctity*	are His Who lives eternally;
ר	Exultation and exaltation	are His Who lives eternally;
ש	Song and praise	are His Who lives eternally;
ת	Lauding and magnificence	are His Who lives eternally.

THE ARK IS CLOSED.

(English)

*A source: Scherman, *The Complete Artscroll Machzor Yom Kippur*, p. 402-403.

GOD AND GOOD

The angels summon one another to sanctify God

״וּבְכֵן נְאַדֶּרְךָ חַי עוֹלָמִים.״

״הָאַדֶּרֶת וְהָאֱמוּנָה״

THE ARK IS OPENED.
Congregation and chazzan:

וּבְכֵן נְאַדֶּרְךָ חַי עוֹלָמִים.

לְחַי עוֹלָמִים.	הַבִּינָה וְהַבְּרָכָה*	לְחַי עוֹלָמִים.	**הָאַדֶּרֶת** וְהָאֱמוּנָה	לְחַי עוֹלָמִים	
לְחַי עוֹלָמִים.	הַדֵּעָה וְהַדִּבּוּר	לְחַי עוֹלָמִים.	הַגַּאֲוָה וְהַגְּדֻלָּה		
לְחַי עוֹלָמִים.	הַוַּעַד וְהַוָּתִיקוּת*	לְחַי עוֹלָמִים.	הַהוֹד וְהֶהָדָר		
לְחַי עוֹלָמִים.	הַחַיִל וְהַחֹסֶן	לְחַי עוֹלָמִים.	הַזַּךְ וְהַזֹּהַר		
לְחַי עוֹלָמִים.	הַיִּחוּד וְהַיִּרְאָה	לְחַי עוֹלָמִים.	הַטֶּכֶס וְהַטֹּהַר		
לְחַי עוֹלָמִים.	הַלֶּקַח וְהַלִּבּוּב*	לְחַי עוֹלָמִים.	הַכֶּתֶר וְהַכָּבוֹד		
לְחַי עוֹלָמִים.	הַנּוֹי וְהַנֵּצַח	לְחַי עוֹלָמִים.	הַמְּלוּכָה וְהַמֶּמְשָׁלָה*		
לְחַי עוֹלָמִים.	הָעֹז וְהָעֲנָוָה	לְחַי עוֹלָמִים.	הַסִּגּוּי וְהַשֶּׂגֶב		
לְחַי עוֹלָמִים.	הַצְּבִי וְהַצֶּדֶק*	לְחַי עוֹלָמִים.	הַפְּדוּת וְהַפְּאֵר		
לְחַי עוֹלָמִים.	הָרָן וְהָרוֹמֵמוּת	לְחַי עוֹלָמִים.	הַקְּרִיאָה וְהַקְּדֻשָׁה*ᴬ		
לְחַי עוֹלָמִים.	הַתְּהִלָּה וְהַתִּפְאֶרֶת	לְחַי עוֹלָמִים.	הַשִּׁיר וְהַשֶּׁבַח		

THE ARK IS CLOSED.

(original Hebrew)

*ᴬ הַקְּרִיאָה וְהַקְּדֻשָׁה — *Summons and sanctity*.
The angels summon one another to sanctify God.

God's 120 Guardian Angels

(note: an alphabetical INDEX follows all the actual ANGELS)

Outline

GATE 1

1. of the LONELY
2. of GRATITUDE
3. of SNOWFLAKES
4. of FREEDOM
5. of MERCY

GATE 2

6. of SUNRISE
7. of CUMULUS NIMBUS CLOUDS
8. of CLEAR STAR-FILLED SKIES
9. of DREAMS
10. of RAINBOWS

GATE 3

11. of GEOMETRY
12. of LIGHT
13. of BUBBLES
14. of EXPLORERS
15. of PASSION

GATE 4

16. of ROMANTIC LOVE
17. of CONFIDENCE
18. of KINDNESS
19. of CHILDREN LAUGHING
20. of ELEGANCE

GATE 5

21. of HOPE
22. of WHITE
23. of BLUE
24. of TIDES
25. of LIGHTING *SHABBOS* CANDLES

GATE 6

26. of COSMIC FULFILLMENT
27. of SEVEN YEAR-OLD BUDDIES PLAYING TOGETHER
28. of FEAR
29. of RAPPROCHEMENT
30. of SENSUALITY

GATE 7

31. of CREATIVITY
32. of RETURN
33. of ENCHANTED EVENINGS
34. of RED
35. of FALLING IN LOVE

GATE 8

36. of LOVE BONDS
37. of MARRIAGE
38. of THE HOLOCAUST VICTIMS
39. of VICTORY
40. of CATCHING THE MOMENT

GATE 9

41. of AVENGING JUSTICE
42. of HONOR
43. of FIRE
44. of FIVE YEAR-OLD GIRLS GIGGLING
45. of LIBERATION

GATE 10

46. of PROTECTING THE YOUNG
47. of *WALKING THE KIDS TO "SHUL"*
48. of FRESHLY BAKED *CHALLAH*
49. of *HAVDALAH*
50. of PUTTING-THE-KIDS-TO-BED

GATE 11

51. of LOYALTY
52. of CIRCLES (including Circles of Love)
53. of COMFORT
54. of KITE FLYING (including tapping-into Cosmic Currents)
55. of ARCHITECTURE (including emotional architecture)

GATE 12

56. of HOLDING YOUR DAUGHTER'S HAND
57. of BUTTERFLIES
58. of IRON MILL WORKERS
59. of ASSAULTS ON THE THRONE
60. of CONQUEST

GATE 13

61. of TRUTH
62. of SNOWSTORMS ON SCHOOL DAYS
63. of TRANQUILITY
64. of SELF-DISCIPLINE
65. of HORSEBACK RIDING along the beach

GATE 14

66. of TWENTY FIVE YEAR+ FRIENDSHIPS
67. of SAILING AGAINST THE WIND
68. of DISSENT
69. of FORTITUDE
70. of SNOW–PEAKED MOUNTAIN RANGES

GATE 15

71. of *JU JITSU* (of parlaying Adversity)
72. of TOUGH LOVE
73. of AWARENESS & CONSCIOUSNESS
74. of COMBATING EVIL
75. of GEMORAH CHAVRUSAHS

GATE 16

76. of STRENGTH
77. of SUBSTANCE & FORM
78. of the DIGNITY OF MAN
79. of REMEMBRANCE
80. of BURYING THE DEAD

GATE 17

81. of OPTIMIZING POTENTIAL
82. of JOURNEYS TO FARAWAY LANDS
83. of GRACE
84. of the ASSASSIN
85. of GENEROSITY OF SPIRIT / COMPASSION

GATE 18

86. of ESCAPE!
87. of INTIMACY!
88. of PLAYING CHESS WITH YOUR SON
89. of PAROCHIAL HIGH SCHOOL MARCHING
BANDS
90. of RESILIENCE

GATE 19

91. of SPIRITUAL CLEANSING
92. of the ROMANTIC LOVE PARTNER
93. of the BETRAYED
94. of SEXUALITY
95. of INTERNAL HEALING

GATE 20

96. of THE LIBRARY OF LIBRARIES
97. of −1, 0, +1
98. of SAGE WISDOM
99. of RESCUE
100. of PEACE

GATE 21

101. of "*AHAVA*"
102. of "*EHEYEH ASHER EHEYEH*"
     (QUEST FOR POTENTIAL∞) [see also #81]
103. of *ALEPH*
104. of THE COSMIC CONTINUUM
105. of ASCENTS IN CONSCIOUSNESS, REALITY
     [see also #73]

GATE 22

106. of "LIFE FORCE" / *CHI*
107. of THE CUMULATIVE CONSCIOUSNESS
     [see also #73]
108. of FLOWS, WAVES & CHANNELS
109. of LURIANIC KABBALAH
110. of FORGIVENESS

GATE 23

111. of *"SHABBAT HAMALKAH"* (The Sabbath Queen)
112. of BREATHING— COSMIC & MORTAL
113. of TRANSCENDENT GOALS
114. of PUNCTUATED EQUILIBRIUM
115. of EARTHLY FULFILLMENT

GATE 24
The Cosmic Warrior's GATE

116 of THE *CHI* BLACK BELT MASTER
117. of GUARDIANS OF THE COSMOS
118. of THE WARRIOR OF THE LIGHT
119. of THE RETURN OF THE PRINCE
120. THE LOST ANGEL

"*An angel is never sent on more than one mission at a time*"

– Midrash

— 1 —
Guardian Angel of the LONELY

I am the Guardian Angel of the Lonely
I try to give them some gentle comfort
Metaphorically, I try to hold their hand
I feel their terrible pain
With no one to share it with
Unable to connect well
with their brother and sister creations

Alone on the raft of life... as they navigate life's
treacherous currents, and drift through its calms
One can be alone in the middle of a crowd
And some find themselves alone even in a marriage

Rich or poor – ALONE is so tough

Alone. So alone.
Almost as lonely as God...

Almost, but not quite as lonely as the original, primal,
dark, empty void
The void
Aching
Which reached out into eternity... through Creation...
through the portal of LIFE...
for RELATIONSHIPS...
and for FULFILLMENT

— 2 —
Guardian Angel of GRATITUDE

I am the guardian angel of *"Modeh Ani"**
The gentlest of prayers
The prayer children are taught first
The prayer adults do not take all that seriously
They should.

I am the prayer of Gratitude

I am the angel of Thanksgiving
Thanks Giving every moment

And Gratitude, of course, suffuses the soul
with cosmic energy
And Gratitude, of course,
wraps us in a metaphysical shield

Gratitude that each and every one of us is at the
epicenter of the cosmos
Gratitude that Life Force flows through each of us,
tracking forward to the ends of time

And tracking back to the *Genesis* point
And perhaps these points converge

Gratitude that we are the recipients of love,
and gratitude that we can give love

Gratitude for each and every person who loves us –
even a bit,

* The early-morning prayer "*Modeh Ani*" gives thanks to the Lord of the Universe for restoring life and spirit for this new day

And gratitude for each and every person who we love –
even a bit

Gratitude that we are Cosmic Guardians of love and
creativity
Gratitude that we have arisen for another day
representing a microcosm of a lifetime – of LIFE

Gratitude for the richness and variety of creation's
potentials
Gratitude, with its implicit theme of Wonderment,
is a "magic vitamin"

It infuses our being with cosmic energy

And rightfully so
Gratitude – given with love –
opens a doorway to greater potential

— 3 —
Guardian Angel of SNOWFLAKES

Yes.

Snowflakes are important.

StarDust.

Each one unique, as every good school child knows.
Each one symmetric, each one adding to the harmony
of the universe.

Each one adding a little artistry and diversity to TERRA.

For DIVERSITY and BEAUTY are important cosmic potentialities.

I have a crew of 7 artists up here approving each and every one;
and logging-in each design for future reference; make sure we never ever duplicate. Else they will trade me in.

My favorite one was one snowflake in quadrant 9708 about a million years before the last Tyrannosaurus Rex. The particular snowflake just had "something about it". It was truly sublime. But the art department up here tells me again and again not to play favorites.

Yes, snowflakes are important. It's kabbalistic, you know.

hey, gotta go, we have a little snowfall scheduled for quadrant 8077...

— 4 —
Guardian Angel of FREEDOM

I am the Angel of Freedom.

My advance is inexorable.
No despotic army of whatever size can withstand my assault.
My battering rams can and will pierce all battlements.

Freedom: A precious gift, which further unleashes
mankind's other potentials.
More valuable than the rarest gem.

Interlinked with man's AUTONOMY.
Interesting, as we are always at-risk
for the Tyranny of the Majority.
And are always at-risk for demagoguery.
Yet, by-and-large, matters seem to work out.

Freedom. Freedom. Freedom.

The tidal wave of history. Liberty.
An idea at the core of the human psyche.
Implanted there at the dawn of time.

Its exquisite and extraordinary offshoot,
Jeffersonian Democracy. Thank you, Thomas.

— 5 —
Guardian Angel of MERCY

Ah, yes

Mercy.

My constituency is the powerless.
The supremely vulnerable.
Often the guilty.
Often those on the wrong side of history.

Certainly those on the wrong side of power.
Yet, on some level, capacity for mercy defines who
we are, doesn't it?

For with Mercy, we make-an-exception –
albeit temporarily – to our Program.
We put aside our usual internal apparent self-interest
guidelines.

We are placed in a position of reaching out to an entity
whose actions are generally unacceptable to us – on
some level – or who does not have a significant claim
on our intervention.

Yet, Mercy, has a unique dimension to uplift us.
To upgrade how we define ourselves, to ourselves.

— 6 —
Guardian Angel of SUNRISE

Rebirth of the earth.

Sublime beauty.

Fresh.

Often crisp.

A daily gift – few unwrap.
Sunrise is a cosmic good-morning smile.

A daily treasure by FedEx early morning delivery.
No signature required.

— 7 —
Guardian Angel of CUMULUS NIMBUS CLOUDS

Yes, it's true.

We got our own Guardian Angel.
They say we add gentle and ever-so-soft beauty and
diversity to the planet.

So, who are we to argue.
We never knew we were so important.
We are just re-configured mist.

And, of course, there are so many other and more
serious and powerful clouds.
We sort of just puff around.

But, it's nice to be valued – and nice to be loved.

— 8 —
Guardian Angel of CLEAR STAR-FILLED SKIES

Crisp.
Eternal.

God's Magic Carpet.

Our instant CONNECT back to civilizations and cultures
of yesteryear.
Our forefathers gazed at them during their Exodus from
Egypt... and so on, and so on...

The constant beacon of explorers through the ages.
The Greeks, Babylonians, Romans, Egyptians all took
their shot at unraveling the skies' mysteries...

Intriguer of little children – and of wise, jaded warriors.

Star shine.
Star bright.
Star forever.

Where infinity and destiny intersect.

— 9 —
Guardian Angel of DREAMS

I am the culprit

Where the subconscious plays out...
It is for your own good, I promise, I promise...

Even those nightmares...

You've heard the reasons...
Helps you guys "work out your issues"
We try to be creative, you know...
Trying not to bore you...

Trying to be interesting...

In our own little Magic Kingdom... No queues...
No lines...

Trying to ease your path... Life is a little fearsome
sometimes, you know...
Have to work on those cold sweats, however...

But, you know, before there was reality
Before there was a cosmos
In the interim between the VOID and CREATION
Perhaps there was... a dreamstate
You never know...

— 10 —
Guardian Angel of RAINBOWS

I mean, you know, we certainly do not want to be
trite...
but, it's really hard to argue with the magic of a
Rainbow
especially those huge ones...

those huge arch – horizon to horizon – ones...

they can almost make you religious :)

— 11 —
Guardian Angel of GEOMETRY

yes,

so elegant

so perfect
so axiomatic
so precise
so lawful
so immutable
so essential
so basic

so Divine...

Note the field Fractal-geometry – which deals with
the concept of recursiveness – a form within a form
within a form... paralleling almost precisely our own
potential within potential within potential... Future
metaphysicians will play with this parallel – and be more
than fascinated.

— 12 —
Guardian Angel of LIGHT

moonlight, daylight, sunlight, morning light, evening
light, starlight, firebug light, candle light, tungsten light,
halogen light, camp fire light (and it's cousin fireplace
light :) and LIGHT

mystery of mysteries
one of creation's most beautiful works
beauty of beauties
not one variation and shade, but a billion trillion of them

the Artist's mark

Let there be LIGHT!

— 13 —
Guardian Angel of BUBBLES

I have the best job

Bubbles are good
Bubbles are fun
Bubbles are cute
Bubbles create rainbows
Bubbles make kids happy
Bubbles are not taken seriously...

except by me...

Just a little too perfect, beautiful, elegant – and
vulnerable

But, it's OK... I'm modest
I'm just a bubble

Some cosmologists (visit the NY Planetarium *Big Bang*
presentation) believe that the cosmos emerged from
one of many microscopic bubbles in the void...
And you just know that bubbles are more profound
than they seem.

— 14 —
Guardian Angel of EXPLORERS

a vanguard of mankind

high, high risk

high reward for the miniscule few who succeed –
of the hundreds of hundreds of thousands who have
embarked over time

aiding and abetting Creation

driven
demanding
iconoclastic
defying the odds
often defying *all* odds
hoping to live to see the tale

God's point-men

May God Have Mercy Upon Them...
Eheyeh is an explorer
Pressing beyond the horizon of the horizon
He is a confident explorer, but be rest assured He holds
his breath occasionally, as well

— 15 —
Guardian Angel of PASSION

PASSION is a big word.

And many of my fellow Guardians have portfolios
intersecting... the guardians of Love and Sensuality
to name but two...
but my portfolio is PASSION in the broader sense...
passion in whatever area...

(even though Passion sometimes gets us into trouble)

For it is passion that drives us forward, passion that
brings forth growth and excellence... passion which will
go against-the-tide...

Passion which gives rich texture.

It is passion that brings out fuller relationship Potential.
And it is Potential which drives the cosmos forward.

* * *

1) There are those who live with Intuition

2) There are those who live life with Passion

3) There are those who have a profound Spiritual
dimension to their lives

4) There are those who live life methodically –
and with discipline

If all are combined properly

In just the right symphonic balance...
One can, indeed, shake the planet

(but remember the Rule guys:
Keep a careful eye on CashFlow)

— 16 —
Guardian Angel of ROMANTIC LOVE

Love, oh Love, Careless Love...

Cupid.

I have my hands full.
There must be an easier way.

So much pain, so much frustration, so many false
starts, so many flame-outs – all for what purpose –
For the purpose of achieving a limited number of truly
fulfilling loves.

Why is it worth all the trouble?
Actually it is the reverse.

The potentiality of fulfilling romantic love is one of the
prime potentialities which activated Creation.

Creation was the separation of Nothingness into
Positives and Negatives, around these opposites: Male

and Female. It is the fulfilling Romantic union of male
and female which consummates Creation...which
brings Creation full-circle.

The elegance is clear – although for some reason,
few have noticed the play.
Thus, Creation needs Romantic love to have been
energized in the first place.
No sacrifice is too great, no pain too severe for the
cosmos to yield on Romantic Love.

For Romantic Love is both a route to a preeminent
cosmic goal, FULFILLMENT, plus an *end-goal*
in-and-of itself.

— 17 —
Guardian Angel of CONFIDENCE

Confidence is the bridge from possibility to probability.
Confidence is magnetic
Confidence is inspiring
Confidence is self-fulfilling
Confidence empowers dreams and goals
Confidence arms the cosmic warrior seeking his
    potentialities
Confidence is key

— 18 —
Guardian Angel of KINDNESS

Kindness.

The best portfolio.
So simple. So powerful.
May I have this Portfolio to the end of time.
So underrated...

So needed and empowering, as each of us navigates
the path of life...
As they say, just a little kindness can have such
profound impact on an individual, and, through that
individual on society at-large

Kindness buffers humanity.
Kindness raises the *chi* level of the practitioner
Perhaps it raises the *chi* level of all humanity

— 19 —
Guardian Angel of CHILDREN LAUGHING

I win all the local popularity contests up here.
I love every minute of it.
No one can touch my popularity
– not Love, not Victory, nobody

I'm holding ACES here

And you can be damn sure I will guard those kids :)

— 20 —
Guardian Angel of ELEGANCE

Yes.

It would seem that I am a cosmic luxury.
But the cosmos also has an ego, you know.
Intellectual elegance.
Mathematical elegance.
Fashion elegance.
Artistic elegance.
Creative elegance.
Architectural elegance.

Cosmic elegance?
and on-and-on we go, don't we...

Who can say whether or not I am dispensable...

But I am here...
and I protect my bailiwick...

— 21 —
Guardian Angel of HOPE

Most of humankind has not had it so good.
The challenges have been daunting.

And ultimately what gives us the strength to go out and
meet daily challenges head-on, even when experience
tells us that our success will be limited?

What drives the parent to struggle, sometimes against
all odds? As we know, it is hope for a better tomorrow,
if not for us, then for our children.

It is perhaps trite, but it is true.
At Creation, the Cosmos had HOPE that FULFILLMENT
was at the end of the journey...
Not only does "hope spring eternal",
From hope sprang ETERNITY

— 22 —
Guardian Angel of WHITE

I am White,
the Angel of White.

Imperious and submissive simultaneously.

I am soft cotton – as well as the terrifying blindness of
an ice storm.
I am the White of Yom Kippur –
and the White of gentle snowflakes.

I am the White of a bride's veil
and the White of a *Shabbos* Table linen.

I am usually good,
usually with the Good Guys,
but every once in a while...

I owe scant allegiances –
and serve as the palette of the universe.

Other entities believe
that they hold hegemony and power
But I am always there

Am not quite sure what they would do
without "lil' ole White".

— 23 —
Guardian Angel of BLUE

Yes

we know
it's bad to play favorites…

but, you know, BLUE is a favorite up here
we liked it so much, we designated the sky as such

Sky Blue
then, of course,

Royal Blue
Midnight Blue
Biblical and mystical *tcheilet* blue
Magenta Blue
Green Blue
Blue diamonds… the rarest of the rare

we sort of get *carried away*…

hard to explain…

— 24 —
Guardian Angel of TIDES

no waves

wavelets

little waves

rolling thunder crashing waves

this is my Guardianship...

century after century

where the seas lip laps the sand... and the sailors find
firm ground...
where lovers walk hand–in–hand
where seashells sunbathe
where little kids build those not–so–perfect sandcastles
where fearsome armadas and navies disgorge their
invaders...

I am there...
eon after eon...

Yes. I oversaw man's ascent from the sea...
the epochal transition...

the heavens themselves stood still...
as man leaped

the heavens themselves uncertain as to this little
epochal forward leap forward...

out from the sea womb... out from Atlantis's Tree
of Life... into/onto another higher dimension Tree of
Knowledge...

the cosmic theme repeated endlessly, in many shapes,
forms dimensions... never to cease...

Womb Tree of Knowledge
to Potential Tree of Knowledge

Birnbaum's Quest for Potential$^\infty$
playing-out in front of my eyes...

Inexorably
Elegantly and Violently simultaneously...
like Childbirth you know...

ask the Tides, the Witness and Notary...

they have seen much, for sure... they talk little...
except to me, of course
– as I protect them
don't you know?

— 25 —
Guardian Angel of LIGHTING *SHABBOS* CANDLES

yes, Candle Lighting has its very, very own Guardian

the other Guardians insisted

they say that Lighting *Shabbos* Candles sustains the
cosmic order

sounds pretty mystical to me
and for my money, I'm more of an Aristotelian

but you know
who can argue with the Crowd

they're a pretty confident bunch

so, enter a parallel universe of grace
tip–toe in gently
because it is, indeed, a gentler universe

but first, the PREP

be sure to polish those beautiful Silver Candlesticks
be sure to be home well in time for *Shabbos*
be sure to gather the children round...
be sure that mom's silk or white cotton scarf is
neatly folded
be sure to protect the household from accidental fire
be sure to protect the kids from touching the flame

and, yes, let dad watch... let him be there... let him witness the Lighting... let him re-visit creation...it may soften his soul...

watch mom strike the match
see the trace of black smoke leave the flame of the match
watch the kindling
watch the flicker

watch the little flames

transport yourselves to another time and place... a spiritual dimension... a more forgiving time... a more forgiving place... in whatever dimension... where there is just a little less mundane... a little less pressure... a little less hurt... just a little more love... a little more forgiveness... transport yourselves there... however briefly...

...transport your soul over the transom through a spiritual door... into the magic of the Sabbath Day

consider putting in a good word for me... I have watched a million billion trillion flickers... do put in a good word for me... children of the Divine

— 26 —
Guardian Angel of COSMIC FULFILLMENT

Yes, I am a VIP Guardian Angel

I am a Boston Brahmin of Angels
Classy
True
Eternal

Fulfillment, Fulfillment, Fulfillment

That sublime attainment
Subtle but wondrous

The true goal – personalized for each entity

Subjective
not Objective

Fulfillment

God Himself was speaking to me
about Fulfillment the other day
He wants an appointment
He wants a session
He wants more Meaning, He's aching
He wants to chat

I told Him I'm booked up the next few years

He's pressing me to squeeze Him in

Suppose I'd better
Who knows what havoc He'll cause if He gets into one
of His God-moods

I need to sit this hombre down –
and read him the *Riot Act*

No more Floods
No more Earthquakes

Cool it

Fulfillment will ultimately be yours, Rough Rider
Fulfillment is the deal

You forgot what got you started in the first place

Be patient
Get a session with Guardian of Patience –
IMMEDIATELY! ASAP!

But what do I tell him when I see Him

He Created a Cosmos to attain POTENTIAL and
FULFILLMENT
And yet,
we've had Hitler and Genghis Khan in the meanwhile

But He's stubborn, *Eheyeh*,
He insists the glass is half full
He insists the gamble has been worthwhile

GOD AND GOOD

Yes, I see the young lovers,
But I also see the smoke of the crematorium
Still drifting heavenward...
I hear their cries in the middle of the night

Eheyeh, we have gambled everything on your gamble
We have gone the distance with you
I've looked into the matter, *Eheyeh*

Yes, you were right to the extent that maximum
fulfillment
Is related to highest possible level consciousness and
emotion and variety and creativity and sexuality –
and TENSION

From this mix, fulfillment reaches deeper
and deeper levels
But TENSION also leads to big, big problems, *Eheyeh*

We know the VOID was lonely,
we know the void ached...
We know "it couldn't take it anymore"

But, *Eheyeh*, reassure us that the pain will have been
worthwhile...
Perhaps we were better off lonely

Perhaps

— 27 —
Guardian Angel of
SEVEN YEAR-OLD BUDDIES PLAYING TOGETHER

of seven year-old buddies playing together

good stuff
solid stuff

practice that baseball pitching
and practice that throwing
practice those basketball lay-ups
and practice those free-throw shots

basics

as good as it gets
the measure of the man

strutting, following, posturing,
tumbling, cajoling, testing
camaraderie in its purest form

almost, never ever to be matched again...
in this lifetime

— 28 —
Guardian Angel of FEAR

FEAR – can cripple

FEAR – the sirens go off

FEAR – crushes

I am just the MESSENGER
I am not the culprit

Too little fear – and the defenses are down
Too much fear – and paralysis sets in

but a touch of fear...
can provide drive and energy and focus

one must ride fear like a galloping stallion

and not be thrown by the horse...

FEAR wears many faces
FREEDOM from FEAR

If only we could get to that point
I fear we never may
I try to TAME fear

To keep it in it's cage

For, if let loose...
FEAR was surmounted at the *Genesis* point
Fear of failure, death, disaster, embarrassment
Fear was trumped by HOPE

— 29 —
Guardian Angel of RAPPROCHEMENT

I am the Guardian Angel of Rapprochement

peace, reconciliation, rapprochement

inter-related cousins
I guard them all

so, so difficult

but, trust me, we work long hours... long centuries

— 30 —
Guardian Angel of SENSUALITY

I am the Guardian Angel of Sensuality

The hardest term in the universe to define
I give them the POWER

Whether they use it for good or evil – or a combination
thereof – I simply cannot control
But that GIFT is integral to the Cosmic Process

The other Guardians really want me to take a one-way
trip to Antarctica

Never to be heard again
Only the Guardian of Emotion protects me –
and believe me, I give him a run-for-the-money

I add the spice
I add the FANTASY
I add to the FULFILLMENT mix

Big time

They need me

For sure
I'm here to stay

No doubt

Remove FANTASY, and the edge-is-taken-off
Take the edge off, and potential FULFILLMENT is at
a lower level

And you know the consequences of THAT

— 31 —
Guardian Angel of CREATIVITY

the most immeasurable of talents...

the most unquantifiable, indefinable
no boundaries

the JOKER in the cosmic deck

when that card is played,
no one can calculate the ramifications
even the Great One has a difficult time ascertaining
the ramifications...

and He invented the term

those who possess the POWER, march only to the
beat of the Creative Drummer
an eternal subculture – with FIRE in their souls
linked to each other through the ages – a tight
fraternity –
who rarely ever once meet each other – sometimes not
even in their own time eras and geographic zones...
they communicate through their creative works...
sometimes via their creative,
psychic energy

passion in their hearts

united in their immortal quests...

now,
one can look at creativity from a totally different angle,
for if we look at creativity as the core component of

what I call the core cosmic dynamic –

QUEST for POTENTIAL∞,

we gain a totally new perspective on it

Meaning,
Quest for Potential∞
Is at the core cosmic dynamic

– and CREATIVITY

is at the core of
Quest for Potential∞

— 32 —
Guardian Angel of RETURN

I am the Guardian Angel of Return

I wield very, very considerable Emotional Power...
more than is generally recognized

We have come back to our land...
never to be exiled again...
We have returned to our roots...
never to chase Pagan idols again
We have returned to the passion of our youth...
never to be sidetracked again...

Return to the womb of love
Return to UNITY

Return to the sublime...

We have achieved *rapprochement* with the memory
of our parents....
After all, what parent does not *ultimately, ultimately*
want to *love their child*....

We have returned to visit the homestead... No, no, no
STOP! – some of us can never come home again...

* * *

I have returned

I am back... to guard and protect you, my dear
children, never to be exiled again
Never to be forced out of the gates again –
for whatever reasons

You are now more fully protected from any harm,
my children
You will now be safeguarded by my more proximate
shield of love
for I have indeed returned, my children, battle-scarred,
returned from the wars...

but indomitable
to protect and shield you...until that day when you are
in a position to guard me,
an old warrior

— 33 —
Guardian Angel of ENCHANTED EVENINGS

I am the Guardian of Enchanted Evenings

Once in every great while

I bring it all together

for lovers... would-be-lovers... loyal lovers...
struggling lovers...

...a cosmic bonus
– a celestial treat

– I let it all just gently fall into place

– for a few magic moments... or minutes... or hours...
perhaps at sunset... or twilight... or star-bright
...and the cosmos themselves wink

— 34 —
Guardian Angel of RED

RED

Crimson red

Sunset red

Blood red

Orange red

Red Red

is there really one red at all

it should be illegal for one color to have so much power

so much energy

so much passion

oh, did I forget biblical and mystical Red Heifer red?

— 35 —
Guardian Angel of FALLING IN LOVE

I'm a snoopy guy

I'm present when the match is lit

I'm rooting both parties on...
when I see it (love :) getting close, you know... and
hoping... wishing and hoping...

I'm just sending them each LOVE VIBES
nice gentle, rippled, love vibes

DO IT
TAKE THE LEAP
MAKE YOURSELF TOTALLY VULNERABLE

GOD AND GOOD

TAKE A CHANCE
LET IT HAPPEN

you know, falling in love is the best, the absolute best...
but God have mercy on us if the other party uses our
love as a power cudgel against us... may the God in
Heaven have mercy...

you know, the cosmos wants us to fall in love
so much
achingly so

love, particularly fulfilling love, consummates Creation,
you know
potential for love–fulfillment, as you know, was a key
cosmic ingredient in the Creation mix
Love is the fuel of the cosmic order
Love is most certainly the Answer to the Answer
Love is a primary route to FULFILLMENT.
To cosmic fulfillment.
It fuels the cosmos in all its glory.
But, back to our young mortals now...
back to our potential lovers, now...
Oh! There they are!
They're coming down the path...

Here they come now... here they come... closer...
closer, now, gently... gently... gently take her hand...
come on now... come on... there you go... atta boy...
she's OK... she's gently smiling... she's so beautiful
when she smiles....

— 36 —
Guardian Angel of
LOVE BONDS/LOVE CONNECTS
AND LEVELS OF LOVE

TRANSCENDING TIME:

Love bonds...
many people don't even know we/we exist...

I'm not particularly visible, you know
but my work transcends time
and, yes,
Love–bonds transcend the cosmos
criss–crossing the cosmos
for all eternity
for ever and ever... and then some...

Neutralize Hate.
Purge Hate.
Kick it out.
Eject it.
It is bad, bad news.

Inter–generational love–flows
coursing through time and space
though thousands of generations
on some level
sustain the cosmos
just as rich red blood coursing through our veins
sustains us on a personal level

The cosmos wants these love–flows as rich and
as healthy as possible

COSMIC BY-PASS SURGERY

one way or another

TOXIC REALITY
must be bypassed

to connect one's core back to eternity

So, allow your internal *Chi* to be connected
(and oxygenated) fully to powerful mainstream cosmic
Life-force currents stretching back to the *Genesis*
point...

— 37 —
Guardian Angel of MARRIAGE

CONSUMMATION:

Marriage consummates Creation.

For, Creation involved un-zipping the cosmic void into
Positives and Negatives, Light and Dark, Matter and
Anti-Matter, Female and Male, etc.

And Marriage is the re-uniting of Male and Female...

Into a sanctified nuclear family unit

Hopefully united in love and commitment

And there-from
Potentially to create new life and love bonds

From
generation to generation, as well

In spite of all the risks and unknowns,

The Sabbath Queen is gently but inexorably
approaching now...
And the children do wish to welcome her in PEACE
search into your hearts
search into your souls...

We have all traveled different roads to get to this point
For sure, wisdom is necessary on all parts

true wisdom

— 38 —
Guardian Angel of HOLOCAUST VICTIMS

we truly feared... at the Creation point... that some
cataclysm of this dimension might someday transpire...
but it exceeded in evil our worst fears... our absolute
worst fears...

that the Forces of Evil would achieve CRITICAL
MASS...

and wreck death and humiliation and abuse and torture
and sadism... almost unchecked...

we shudder
we tremble
we dare not speak

perhaps we indeed erred in creating the Universe

in creating Man
in creating Light... for in doing so, we simultaneously
also create Darkness
and who, indeed, can measure the suffering of a
5 year old girl torn from her mother and sentenced
to abomination after abomination... for being born

we stand mortified at Creation

uncertain if we did the right thing

if we made the right call

in lighting the initial spark...
may god have mercy on our eternal souls...
may God have mercy on the souls of the victims
hallowed be thy names...

— 39 —
Guardian Angel of VICTORY

I am the Guardian Angel of Victory

I stand triumphant

over battle, over the challenge, over the quest,
over my indomitable quest

I stand, pulsating with triumph – proud – unbowed

Victorious – and Triumphant
I discern the path of least resistance
My stratagems, tactics, talents and assets proved
superior
But ultimately it was my WILL which prevailed

I pushed aside all remaining obstacles
I swept aside all hindrances

For the moment, I am at the pinnacle

Savoring my triumph

There is no substitute for Victory –

except –

except for Dignity
except for Morality
except for Defense of Principle
except for Acts of Conscience
except for protecting the weak
except for Loyalty

except for... so, so many things

GOD AND GOOD

Alternate victories, ultimate victories?

I am aware of the issues
I am aware of the pain
I am aware of the compromises
I am aware of the price
I am aware of the suffering
I am aware of the dead
I stand, pulsating with triumph

Beware of the victorious

Seek me

Be wary of me

I will intoxicate you
I will seduce you
I will suffuse you with hubris

Beware of me, all yea who seek fulfillment

Seek me
Impress me
Cajole me
Trump me

if you can

There is nothing, absolutely nothing, like pure Victory

— 40 —
Guardian Angel of CATCHING THE MOMENT

I am the Guardian Angel of "CATCHING the MOMENT"

subtle but important

"subtle" is my middle name...
now, to us up here,
it is so clear
it is so obvious
but most will miss it...
the moment.

at the inflection point of the great PAST and the infinite
FUTURE

"k'heref eyin" – as the blink of an eye

few will fully savor it
the multifold pleasures and fulfillments which surround
us on a regular basis
the gift of life
of spirit
notwithstanding most travails

rich or poor
strong or weak

in our determination to improve and advance... while
also most certainly an excellent trait, we sometimes

miss catching the life we already have
not just *carpe diem* my friends, but *carpe moment*

simple pleasures
basics

don't get too fancy, hombre

and,
next time there is a potential HUG on your radar-scope,
do maneuver for it my friend – and enrich your soul...
for life "is but a dream" – flowing swiftly

– and whatever you do, absolutely, positively, DO NOT
sweat the small stuff :)

— 41 —
Guardian Angel of AVENGING JUSTICE

I am the Angel of Avenging Justice

And my celestial sword is sharp

IN THE NAME OF THE FATHER...

On behalf of humanity,

I am the avenger

I do hunt down evil souls

to the farthest reaches of the cosmos

.....HALLOWED BE THY NAME

They are quite terrified of me – and rightfully so
Their ending is not quick – and it is not swift – and it is
not painless

I avenge Mankind
I avenge the innocent, the murdered, the tortured

THY KINGDOM COME

Justice is done.

Without mercy

And with brutal Finality

THY WILL BE DONE.

Matters *'cut-both-ways'*, my dear young godfather

— 42 —
Guardian Angel of HONOR

I am the Guardian Angel of man acting with Honor.

One individual can ennoble an entire society – and
through that society, all of humanity.
Every once in a while, an individual rises above
immediate self-interest – for the sake of integrity and/or
the greater good – and/or the truth – and/or justice.

Honor transforms all those within this individual's
penumbra

Honor honors mankind
L'Alom va-ed
Now and forever more

— 43 —
Guardian Angel of FIRE

I am the Guardian Angel of FIRE
Prometheus the extraordinary is my Greek alter ego
I changed the planet immediately and forever more
The way people eat, sleep, live, travel... for starters.
I am both LIBERATOR... and DESTROYER
...so important ...and so dangerous
...so constructive ...and do destructive
generally a blessing ...but sometimes a curse
...so beautiful ...and so deadly
On some level,
human history commenced with FIRE'S discovery
Hopefully human history will not end in nuclear fire

— 44 —
Guardian Angel of
FIVE YEAR-OLD GIRLS GIGGLING

the heavens smile
the stars in the sky take a break from twinkling to watch
rainbows take a recess to catch a glimpse

angels *"take-5!"* to watch them
olympians break from practice
candidates stop squawking
ducks stop quacking

— 45 —
Guardian Angel of LIBERATION

I am the Guardian Angel of Liberation

Liberation, Hallowed be thy name
I am the soul of the black US Army sergeant liberating
the inmates of Bergen Belsen...
I am the soul of the Supreme Allied Command
liberating an entire continent of the Nazi scourge

Yet my mandate is limited... I can only hope to inspire...
I cannot overtly...
interfere...
                    Semper Fi

--

* *Semper Fi* is the motto of the U.S. Marine Corps,
from the Latin, *Semper Fidelis*, "Always Faithful"

— 46 —
Guardian Angel of PROTECTING THE YOUNG

I am the Guardian of Protecting the Young

from fear
from injury
from hunger
from terror
from poverty
from humiliation
from bullying
from all abuse

I wish that they had given me more power;
We never meant to allow them any harm...

— 47 —
Guardian Angel of *WALKING THE KIDS TO "SHUL"*

so magical
so wondrous
so transcendent

may god grant us the health and the healthy children...
and the freedom

open our eyes to grasp its enchantment
open our hearts to gently listen to their souls

as we walk ensemble to *shul*
spring, summer, winter and fall

rain or shine
even snow

do not underestimate its power
do not underestimate the gift

their hearts will rarely be as pure – as when they are
walking to shul with their parents
united in their goals
protected and nurtured every–which–way

an enchanted SPACE within the wider enchanted
SPACE of *shabbos*
not necessary to dissect it fully
just gently... ever–so–gently enjoy the moment

if they still let you, hold their hand
if not, just hold their love,
but whatever you do, don't *mess it up*

this is your moment – for all of you...
aliyah (ascent) of sorts to the *Bet Hamikdash* (Holy
Temple)... ascent to Holiness... together...
does it get much better?

winter: wrap that scarf well... make sure you have
good gloves in your pocket
spring: look at those azaleas, rhododendrons, roses,
behold God's wonders
summer: oh, I can't believe it's so hot, dad...
fall: Rosh Hashonah the leaves are turning and falling
off, so all must be right with the world, children...

may God give us the wisdom

to treasure the moments
to treasure the gift
to treasure the memory
to treasure our good fortune
to treasure the treasure

ask them about life
ask them about God
ask them about their dreams

and their dreams will come true.

— 48 —
Guardian Angel of FRESHLY BAKED *CHALLAH*

[**Challah**—(plural, *challot*)—Hebrew for "dough offering." Bread used in festive meals on the Sabbath and holidays. There are always two *challot* for each Sabbath meal, to remind Jews of the double portion of *manna* they received on Fridays in the desert so they would not have to gather food on the Sabbath. – Haim Sabato]

Who can unravel some mysteries
who can unravel some pleasures

let your senses and psyche just try to even partially
absorb it...
and transcend the mundane...

enter a portal to Heaven

for, who can so easily absorb 150+ generations of
Masorah...

pause for *Shabbat* – and enrich your soul
pause for *Shabbat* – and center your soul
pause for *Shabbat* – and *hitch a ride* to eternity

Dad's cutting the *Challah* now......

smells sooooooooooooooooo good.......
ummmmmmmmmmmmmmm
5 super fresh pieces......one for each of us...
now he's sprinkling a little salt......

OK, OK .... I'm ready

personally handing a small slice to each of us........
ahhhhhhhhhhhhhhhh

take a full bite out of eternity

— 49 —
Guardian Angel of *HAVDALAH*

[**Havdalah**—ceremony marking the end of the Sabbath. It employs a
lit braided candle and consists of blessings over the Creator of wine,
the Creator of spices and the Creator of fire, as well as the over-riding
blessing over the Creator of the universe, who divides the cosmos
between the Holy and the profane.]

the divide between the Holy and the mundane,
the Jews like to demarcate it with fire

Sabbath candles preceding the Holy...
a *havdalah* candle following...

don't rush it
it is a sacred ceremony

listen... *"He-nei El yishosy evtach v'lo efchad..."*
in God, my strength I will believe,
and I will not be frightened...
back into the harsh reality of the world
out of the spiritual cocoon of the Sabbath
sip the wine
sense the *bisumim* (spice) fragrances
watch the flame – uniting you to a million trillion
households past present future
grasp its simple power
its simple elegance
its simple statement
look at the flame one last time for this week this
shabbos night... let your soul savor it's

primal beauty and elegance...

— 50 —
Guardian Angel of PUTTING–THE–KIDS–TO–BED

tuck them in
ever so gently

just listen to their wisdom
absorb their beauty

hint to them that you will guard them
that you will protect them from any monsters –
and then hope and pray that you will always be able to

listen to them bless their family and friends
listen to them say the *SHEMA*
(core Jewish prayer...*Hear O Israel*...)

and thank God that you are alive
to have deserved this magic moment

— 51 —
Guardian Angel of LOYALTY

stand by me
stand by me

power and fortune wax and wane
and beauty peaks
through the glorious highs – and the devastating lows
through advances and retreats
so please please my friend

STAND BY ME
requite my trust,
ennoble yourself –
enrich the cosmos

and together we will transcend all eternity

— 52 —
Guardian Angel of CIRCLES

the primary geometric of the cosmos is the SPIRAL....

perhaps a double-helix spiral
but CIRCLE comes close

* a simple circle *
so at the next *simcha* (festivity)
do join that circle
grab that hand
join the circle–dance
and celebrate it all: life, health, joy, the bride & groom,
the smile your first love once gave you – and a better
tomorrow, for sure
and give just give that random hand you're holding
an ever–so–slight squeeze

— 53 —
Guardian Angel of COMFORT

comfort him
he has just lost his wife
and he feels lost

comfort him
for he has just lost his job
and he is secretly scared

comfort him
for he has just lost his love
and fears that there may never be another like her

comfort him
for he has just lost his dream
and may now be relegated to the mundane

comfort him
for he has just lost his friend to betrayal
and his roots are shaken

comfort him
because he has just lost his son
and his world has ended

comfort him
for he lost his faith
and an emptiness gnaws away at him

comfort him
- because he has no one left to comfort

— 54 —
Guardian Angel of KITE FLYING

Feel the tug thrust your torso
connect with the wind
connect with the sky
connect with your core
connect with your planet

do it with your kids –
they'll remember it when...
in their sunset days

it's really good stuff
do it at the beach
but not too close to the ocean...
the wind will be too strong
you will lose your kite
to the ocean's vast personal collection
deal with the strong tugs!
deal with the sudden slack!

a good metaphor for life

do not let the string break!!
ease up!!!
do not let the kite crash!!
exert more pull!!! *quickly*

— 55 —
Guardian Angel of ARCHITECTURE

the space between engineering and art
they were reluctant to give me my own portfolio
but they saw Lloyd Wright's works and sighed

architecture – often defining mankind

to ourselves, to our children, to the gods

sometimes we are truly just struck in awe

— 56 —
Guardian Angel of
HOLDING YOUR DAUGHTER'S HAND

...if she will still let you...
remember when she was three, four, five
so vulnerable

and now, a young lady, of course
but will she still let you hold her hand
if you walk with her?
would she take it the wrong way
would she understand that you just want
to be her dad...

forever

— 57 —
Guardian Angel of BUTTERFLIES

so dainty
so superfluous
so vulnerable
so whispy

no "survival of the fittest" apparent here
but in their superfluousness, so crucial
for we need some gentleness, some fragile and dainty
and beautiful entity to remind us that power
is not the end-all,

and we need some gentleness, some fragile and dainty

and beautiful entity to calm our collective souls
and we need beauty and grace – for their own sake

the Goddess of Cosmic Fulfillment has her
prerogatives, as well

— 58 —
Guardian Angel of IRON MILL WORKERS

we work
long, long hours
in harsh conditions and often-extreme heat
in considerable danger

we just want to provide for our families
we give it our best

just like our fathers before us did
day after day
year after year

hoping that we do not see that dreaded pink slip

pass me that beer, will ya'

— 59 —
Guardian Angel of ASSAULTS ON THE THRONE

tactical
measured

analytical
willful
determined
steel
flexible
cunning
arrogant
indomitable
only one chance

the stakes are high

I, Natasha Levy of PS 152 will win the 4th grade
POETRY contest!

— 60 —
Guardian Angel of CONQUEST

my soul needs it
my entire being is geared for it

I have studied those before me
I have read their notes
I have read their notices
I have learned their axioms

and visited their monuments
and I just wait for an opening

I lie in wait

I want "the rush"

— 61 —
Guardian Angel of TRUTH

Ve ri tas
Harvard's logo

Truth

So very elusive
Even those who profess it to be sacrosanct

so often mangle it
so often color it
so often trample on it

. Truth has so many facets

More than a perfectly–cut 58–faceted diamond
but be true to thyself, my friend

or all is lost

interesting that TRUTH is not a mitzvah (Jewish precept)
(although ACCURATE WEIGHTS are hyper-strictly decreed)

as TRUTH is not always desired
(doesn't she look beautiful?)

TRUTH is more of an ideal – in ideal circumstances

Amazing, right?

— 62 —
Guardian Angel of
SNOWSTORMS ON SCHOOL DAYS

SIX INCHES!!

gr8
they've gotta cancel now
cool
day off

gotta call Jonathan
we gotta sled down his hill

maybe I'll make a Snowman with Simone
hope she gets outta bed before noon

gotta get snow–proof gloves – Dad will go crazy if I
start getting frostbite again

hope the sled is in the garage
hope Jonathan is up
hope Simone gets outta bed

— 63 —
Guardian Angel of TRANQUILITY

the universe was created in a storm
but I am the Guardian of Tranquility
tranquility in the face of provocation
tranquility in the face of betrayal
tranquility in the face of danger
tranquility in the face of evil

now, tranquility is not always the answer
indeed, in some cases, it is precisely the wrong answer
but tranquility has its moments
gracious and exquisite moments

— 64 —
Guardian Angel of SELF DISCIPLINE

so difficult
especially with all these Type-A Personality Guardians
floating around
seems to contradict the *play-at-the-edge* theme, which
sometimes seems to permeate this place

but you know,
without self-discipline we are ultimately lost
we will inevitably overreach and overplay our hand

however formidable our hand
when we have self-discipline, presumably we control

the limits of our forays
in whatever domain

so, be careful my extraordinary friends
for if you overplay even a strong hand,
you may lose your seat at the table

— 65 —
Guardian Angel of
HORSEBACK RIDING ALONG THE BEACH

can't explain it
can't justify my inclusion

I just know that I received my Certified Letter from the
Great One to show up – and I'm here

now, I'm not complaining, mind you
there is definitely something special about my portfolio
and, indeed, who has not been reborn by the
experience

but, it seems something of a luxury
even, if at some level, it is still just a simple pleasure

but more accurately,
a not-so-simple pleasure

By the way, at sunrise is optimal

and along Bermuda's pink-white beaches, is not bad…

— 66 —
Guardian Angel of
TWENTY-FIVE YEAR+ FRIENDSHIPS

formidable
loyal
great
equilibrium
enhance society
special ingredients
smart people
have overcome many hurdles
steady players
people worth knowing
watch out for that second wife!

— 67 —
Guardian Angel of
SAILING AGAINST THE WIND

overly romantic, quixotic

what happened to caution, self-discipline,
measuredness
how can you justify – to the kids, in particular

hard to explain
hard to justify

but, of course, sometimes it just needs to be done
it just must

no matter what the price
the "greater good" – that dangerous "siren song"

a loving mate is helpful in these circumstances :)

— 68 —
Guardian Angel of DISSENT

Dissent

the Jews are too good at dissent
perhaps they should *cool-it* a little
always challenging the establishment
goes back to Abraham and Terach's idols
follows through to the Russian revolution
nothing gets these guys down
and, of course, the new establishment is the first to
victimize them in any event
but it's in their Jewish blood

liberté, egalité, fraternité
you'd think they invented the slogan
they bequeath these gems to the populace –
and then have their synagogues burned to the ground,
hopefully not with themselves inside

but as we alluded to,
Judaism was itself a revolution
and the exodus a rebellion
as were the Maccabees,
the Masadas and pretty much,

in one form or another,
nearly every episode
we hold dear
so it is not a question of whether,
it is just a question
of when – and how

choose worthwhile targets my children,
because more often than not,
you will succeed

Dissent

Eheyeh said it could be done
That we could *leverage–buyout* the cosmos
That we could leverage future Potential / Fulfillment
into Creation

Eheyeh saw what we all did not see

— 69 —
Guardian Angel of FORTITUDE

no one ever said things would be easy...

no one promised a rose garden... indeed,
quite the opposite
one challenge after another

and if born "with a silver spoon",
that comes back to haunt, as well
Fortitude

Pearl Buck's "The Good Earth"
of course, a nurturing household, talent, education,
work ethic, luck, minimal risk path, a good love–
partner, the right place, the right timing
can, in-combination indeed set you free...
but remove a couple of these components –
or take the edge off of them – and,
especially over the long run,
it gets dicey

sometimes very dicey

— 70 —
Guardian Angel of
SNOW-PEAKED MOUNTAIN RANGES

raw, unfettered natural wonder
watch with awe – and gasp
at creation's wonders

tracking straight-back to the beginnings of time
essentially primal, elegant, smooth, sparkling,
crystalline, dangerous, beautiful, wondrous, powerful,
forbidding, untamed, changing, seductive
all simultaneously

conquer me

sound somewhat familiar?

not bad for an entity

— 71 —
Guardian Angel of *JU JITSU*

not just ju jitsu at the dojo
life itself *ju jitsu*

leveraging your opponent's weight against him
turning a disadvantage – into an advantage
turning a negative – into a positive
turning a weakness – into a strength
turning a setback – into an advance
turning pain – into personal growth

we all face adversity and setbacks and challenges
but to whatever extent we are adept at

ju jitsu-ing adversity for growth and energy, we win
if we become adept at "turning" these situations, we
win at the game of life

basically,

if things turn out good, we're fine
and if we face adversity, we may still be fine –
if we can parlay the energy of the adversity

as you know, we posit that at the *Genesis* point itself,
the cosmos jiu-jitsued potential into REALITY

if you encounter a major setback
attempt to use the pain-fire to raise your level
your level of consciousness, awareness
– and you will emerge triumphant

* * *

if you encounter a major setback
pivot off of the setback,
much as a swimmer
pivots off the wall
– and you will prevail over previously un-prevail-able
situations

if you encounter defeat and/or massive pain
do not allow it to crush you or to burn through you
rather, open your arms... smile at the soul of the beast
and employ the adversity–energy as a tail–wind to
propel you forward
with velocity and power

* * *

do not seek adversity

but if you encounter it,
turn it into a ('black') energy source

to trump other challenges...
employ the adversity–power and the adversity–pain
to sharpen your senses,

to optimize your awareness and tactical skills
– and to charge your will

— 72 —
Guardian Angel of TOUGH LOVE

I am the Guardian Angel of TOUGH LOVE

now, my friends, we wish to produce gems
multi-faceted gems, which sparkle
now – and 75 years from now
not princes and princesses – who will inevitably leave
pain and destruction in their wakes

kindly do not live under any illusion that pampering will
produce a good result

and no physical please, no trauma
nice and gentle – but firm
gentle and firm – until you drop

and, as an aside, please send correct signals *vis-à-vis*
money
achievement
relationships
standard-of-living

try not to mess up, please

and lead by example, please
and most definitely do not come crying to me later

I really, truly will not be receptive

you have been clearly alerted and forewarned
go now... here come the kids... nice, firm, and gentle,
now...

— 73a —
Guardian Angel of
AWARENESS (half-brother of SENSITIVITY)

listen

just listen

listen like a baby – with the sensory gates wide open –
and you will be rewarded with extraordinary treasure...

allow your entire system to listen,
to hear what is being said
hear what they are TRYING to say

then hear what your own system is saying
hear what your body is saying
hear what your emotions are saying

listen – and you will prevail

listen – and the world is yours

— 73b —
Guardian Angel of CONSCIOUSNESS

Consciousness (a first cousin to AWARENESS) is key
Because as we ascend in consciousness
we "ascend to the gods"

The *Lubavitcher Rebbe* zt'l operated at an

extraordinarily high level
But if mankind is inexorably ascending in
consciousness,
A thousand years from now,
the Rebbe's level may just be considered average
and if mankind is indeed inexorably ascending
in this sphere,

where, indeed, will it lead...

But, for sure, as we ascend in consciousness,
We become attuned to our CONNECTEDNESS
To humanity – present, future and past

With the attendant flows connecting ALL
As we are all connected as a unitary consciousness

But, in particular,
the next higher level of consciousness of Man
And, in concert, the next fuller level of Reality

The cosmos seeks to reach its fullest variety and
richness,
In concert, the cosmos needs Man to ascend to
increasingly higher levels of consciousness –
to perceive, observe and even potentially,
explore the cosmos

Why? Because, among other reasons, cosmic reality,
however extraordinary, needs a conscious observer
to give it fuller reality

As there are, indeed, levels of reality
Just as there are levels of consciousness

— 74 —
Guardian Angel of COMBATING EVIL

"timche et zecher Amalek"

erase all trace of the (gratuitously) evil Amalekites
evil festers and infects
it never stays stagnant

turn a blind eye at your peril

evil will rise like a medieval monster – when you are
most vulnerable – and
destroy your life's work

hearken unto my words

— 75 —
Guardian Angel of GEMORAH *CHAVRUSAHS*

[A *Gemorah Chavrusah* is a tradition whereby students are
encouraged to study *Gemorah* (Talmud) in sort of a buddy
(*Chavrusah*) system, i.e. students break up into 2-man groups,
and the 2-student *Chavrusahs* study it together, and try to
maintain the same precise ~'buddy' setup ongoing, even for
several years ongoing.]

yes, I know, old school
a little European

not quite politically correct
what can I tell you

GOD AND GOOD

I play to win
not to draw

I go for the finer points

there is something special and unique about it

I know, you want to turn the page

that's OK

just think about it...
tuck it into the back of your mind...

I'm a pretty smart guardian

* * *

a *chavrusah* is a peer partner in study, generally
talmud study

meaning twosomes are set up to study the dialectic
of the talmud together

the talmud may have its faults,

but studying it via a *chavrusah*, is not one of them...

— 76 —
Guardian Angel of STRENGTH

strive continuously to deal always from strength
moral strength, spiritual strength
intellectual/academic strength
emotional strength
relationships strength
financial strength
political strength
military/security strength

all else is dependent on these pillars –
on both an individual and political level

no one says it will be easy

but to the extent, you solidify these pillars –
you will withstand the vicissitudes of time

— 77 —
Guardian Angel of SUBSTANCE & FORM

both are necessary

different societies put different weight on the respective
importance
of each pillar
so best to assiduously cover both bases

SUBSTANCE you know all too well
but FORM is important as well

reach out and seek out guidance, continuously

FORM has not always been your forté
do not lose the battle for lack of the right pennant

— 78 —
Guardian Angel of DIGNITY OF MAN

Judaism's universal contribution...

two thousand years before the 14th amendment to
America's extraordinary Constitution
freeing America's Black slaves.
another document set forth the equality
– and entitlement to dignity – of all races

and, punctiliously over the centuries, there has been
no wavering over this key issue

the cosmos was created for man to reach his
glorious potentials –

ALL men, ALL potentials

period.

— 79 —
Guardian Angel of REMEMBRANCE

the baton is handed on...
generation to generation...

father to son, father to son

the 'shalshelet', the chain
but, within proportion, the past must be remembered
and sometimes sanctified
for to do otherwise, would negate their contribution
to ascending knowledge, spirituality, consciousness
to civilization's advance
therefore, while everything has its measure

Remembrance is important

But like all matters, with appropriate measure

— 80 —
Guardian Angel of BURYING THE DEAD

I am an old soul...
I seek dignity and closure
I see the denouement....

they are all fairly equal before me
fairly equal

at their journey's end
I see death – and have a consuming passion for life

— 81 —
Guardian Angel of OPTIMIZING POTENTIAL

a fine line
press too little, and life is just mundane and *humdrum*
press just a little too hard, and you are a quixotic failure
press to just the OPTIMAL point,
and FULFILLMENT is yours

We pivot our entire hypothesis on the proposition
that Quest for Potential∞

Is the underlying motif of the cosmic order,

indeed, that it IS the cosmic order

So, optimizing potential
emerges as a primary imperative,

if not "THE" primary imperative,
on multiple levels

— 82 —
Guardian Angel of
JOURNEYS TO FARAWAY LANDS

add a little spice to your life drama
see how the *other half* lives
see how we've done in the other districts
visit your *35th–cousins*
get a move on

break that inertia
make it happen
bring a good digital
but what is happening in this picture?
probably more than the author realizes...

— 83 —
Guardian Angel of GRACE

yes

I know
it is good

may god shed his grace upon thee

sublime

not a theme usually focused on in Jewish discussion
but a legitimate – and most powerful – universal theme

a gentleness
a forgivingness

which restores our inherent humanity

which brings us back to the sublime component of
our roots

— 84 —
Guardian Angel of THE ASSASSIN

I change the course of history –
instantaneously all bets are off
do not be smug
you cannot stop me – if I am prepared to die
and I AM prepared to die

I have but one *raison d'etre*
to smite with one stroke

I am a guided missile
and I will wreck the best-laid plans
and best-laid kingdoms
and best-laid tyrannies

but, trust me,
I'm not all that picky

— 85 —
Guardian Angel of
GENEROSITY OF SPIRIT & COMPASSION

a.k.a. big hearts
lev tov lev shalem
the Godforce in full force;
of Compassion

Compassion's spiritual energy unites us all,
to the far ends of the cosmos

Compassion is a complex emotion,
making us vulnerable and strong simultaneously

plus profoundly connecting us

— 86 —
Guardian Angel of ESCAPE

escape from tyranny!
escape from persecution!
escape from tormentors!

escape from checkmate!
escape from a quagmire!
escape from the enemy!

escape from the void!

trust me, it wasn't easy

— 87 —
Guardian Angel of INTIMACY

I am the Guardian Angel of INTIMACY

Perhaps, I must first earn your trust,
because I will ask you for vulnerability

I must make myself vulnerable first,
to show you I am serious

I will cherish your soul – and embrace your spirit

I promise to guard your secrets
– and to overlook your weaknesses

I will let you test me – to assure you I will not hurt you

I understand the leap you must make

I will give you solace – and *shelter-from-the-storm*
I will take you to a safe place

I will take you deep into-my-womb

deeper and deeper into my soul

let me take your hand into mine

— 88 —
Guardian Angel of
PLAYING CHESS WITH YOUR SON

Sun Tzu's
The Art of War

in a different modality
and now, for our Western friends,

Sir Basil Liddell Hart
his 20th century successor
would approve

Move
Counter-move
Maneuver for position
Pocket even small incremental gains
Erect a flexible defensive line
Probe for the *path of least resistance*
Use your enemy's strength against him
Tenaciously parlay a slight advantage
Advance those pawns
Maneuver with your knights and bishops
but, above all else

Maneuver for sudden checkmate

but
how aggressively do you play against your
9 year-old son

especially as you are teaching him

for
too gently – and you are patronizing
too aggressively – and you will scar his ego

Well, big time strategist
Figure out your strategy surrounding your strategy

Keep your eye on which game is higher stakes, papa
Don't checkmate yourself on this plane, big shot

I thought you were such a great tactician,
Alexander the Great incarnate...

Certainly you can handle this one, Big Dad
You hold all the cards, Mr. Confident

You do, don't you?

— 89 —
Guardian Angel of
CATHOLIC SCHOOL MARCHING BANDS

Feel the cadence
Feel the drum roll
Feel the ground vibrate
Feel your soul respond
Hear the drum roll
the powerful and finessed drum roll
Feel the power
Feel the beat

Track back TWENTY centuries to the inexorable Roman
legions advancing
Battle Legions on the march
Red battle pennants flowing
The Holy Roman empire on the march

Feel the earth tremble
Feel the earth shake
Feel the earth quake

See those varsity majorettes

Feel their sexual energy
Feel the beat

Feel the pounding
Feel the tympani
Feel the impending crescendo

Gaze upon those Roman armies advancing

Slave platoons *on the chain*
See the advancing legions
Helmets glistening
Blood-encrusted swords dangling
Hear their trumpets blaring
Invincible, cadenced, marching

Feel our power
Listen to our drum roll
Tremble at our might

Empires to be carved
Nations to be dominated
All roads lead to us

To us
To Rome

— 90 —
Guardian Angel of RESILIENCE

...the Phoenix

of those who rise from almost total annihilation
to live

GOD AND GOOD

to strive
to advance
to re–build
to defy the obstacles
to leap over the pain
to bypass the destruction
to only glancingly look back
to assemble the building blocks,
one by one, piece by piece
to leave the destruction behind
not to "have time for the pain"

to strip down to basics
to laser-focus their next priority repeatedly
to advance, inch by inch,

inexorably

to follow their destiny
to reclaim their birthright
to provide for a better tomorrow

"anu ba-nu artza livnot u-l'hibanot bah"
we have come to the land of Israel,
to build and, ourselves, to be re-built by

blood, sweat and guts

on an individual – and collective level

I am the Phoenix;
I have arisen from the dead

I have risen above the pain
above the destruction

I have come to re-claim my eternal birthright

with you – or without you,
I will survive,
and I will prevail

* * *

I will run interference for her,
but my granddaughter,
if she so chooses,
will become a physicist,
and my grandson will write,
a fine work of poetry,
and all will be well on this godforsaken planet

— 91 —
Guardian Angel of SPIRITUAL CLEANSING

in Christianity I help out with exorcisms...
in Judaism, I help excise *dybbuks*

I cleanse souls
sadism, evil, torture, evil all unfortunately leave their
tangible imprints on god's children
saddling them with heavy weights to bear
skewing their vision
hobbling their potential
we seek to excise these evil imprints

GOD AND GOOD

to set god's children free
so that they may sparkle bright and unfettered,
yet once again
but these excisions of evil are long and arduous
processes... sometimes even a lifetime
is simply not enough...
care must be taken

love, patience, timing, epiphany, will, and ultimately
– their daring – will set them free

I seek
to liberate their souls
to free the sunshine in their hearts
to have them re-born

and take their proper place
in the constellation of man

good morning, Starshine
be on your way

you have transcended evil and all pain
you are free now

say a little prayer for us,

if you might

pray that a new day has dawned

for us all

— 92 —
Guardian Angel of ROMANTIC LOVE PARTNER

do not play with her heart, for you will lose it
do not confuse being loved, with being powerful
do not walk through the manipulation portal
do not enter that zone
do not go there; you will not win
do not play with her love, because she will rescind it
do not play with her vulnerability, for she will close it
do not emulate a poor model, for you will suffer his
cold fate
do not take her kindness as weakness
for you will forever regret it

do not play with her psyche,
do not play with her love

— 93 —
Guardian Angel of the BETRAYED

I try to give them comfort
I try to give them some peace
I try to give them some solace
I try to provide some balm to their scarred souls
I try to provide some healing to their psychic wounds

we all know they will never be the same again

— 94 —
Guardian Angel of SEXUALITY

they have me veiled and cuffed

JUSTICE has a 'Restraining Order' out on me
VENGEANCE sometimes makes angry moves in my
direction

POWER wants me shackled hand-and-foot
TRUTH trembles whenever I pass close

but, frankly, only Summa fully has my number
and only he and his DELETE key give me pause
the rest of the crew I have dealt with for several
thousand years; ultimately they always back off

Summa, however, is possibly another story
He says he'll just enhance SENSUALITY if I mess
around... give her a better piece of the action...

I don't know why they get so uptight with me
You'd think I made empires crumble :)
You'd think I made grown men act like uncontrollable
little boys :)
You'd think I have this extraordinary hold on otherwise
dignified individuals :)
You'd think I had more power
than the King of England :)
You'd think I could make-or-break regimes :)
You'd think I brought out the primitive in mankind :)
You'd think all the mighty and powerful just crumble

when I give a coquettish smile :)
You'd think they almost all lose total control
when I'm at my peak :)
You'd think there was nothing else to think about
but me :)

Hope he doesn't press that DELETE key...

You just never know when Birnbaum
will 'call-your-card'...

He's a cool number...

Gotta find his weak point...
zero–in on his fantasy...
Find the achilles heel in his soul

Lock his DELETE key...

get a hammer-hold on his Harvard psyche...
imprison his soul...

ambush this idealistic *boychik*

show this sweet boy a real *Cosmic Tango*

aieeeeeeeeeeeeeeeeeeeeeeee....

D– E– L– E– T

— 95 —
Guardian Angel of INTERNAL HEALING

I am the internal healer
I help mend souls

often it takes very substantial time
many, many decades

for abuse wreaks very serious damage

the road to recovery must be navigated very carefully
and very diligently

the protagonist must have an indomitable will

then, we have a fighting chance
then I can practice my profession
then I can help with the timing of the moves
then, it is a race against time

and a lifetime is more-often-than-not insufficient time

often they see what mortal men cannot;

they carry 2-ton weights on their shoulders,

they are my charge
where they go, I go
tucked into their core

I'm along for the journey

along for the duration
god is embarrassed to *look them in the eye*
the cosmos has let them down
deprived them of their rightful due
made them suffer for all humanity's shortcomings

I am their internal healer
the work is not easy
fixing shattered glass would be an easier task

for, the glass has not been betrayed

— 96 —
Guardian Angel of LIBRARY OF LIBRARIES
(the Collective Human Consciousness
as "repository")

I am the ORGANIZER and REPOSITORY of all acquired
knowledge and insight and information
I have the ability to organize and make sense of
ceaseless data and information
This ability comes from within the cumulative human
consciousness
I organize all acquired knowledge
I am a truly great ORGANIZER
I am the cosmic librarian

yes, all the billions of books are in my stacks
all the books ever, ever written
all the manuscripts ever penned

GOD AND GOOD

all art
all creativity
all discovery
all history
all learned insight
all conjecture
all emotion
all hypothesis
all fears
all hopes
all dreams
all intuition
all despair
all aspirations
all thoughts

continuously inexorably evolving and expanding
every milli-milli-second
a roaring tempest of knowledge accumulation
a calm cosmic storm of wisdom acquisition

for I am the
COLLECTIVE HUMAN CONSCIOUSNESS
and
I am vast
and
I am profound
and
I am, indeed, quite real

— 97 —
Guardian Angel of -1, 0, +1

yes, specifically these three digits
three gentle seemingly lightweight digits
heaven's building blocks
god's mortar

they are my charge

my mandate is to vigilantly protect them from all harm
to protect their integrity
very few realize
that so very much hinges on them
for, at the *Genesis* point

0 was divided
into -1... and +1...

this is the essence of creation
at the *Genesis* point

Nothingness was divided into
pluses and minuses
a radically different spin on the classic phrase
Creation ex Nihilo
and from that division, into pluses and minuses,

onward
positive and negative
good and evil

blessing and curse

GOD AND GOOD

male and female
advance and retreat
dark and light
and on and on and on...
simple but powerful
powerful enough to create a universe

or perhaps a universe and an anti-universe
or perhaps powerful enough to create a Divine to create
the cosmos

and then

the same three digits
gifted to mankind;
for the BINARY system of 1s and 0s
the foundation, as well, for the vast computer and
telecommunication universes

the foundation, as well,
for the DECIMAL system based on 10

so simple
so pure
so powerful

I must be vigilant
for all of infinity

I live and sleep 1s and 0s;
sometimes I wish they had given me RED instead

— 98 —
Guardian Angel of SAGE WISDOM

Wisdom is embedded
And wisdom flows
Multi-tiered and multi-dimensional
Transmitted from generation to generation
and flowing in the here-and-now through cosmic
consciousness
Inherent in our overarching Quest for Potential∞

— 99 —
Guardian Angel of RESCUE

I am the Guardian Angel of Rescue

I defy power and danger
– and "the odds"
to rescue my fellow members of mankind
from danger, from evil, from bondage...

My instincts need be sharp...
my arrow must find its mark

I must succeed
For the repercussions if I fail are serious
But if, *against-the-odds*, I do succeed,
in addition to the lives rescued,

I lift ALL of mankind's spirit

well beyond the circle of the immediate rescuees
well beyond the particular time frame in which I operate

But I am, indeed, the last resort
I seize life from the jaws of darkness

My instincts had best be sharp
My cause had best be true
Be sure my friend

To be possibly WORTHY of my hi-risk endeavor

I am the Guardian Angel of Rescue

I was there at DUNKIRK – on the English Channel –
in June 1940 when – called upon by Her Majesty –
hundreds of valiant British fishing boat captains rode
to the incredible rescue of 338,000 trapped British and
Allied soldiers on the beaches of Dover

*

I was there at ENTEBBE airport in Uganda in July 1976
when an airborne Israeli commando force electrified the
world with their creativity and daring – and success

* * *

And I was there on duty with the *noble brigade* –
on a bright sunny morning in Manhattan,
September 11, 2001....

300 strong they were
NY's "bravest", NY firefighters

Dispatched into Tower Two
by the *'powers-that-be'*

...To the rescue

When Commanders gave the order to charge;

Up into the vertical valley charged the 300;

Billowing smoke to the right of them

Lapping flames to the left of them;

When communication seemingly went awry;

Up the gasoline-stenched stairwells they charged

Charging up, while thousands were fleeing past them
down;

New York's fire-warriors;

Man for Man

Warrior for warrior

Valiant and physically strong

Volunteers, all, for the gallant rescue

Upward, flight after flight
Some charging-up 80+ flights

GOD AND GOOD

in full "battle-gear"
they charged
The bravest brigade

oxygen-tanks and all
upward, upward, upward
and onward
charged the 300

billowing smoke to the right of them

lapping flames to the left of them
up the stairwells of doomed Tower Two

upward and onward charged the immortal brigade;
a rescue attempt *ad extremis*

boldly they rode and well;

Into the jaws of Hell

charged the 300

was it mythological lore or real
The charge of the *bravest of the brave*
up the vertical valley of danger

into the *line-of-fire* of death

the *fighting Irish* –
the bravest brigade of all –
charging ever upwards

sweating badly now
exhausted, exhausted
communication now cut off
they had a *rendezvous with immortality*

billowing smoke now surrounding them
billowing smoke to the right of them
flames now lapping at them to the left of them...

boldly they rode and well,

Into the jaws of Hell

onward and upwards charged the 300

the gasoline stench increased; the oxygen decreased

Hope the "little woman" will be OK *y'know*
take care of the kids *will ya'*

onward, onward, upward, charged the 300
the immortal brigade

muster all the guts you've got in *ya'*...

The brotherhood believes in *ya'*

Onward, onward, upward, charged the 300
Onward, skyward to impact floor 80 now
charging upward, forward and onward
charging well
right into the gaping jaws of Hell

GOD AND GOOD

onward, forward, upward, charged the brave 300;
into Dante's looming inferno

Doomed, doomed were the 300

Their commanders had not intuitively grasped
the lethal trap
Not *a chance in hell* protected the brigade

As they valiantly *plied-their-trade*

Remember us to the Brotherhood *will ya'*
I kept the faith, dad, I kept the faith

Now and forever
..."the BROTHERHOOD"

Doomed they were

charging into ETERNITY

rode the 300

— 100 —
Guardian Angel of PEACE

'Yisa Hashem Panav elecha'
May God turn His countenance to you
'v'yasem l'cha shalom'
and establish for you Peace
(Numbers 6:24-26)

'Sim shalom'
Establish peace

'tova uvracha'
goodness and blessing

'chain va-chesed vi-rachamim'
graciousness, kindness and compassion

'l'varech et amcha yisrael'
to bless your people

'b'chol et u'vchal sha-a'
at every time and at every hour

'b'shlomoecha'
with Your peace

— from the *Siddur* (Jewish prayer book)

— 101 —
Guardian Angel of '*AHAVA*' (Love)

'*Ahava*' – LOVE, the same '*gematriyah*' (letter valuation)
as

'*ACHAD*': Oneness/unity
For '*ahava*'–love and only '*ahava*'–love –
makes the cosmos WHOLE.
For initially the Void was unzipped into

Positives and Negatives,
White and Dark,
Male and Female.
And, in Love –
And In Relationships –
And ultimately in Marriage–union
Does the Cosmos re–Unite.

Seeming linearities,
Consummate circularities.

The cosmic ring is completed
May the love be rare and pure

Simple, but profound
Simple, but true

In Marriage,
All polarities

Re–Unite
That is the profound and powerful
Cosmic drive
Impelling us all to take that leap–journey
From Biblical times – through the present.
Attempting to make not just ourselves,
But the entire Cosmos, Whole.

Come with me for a full journey! Love beckons
Come with me for a death-defying Leap! Love entreats

I will complete your Soul
I will quench your Heart
I will re-Unite the entire Cosmic order

You will single-handedly effect
'COMPLETION–of–CREATION'

ahava, ahava, ahava
Love in its many, many forms
Love, oh Love

Careless Love

I am the "middle-child" Guardian Angel

as far as the establishment was concerned
I was not given enough attention...
Almost always a peripheral supporting role

I was over-shadowed by the others for centuries...
I pleaded with them to pay more attention to me...
They did not listen

Then, Hillel and, in his footsteps,
the shepherd entered the picture
With LOVE center-stage...

— 102 —
Guardian Angel of "*EHEYEH ASHER EHEYEH*"
(Quest for Potential)

"I WILL BE THAT WHICH I WILL BE"
the primal name of God
Holy potential
Quest for potential$^\infty$ of potential$^\infty$ of potential$^\infty$...
ad infinitum... an infinite spiral...

The core dynamic
actually bordering on the abstract

the Holy Grail of metaphysics

Quest for Potential$^\infty$ squared infinitely
(*Eheyeh Asher Eheyeh*) to the infinite power

the sole explicit hint of the underlying motif of the
universe
concealed within a burning bush

wrapped within the history of Israel

connected to the saga of Liberty
to Moses – who set us all free
The name of God is actually POTENTIAL
For they are, indeed, one
Inextricably intertwined

Ascending levels of potential/consciousness/reality
Cosmos after cosmos unfolding...
molting and emerging...

Metamorphosis ongoing...
Holy Quest for Potential

Eheyeh Asher Eheyeh

The inexorable cosmic unfolding...
Seeking after its own infinite perfection and fullness

At the core of the Divine
The key cosmic potentiality catalyst
The spark of the Divine

Eheyeh Asher Eheyeh
One name / Three words / The Cosmic Essence
Tremble at its simplicity
Shudder at its clarity

Front-and-center at the core of the key biblical

narrative
Staring at us...
for three thousand very long and arduous years
Potential / Freedom / Liberty / Meaning / Spirituality

All one infinite spiral

Man, the spearhead
Moshe Rabeinu [Moses our Teacher] – the point of the
tip of the metaphysical spear...

Advance... inexorable advance

Freedom

And Upliftment

— 103 —
Guardian Angel of "*ALEPH*" (1)

(the first letter of the Hebrew alphabet)

I am 1.
I am first. I represent unity.
I am inherently so Powerful.
The cosmos was created with Beth
- the second letter of the alphabet
So as not to DEIFY me
I am First – and, on some level, in a cosmos predicated
on circularity and unity, I am last.

First there was First–*Aleph–Achad: Eheyeh Asher
Eheyeh* Infinity
And intertwined with the above was Love–Hope

Then there a wait... a very long wait
Then there was Despair
Then there was an Insight
Then there was a pause

Then there were the equations... many equations
Then there was a Focus
Then there was a Determination
Then there was a Yearning
Then there was a Will – a very strong Will
Then there was the cumulative potentiality Catalyst
    drawn from infinities to come
Then there were ascending levels of
    Consciousness and Reality
Then there was a Flicker
Then there was a transcendental Flame
Then there was a Creation–Storm
Then there was Aleph

Then there was Life

— 104 —
Guardian Angel of
THE (REALITY (POTENTIALITY CONTINUUM

(Reality (Potentiality... infinity
is a continuum

No man is an island; He is a continuum
Tracking forward to infinity... Tracking backwards to the
Genesis point

[See the mathematician Mandelbrot's fractiles]

and, to the timeless mindbending Question:
Which came first: The chicken or the egg?

Answer: They both emerged simultaneously...
>> at the birthing point <<
as part of a flowing continuum

— 105 —
Guardian Angel of ASCENTS
(in consciousness and reality)

The cosmos is in a never-ending ascent of
consciousness and reality
It is a work-in-progress

Emerging from a nether-world of potentiality into
ever-increasing reality

Points on infinite continuums ever-so-gently emerging

Reality on some level defined by the level of
consciousness of the observer (see The Quantum)

— 106 —
Guardian Angel of
"LIFE FORCE" / *CHI*

I flow through the cosmic seas
Tracking forward to infinity
Tracking back to the origins of origins
Of course these two points converge
But that is my secret

I connect all life – past, present and future
Tap into me – and you soar
Disconnect from me – and you are relegated to the
mundane
I surge through Man
I breathe LifeForce through him
I energize his potentialities

Sense me – and tap into me
For I am the spark of the Divine
The river of infinity
Coursing through Man

The ancient Chinese got a handle on the (Life Force)
situation
More powerful than gunfire, which they are also
credited with discovering

Does *CHI* interconnect all cosmic organisms –
with an entire array of wavelengths and channels?

— 107 —
Guardian Angel of
THE CUMULATIVE CONSCIOUSNESS
(as "decision-maker")

We are all interconnected
Across the planet
And on some level, through time
The Cumulative Consciousness...
flows throughout the cosmos
all part of a large miasmic sea
of consciousness

And when *critical mass* of consciousness is attained,
humanity takes a leap forward and onwards

It is this Cumulative Consciousness impacting
critical cosmic and evolutionary decisions

— 108 —
Guardian Angel of
FLOWS, CHANNELS, WAVES & MERIDIANS

Flows make the universe "go round"...

Life-force flows
Hereditary *chi*
Potential *chi*
Meridian *chi*
Blood *chi*

Aura *chi*
etc.

Emotional / Love / Relationship flows
Grandparent-Parent-child
Child-parent-grandparent
Sibling-sibling
Fraternal-Fraternal
Mentor-disciple
Person-world
World-person
etc.
Spiritual / Religious / Piety-driven / Meditation-driven
flows

Energy flows

Communication flows

Intellectual flows / Artistic flows / Music & Harmonic
flows / Creative flows / Fashion

Consciousness flows

Physical flows
Cosmic / Planetary / Time /
Terrestrial / Electromagnetic / Light spectrum /
Gravity-related / Tidal / Ocean current /
Weather currents /
Celestial / Seasonal
Internal Bodily / Electrical / *Chi* /
Respiratory / Circulation /

Reproductive etc. /
etc.

Other flows
Unknown
Unknown
Unknown
Unknown

Kindness-driven / Empathic–driven / Self-sacrifice–
driven / Forgiveness–driven / Mercy–driven /
Generosity–driven / Compassion–driven /

Hope–driven / Passion–driven / Creativity–driven /
Liberation–driven / Loyalty–driven / Will–driven

Airwaves / light waves / radio waves /
TV channels / micro waves
Geological–continental drift, rocks being recycled
Carbon–plants, eating, decomposing /
food chain flows
Oxygen–photosynthesis
Krebs cycle, other metabolic cycles
Information flows (maybe most important)
proteins – * DNA – * RNA – * proteins
Stellar cycle
Computer revolution–faster, more complex, Artificial
Intelligence, simulations
Money flows...
People migrations
Climate flows...ice ages, etc.

— 109 —
Guardian Angel of LURIANIC KABBALAH

(the Kabbalah of Rabbi Isaac Luria in the Middle Ages)

hypothesizing stages of Divine emanation
Tucked into Jewish lore for 15 centuries
later, Birnbaum's primordial quests for potential
...*Summa* would pluck me out of MYSTICISM and tuck
me into METAPHYSICS

Were these, as well, stages of consciousness
Were these, as well, stages of REALITY
Were these, as well, the infinitely spiraling cosmic
equations

Spiraling closer and closer to Creation?

— 110 —
Guardian Angel of FORGIVENESS

Summa inserted me almost last
It was not his natural inclination to include me
in the first tier
Forgiveness is complex

And forgiveness is indeed dangerous sometimes
Indeed forgiveness is not always in the cosmic interest

And sometimes destructive
But if the overriding and overarching intent of the

original perpetrator was basically benign and non-
destructive, forgiveness of the particular action is
usually appropriate

Not only for the usual *karmic* reasons
But as well

Because forgiveness re-opens a CHANNEL
A life-force flow back through that person
A (LOVE) *chi*–channel through that person, if you will –
And through that party – to their entire network...
And to the extent that we open life-force channels

We empower ourselves
And reach fullest life and cosmic vitality
And therefore,

At some point we must consider
"forgiving" even our dear parents :)
The "sins" they may have perpetrated against us
Most probably unknowingly

Either in zealousness
Or replicating their own difficult experiences

For all parents, of course, inherently love their children
And certainly mean them no harm
There are plentiful opportunities – and tension points

Along the journey
With potential for mis-steps

So, feel the eternal cosmic flows flowing from Eden...
feel the metaphysical FLOW which has always been
waiting your GO AHEAD to bathe you... allow this
subtle but profound cosmic dynamic to nourish your
soul... forevermore... and, perhaps at some point,
say a gentle prayer of thanks to have reached this
point of LIGHT

— 111 —
Guardian Angel of "*SHABBAT HAMALKAH*"
(the Sabbath)

The Sabbath Queen

In my own way, I complete Creation
I center the cosmos
I calm the storm
The cosmic storm
The human storm
Y'kum purkun min sh'mayah
May Salvation come from Heaven
And, indeed, it does
And I am indeed but one vehicle
But a weekly vehicle, at that.
Come, my children
Prepare for peace
Prepare for a spiritual island in the midst of the storm
Prepare for the Sabbath Queen
For she will bring you an interlude of peace
An interlude of higher level spirituality
A moment of sublime grace

To connect with the Divine
To connect with your soul
To center your core
To elevate your spiritual level
To be at harmony with the universe
To enter a bubble of grace with your families

— 112 —
Guardian Angel of COSMIC BREATHING

Love in
Love out

Breathe in receiving love;
Breathe-out giving love

Breathe in GRATITUDE;
Breathe-out COMPASSION

Breathe in THANKS for god's bounty;
Breathe-out GENEROSITY of SPIRIT

Breathe in some of the LOVE you potentially may
have received;
Breathe-out bountiful LOVE you might potentially
have given.

Breathe in ascending levels of desire and love and
pleasure;
Breathe-out an explosion of lovingness and
givingness.

Breathe in oxygen to luxuriate every cell of your body
Breathe-out carbon dioxide, food for every plant on
the planet

Breathe in the wonders of the world
Breathe-out guilt and toxicity

Let this *nutritious* breathing cleanse your heart,
and cleanse your soul of *toxins* and *blocks*

The bronchi of the human lung are self similar over 15
successive bifurcations – meaning the same pattern is
repeated under 15 successive microscopic levels –
as they are the products of – and the energizers of –
POTENTIAL – i.e. *potential within potential...within
potential... ad infinitum*

An ancient Hindu (Eastern) myth known as the "Breath of
Brahman" has God EXHALING, i.e. creating the cosmos
(via the Bang Bag as we lately came to learn), and, then,
trillions of light years later, INHALING, i.e. contracting
(imploding) the cosmos... They, the Hindus were half-right
[the first half :)]

— 113 —
Guardian Angel of TRANSCENDENT GOALS

The Cosmos Itself has goals – transcendent ones

Its quest for infinite potentialities is, of course, its goal

GOD AND GOOD

This quest is its own *raison d'etre*
The cosmos is sustained not because it necessarily
reaches its goals,
but because it is true to its eternal quest
The quest allows the cosmos to defy not just the void,
not just inertia, not just gravity, not just entropy;
The quest allows the cosmos to avoid cosmic death.
The quest sustains cosmic *CHI* – cosmic life force.
This quest drives the cosmos.

On an individual level,
It is our transcendent quests, which sustain us:
Quests for love-giving to our family and close friends
Quests for spirituality
Quests for growth – in whatever realms

When we continue to reach ever-higher,
we tap into cosmic flows
We tap into eternity
We become almost immortal
We can transcend severe pain, riveting betrayals,
enormous defeats, setbacks and losses

Why? Because we remain tapped-into the vital
life-affirming currents of the cosmic order
Because we remain plugged–into eternity and infinity

— 114 —
Guardian Angel of
METAMORPHOSIS / PUNCTUATED EQUILIBRIUM

I am the invisible Guardian Angel

inextricably linked to the abstract dynamic
Quest for Potential∞
When the cosmos is ready for its next leap,
I am the catalyst
When Mankind emerged from the Eden void of Bliss
When the Dinosaur Age ended
When humanoids emerged from the sea
I presided
As Vicar for the Divine

Eheyeh Asher Eheyeh

L'olam va-ed (eternally)

My code name:
"PUNCTUATED EQUILIBRIUM"
(that is, "Sudden Leaps" across species lines)

Yes, I know
You heard this term before –

In relation to a critique of Darwin's Theory of Evolution
For there seemed to be this FLAW in his theory
There seemed to be sudden jumps across entire
species – unaccountable by Darwinian theory
And, of course the FLAW does exist

GOD AND GOOD

But Punctuated Equilibrium's main claim to eternal fame is
not that it is a flaw in another's theory,
But, rather, that it is the tip of the iceberg of the actual
primary cosmic dynamic

It is the "Work-in-Progress" of Quest for Potential$^\infty$

As the entire cosmos leaps forward –
as the cosmos metaphorically re-invents itself
Reaching to the NEXT higher level across one or more
species simultaneously

All components initially emerge – and then continuously
advance – in an inter–related advance
They are all part of an inter-related dynamic –
Man's consciousness / more advanced human states /
cosmic richness / cosmic levels of reality

All advancing and periodically leaping forward in-sync
Across entire cosmic frontiers
Initially from out of the Void
And from thence onward to eternity and infinity

But how do leaps occur across an entire species?
Summa hypothesizes that multiple and potentially
powerful, albeit generally latent, channels connecting us
all exist

As the cumulative cosmic consciousness selects a "route
forward" for the ADVANCE of Life,
a sort of DIRECTED EVOLUTION occurs,

Whereby a particular channel or channels are given
priority

While other channels are allowed to terminate

Thus it is the cumulative consciousness directing these
punctuated equilibriums
it is "survival of the fittest" only in terms that the
collective human consciousness deems this channel
to be the fittest

— 115 —
Guardian Angel of EARTHLY FULFILLMENT

In going through the Museum of Natural History
in New York,
and viewing the various exhibits and charts
of life through the ages,
one is always struck by the
hi-definition *key components*:

permeating –

**inexorable advance + richness + beauty
+ wondrous variety + elegant complexity
+ exquisite inter-dependence + all-pervasive
sexuality/mating/reproduction + life-questing
diversity**

and one must presume

that these CONCEPTS are key goals

– whether intermediate or final – of Creation

— 116 —
Guardian Angel of *CHI* BLACK BELT MASTER

The *CHI* black belt wants to be constantly GIVING and constantly emitting POSITIVE emotional flow; he wants to tap into CREATION – the Cosmic GIVING.

The *CHI* black belt wants to tap into the *CHI* of his fellow Man...and overall cosmic *CHI* (however vague that concept is)
This GIVING approach of the *CHI* master will keep super-charging his *CHI*. The *CHI* master does not want any toxic emotion blocking his ability to be GIVING and FLOWING towards fellow MAN;
When he feels internal ANGER, he shifts gears and emits COMPASSION;
when he senses internal VENGEFULNESS, he shifts gears and emits FORGIVENESS;
when he senses internal JEALOUSY, he shifts gears and emits ADMIRATION;
when he senses internal HATE, he shifts gears and emits...what does he emit?... I'm not sure... But perhaps he emits EMPATHY for the circumstances that drove his fellow MAN to evil + HOPE for a better tomorrow where such evil does not walk the face of the earth. EMPATHY and HOPE will have to do here. EMPATHY and HOPE are about as positive as we can get in replacing HATE.

But EMPATHY and HOPE will do.

The *CHI* Master knows that he cannot control the emotions of his fellow Man towards him; But he can control his emotions towards his fellow Man – and therein lies his Victory. For the ultimate GIVER is the ultimate Victor.

The *CHI* master understands that "initially" the VOID divided into positive and negatives...that although there is not necessarily a 1:1 polarity correspondence between specific emotions, on a broader basis, there is a polarity. The *CHI* Master will counter Negative with Positive. When Negativity is directed towards him, he will deflect it. The *CHI* Master will, as a matter of regimen, substitute Positive emotion for any of his own internal Negativity. He does not repress his Negativity. He accepts it, feels it, and then substitutes it out. The *CHI* master is a master of his emotional flow to his fellow MAN. He is empowered, enriched, enlightened. He is so extraordinary. He is almost at the level of a BABY.

— 117 —
Guardian Angel of GUARDIANS OF THE COSMOS

We are all – each of us – Guardians of the Cosmos Understand that each individual is a Guardian of Cosmic Potential.

...of Creativity ...Liberty, Love, Mercy, Kindness,

Intellectuality, Spirituality, Consciousness *et al*.
Some are particularly Guardians of Cosmic Beauty
and Grace
We each protect, elevate and advance these cosmic
treasures

We each can potentially breathe life into these
attributes
We each can transform and elevate them
(Would that we had enough time in the day, for sure)

And each transformation impacts the whole–of
humanity–and the cosmos
Therefore, do not underestimate your individual
importance in the cosmic design of matters
Being a 'Guardian of Cosmic Potential' is heavy and
heady stuff

We need you!

— 118 —
Guardian Angel of the
WARRIOR OF THE LIGHT

The Warrior of the Light (see late 20th century book by
this name by the Brazilian author Paul Coelho) stands
upright and confident, his magic sword by his side.
He has a vision for the future, but is well grounded in
the present. He is armed educationally, intellectually,
emotionally, tactically, spiritually, possibly religiously.

He follows his star. He has a feel for his short-term,
medium-term and long-term goals, subject always
to fine-tuning.

He is a good friend to his allies; and a tenacious
enemy to his foes.

He does not always play-it-safe, for then he would
have to lower his Sights considerably. He assesses
and re-assesses the limits of the plausibly possible.
The plausible limits. That is his turf. But what does
PLAUSIBLE mean? He must trust his gut. Totally. He is
a Warrior. He can indeed possibly fail and fall – possibly
never to rise again.
If he sets his Sights too low, it will be a life unfulfilled.
He will have let himself down in his most important
mission.
If he sets his Sights too high, he will be relegated to
the realm of naïve dreamers. He must not over-reach.

If he sets his Sights just right, he may suffer along the
way, and he may bleed, and he may, from time-to-time,
kick himself for starting out on this possibly-too-bold
journey – but he will ultimately prevail – and the angels
of the cosmos will rise in unison – and applaud his
daring quest.

The Warrior of the Light is tranquil in the face of myriad
obstacles and challenges and, indeed, threats. But he
does have his magic sword by his side... and, deep in
his gut he knows, he knows, that one way or another,
he will, before his dying day, prevail...

— 119 —
Guardian Angel of the
RETURN OF THE YOUNG PRINCE

Battle-scarred and wizened, he gazes at the distant Port. The Port of his hometown, which he left so many months ago. When times were simpler. When he was not particularly familiar with the term 'defeat' or "major setback".

The odyssey of the fleet was far more perilous than anticipated. He had overestimated the power of his "magic touch". The journey was to prove far more brutal than anticipated. The "strategic ground" had radically shifted...and was to shift again several times before the end of the mission. The multiple betrayals, as well as the blunders by hangers-on were extreme. The losses along the way were heavy, quite heavy. There was almost to be no return at all. Were it not for some unanticipated change in the weather subsequent to the ambush, the fleet would have been annihilated on the first day of the surprise attack. They had been ambushed by the 35-ship Pirate Fleet. And were it not for the valor of the daughter of his Personal Secretary, the Fleet would have been decimated on Day 14. And he himself would ultimately have been either captured or killed. The Personal Secretary's svelte daughter, Amanda, had feigned betrayal and desertion to gain an eventual audience with the curious Pirate Commander – and then drove a stiletto into his throat...shortly after midnight.

Close. Very, very close.

When the initial alliances had broken up, the treachery and betrayals followed almost unremittingly. And when the pirate raiders scanned him through their eyepieces, they did not particularly care that in his youth he had been a local hero. They just came to plunder and torture and kill. But the pirates also underestimated his resourcefulness – and his cunning.

He now knew quite clearly who his friends and enemies were. He had been about 90% on-target before the journey. But the 10% miscalibration almost cost him everything.

He scanned from side to side. The now-smaller Fleet. Pennants billowing. White sails filled with wind. Heading homeward. Getting closer to Port now. 40% of the principality's Fleet at its peak. Two of his three original top lieutenants were now dead.

He was DOWN 2 top lieutenants and 60% of his fleet, and UP one treasure map. The trade-off had been brutal. His destiny would now seem to rest with the map. A searing 11" scar now crossed from his left shoulder across his chest. The initial intent of the mission was to return with awesome treasure. The updated goal was to survive the assorted treachery – and the seismic shift in alliances. No empire. No treasure.

For the time being, "live to play another day". But the home Port would be independent – and free from attack – for now. And he, himself, was now forged-in-fire. And was a now a very, very fine-tuned warrior. Emissaries from a faraway kingdom had – almost magically just the week before – come by pilot ship with exquisite news...offer of a potential alliance of exquisite opportunity... far surpassing that of the previous odyssey...the Phoenix Prince they had called him. The Emperor of the faraway kingdom had apparently been tracking recent events. And the distant Empire had been intrigued. And the distant Emperor was now apparently considering the possibility of offering a Golden Alliance.

Fate or Mirage? Destiny – or pie-in-the-sky?
The battle-wizened Prince was returning home now.

The young Prince needed time... some time... some time to analyze the latest overture and think this through... to re-gather his strength... to properly dress his wounds... to re-center himself... to touch base with his allies... to walk in his garden... and trek the tree-covered paths of the mountain's of his youth... to interact with some of his boyhood friends... to gather Life-Force from his Inner Circle and family ...and then... to plan...

— 120 —
the LOST angel

* * * * end of Angels * * * *

GOD AND GOOD

AFTERWORD to 120 Angels

"Holy quest for potential is the underlying core
dynamic of the cosmic order.

Holy quest for potential is the "primal scream"
of the cosmos. Holy Potential, emanating through
and from the Divine essence, radiates through the
universe – questing, pulsating, exploding, reaching,
energizing, expanding, in time and out-of-time.

It is at the core of the holy/natural drive of the cosmos.
It is the "primal engine" of cosmic existence."

> – from the work
> *God and Evil*
> PART TWO, Section 200.00

* * *

"V'hassneh einenu u'kkal"

"But, the bush is not consumed"

The Biblical author (the GODHEAD of the infinite "holy" human/Divine consciousness) was keen to the mysteries of the cosmos, but his audience was simply not ready....

It was three and a half thousand years premature to unveil the cornerstone secrets of the cosmic order....

Instead, the Biblical author wrapped the key cosmic secret – *Eheyeh Asher Eheyeh* – the key to the Cosmic Code – in an enigmatic Burning Bush at the epicenter of the saga that liberated the Jews – a saga that would be re-told year after year at Passover at a minimum, decade after decade, century after century, millennium after millennium by an indefatigable – and truly eternal people.

end of 120 Angels

INDEX (alphabetical)
to 120 Guardian Angels

	ANGEL	ANGEL #
	of -1 ,0, +1	97
A	of *"AHAVA"*	101
	of *"ALEPH"*	103
	of ARCHITECTURE	55
	of ASCENTS	105
	of ASSAULTS ON THE THRONE	59
	of the ASSASSIN	84
	of AVENGING JUSTICE	41
	of AWARENESS	73a
B	of the BETRAYED	93
	of BLUE	32
	of BREATHING	112
	of BUBBLES	13
	of BURYING THE DEAD	80
	of BUTTERFLIES	57
C	of CATCHING THE MOMENT	40
	of CATHOLIC HIGH SCHOOL MARCHING	89
	of *CHI* BLACK BELT MASTER	116
	of CHILDREN LAUGHING	19
	of CIRCLES	52
	of CLEAR STAR FILLED SKIES	8
	of COMBATING EVIL	74
	of COMFORT	53
	of CONFIDENCE	17
	of CONSCIOUSNESS	73b
	of CONQUEST	60
	of COSMIC FULFILLMENT	26
	of the COSMIC CONTINUUM	104

ANGEL	ANGEL #
of CREATIVITY	31
of CUMULUS NIMBUS CLOUDS	7
of the CUMULATIVE CONSCIOUSNESS	107
D of the DIGNITY OF MAN	78
of DISSENT	68
of DREAMS	9
E of EARTHLY FULFILLMENT	115
of "*EHEYEH ASHER EHEYEH*"	102
of ELEGANCE	20
of ENCHANTED EVENINGS	33
of ESCAPE	86
of EXPLORERS	14
F of FALLING IN LOVE	35
of FEAR	28
of FIRE	43
of FIVE-YEAR-OLD-GIRLS GIGGLING	44
of FLOWS, WAVES & CHANNELS	108
of FORGIVENESS	110
of FORTITUDE	69
of FRESHLY-BAKED "*CHALLAH*"	48
of FREEDOM	4
G of "GEMORAH CHAVRUSAHS"	75
of GENEROSITY OF SPIRIT	85
of GEOMETRY	11
of GRACE	83
of GRATITUDE	2
of GUARDIANS OF THE COSMOS	17
H of "*HAVDALAH*"	49
of HOLDING YOUR DAUGHTER'S HAND	56
of HOLOCAUST VICTIMS	38
of HONOR	42

	ANGEL	ANGEL #
	of HOPE	21
	of HORSEBACK RIDING	65
I	of INTERNAL HEALING	95
	of INTIMACY	87
	of IRON MILL WORKERS	58
J	of JOURNEYS TO FAR-AWAY LANDS	82
	of JU JITSU	71
K	of KINDNESS	18
	of KITE FLYING	54
L	of LIBERATION	45
	of the LIBRARY OF LIBRARIES	96
	of "LIFE FORCE" / *CHI*	106
	of LIGHT	12
	of LIGHTING "*SHABBOS* CANDLES"	25
	of the LONELY	1
	of the LOST ANGEL	120
	of LOVE BONDS	36
	of LOYALTY	51
	of LURIANIC KABBALAH	109
M	of MARRIAGE	37
	of MERCY	5
O	of OPTIMIZING POTENTIAL	81
P	of PASSION	15
	of PEACE	100
	of PLAYING CHESS WITH YOUR SON	88
	of PROTECTING THE YOUNG	46
	of PUNCTUATED EQUILIBRIUM	114
	of PUTTING-THE-KIDS-TO-BED	50
R	of RAINBOWS	10
	of RAPPROACHMENT	29
	of RED	34

ANGEL	**ANGEL #**
of REMEMBRANCE	79
of RESCUE	99
of RESILIENCE	90
of RETURN	32
of the RETURN OF THE PRINCE	119
of ROMANTIC LOVE	16
of the ROMANTIC LOVE PARTNER	92
S of SAGE WISDOM	98
of SAILING AGAINST THE WIND	67
of SELF DISCIPLINE	64
of SENSUALITY	30
of SEVEN-YEAR-OLD BUDDIES	27
of SEXUALITY	94
of *"SHABBAT HAMALKAH"*	111
of SNOWFLAKES	3
of SNOW-PEAKED MOUNTAIN RANGES	70
of SNOWSTORMS ON SCHOOL DAYS	62
of SPIRITUAL CLEANSING	91
of STRENGTH	76
of SUBSTANCE & FORM	77
of SUNRISE	6
T of TIDES	24
of TOUGH LOVE	72
of TRANQUILITY	63
of TRANSCENDENT GOALS	113
of TRUTH	61
of TWENTY FIVE + YEAR FRIENDSHIPS	66
V of VICTORY	39
W of *WALKING THE KIDS TO "SHUL"*	47
of WHITE	22
of the WARRIOR OF THE LIGHT	118

The final section, The Lost Manual,
is built on two Parallel Tracks:

A "Wisdom Book"

and a

"Self-Actualization Book"

Simultaneously, implicit in this body of work is another
key proposition and theme: namely, that what is true on
a cosmic level, metaphysically is also true, in parallel,
on a personal level "self-actualization-wise", and
vice versa.

Meaning, by understanding one, we achieve a fuller and
more profound understanding of the other.
Each can provide crucial clues as to the other. I operate
under a related corollary of mine – that gaps in one can
be filled-in, by examining the other. I propose that this
elegant – and awesomely powerful –
"cosmic detective tool" will enable philosophers and
metaphysicians to fill in gaps or fine-tune aspects of
Metaphysics.

I posit that metaphysical themes which play out on a
grand cosmic level, driving the cosmos, have direct,
usually 1:1 parallels with mortal dynamics.

Inasmuch as I also posit that every single human is a universe, albeit physically smaller than the grand Universe which we operate in, the parallel works elegantly and powerfully.

Unlocking the cosmic code is not just an ivory tower academic enterprise. For, the stakes are, of course, great. For, to the extent that we unlock the cosmic code, we also understand ourselves, our children, our purpose, our inner drive, our universe, our planet, our civilization, our struggles and triumphs and our ultimate meaning. We can better prioritize and put matters in perspective. We can achieve higher and higher levels of self-actualization, and, indeed, consciousness. We can empower ourselves and optimize our lives. We can better set goals for ourselves and for our children. We can prevail better over adversity and inevitable setbacks, and, indeed, prevail better over success. We can advance forward with deliberate confidence. As noted, The Lost Manual is also a "Wisdom Book", offering either explicit or implicit thoughts about life –
from the perspective of 'the perpetrator' of this particular overarching metaphysics. The underlying motif is that there are really no simplistic ABSOLUTES. Rather, life is more nuanced, more textured. Some of the "wisdom themes" offered, are spins of classic themes, but with more nuance, and with an occasional dose of pop culture.

GOD AND GOOD

Part III:
The Lost Manual

GOD AND GOOD

Part III: The Lost Manual
TABLE OF CONTENTS

Introductory to The Lost Manual   360

The Lost Manual   361

Introductory to
The Lost Manual

*Fable has it
that in ancient times
a timeless MANUAL existed,
which, along with the Ark of the Covenant,
had been lost...*

The Lost Manual

The only CONSTANT in the universe is CHANGE
He who masters CHANGE, masters the universe

*

Advance, continuously advance
– on all fronts

Incrementally is OK – but steadily

An occasional leap is not a bad idea, as well.

*

With PASSION
comes both greatness and pain

With GREATNESS
comes danger

With PAIN comes opportunity

*

GOD AND GOOD

There is nothing,
absolutely nothing
more powerful than
– "an idea whose time has come"

Power must be anchored in justice
Justice must be anchored in power
Justice is elusive

                    *

Power must be used with finesse
ditto, Wealth

                    *

Seek after your own Potential –
steadily and inexorably

– and you will energize your entire being
every hour, every day, every year
– to the day you complete your work here –
in this form

                    *

Life is great
Life is difficult

Giving your life MEANING & GOALS,

tips the scales towards one or the other

*

All good relationships are profound

They connect us with all eternity
They fill our souls
and elevate us as humans

*

Treasure,
enhance and protect
loving relationships

Stay close to entities
which seem to bring out the best in you,
which seem to actualize your potential

*

All individuals,
situations and greater contexts
are unique –
- and therefore
few "sage wisdoms" universally apply

*

Multi-generational connecting,
meaning grandparent > parent > grandchild
connecting with love and care and respect,

will tend to enhance *potential-life-force*.

GOD AND GOOD

*

Entities and people
morph themselves every year.

Just follow the play.

- and be self-supportive of a *positive morph.*

*

Play the cards you are dealt;
Do not lament cards you were not dealt;

*

The ability to "listen"
is a pre-requisite for success
in business, romance, all relationships
(and metaphysics)

*

The ability to *discern* and then
deliver-to-the-other-party
what they desire and need most
is a pre-requisite for success
in both business and romance
(and metaphysics)

*

Recent incarnations are more important than
prior incarnations. *Move on!*

Of course,
old realities and projections
only recalcitrantly fade.

But, they are supplanted.

*

Just concentrate on OPTIMIZING

the play –

and you will achieve success and fulfillment

*

Strive to become
the embodiment
of (the unisex) values
you wish
your Dream Lover
to be –
and you will reach fulfillment
on multiple levels

*

In weakness there is power;
in power, weakness…

GOD AND GOOD

corollary: His strength is also his weakness
corollary: In crisis, there is opportunity

*

Don't be too fancy;
Don't be too simple

But, you can be fancy with *generosity,*
and can be simple in saying "yes"

*

One can grow
through "good fortune" –
with gratitude and generosity;

And one can grow
through "bad fortune"
– if one can *ju jitsu* the toxicity.

If you can be adroit enough
to parlay both eventualities,
you will find yourself advancing
very steadily and quite inexorably

*

Timing, Timing, Timing
Location, Location, Location
Preparation, Preparation, Preparation
Focus, Focus, Focus

Creative, Creative, Creative
Tenacious, Tenacious, Tenacious
Prioritize, Prioritize, Prioritize
Flexibility, Flexibility, Flexibility
Versatility, Versatility, Versatility
Diplomatically, Diplomatically, Diplomatically

Nimble, but ultimately, DECISIVE

*

Low risk,
High potential reward: dream situation
High risk,
Low potential reward: disaster-in-the-making

*

Be truthful to yourself,
Believe in yourself,
Follow your star
and go for VICTORY

*

If you segue from a *dark universe*
(say, an abusive household)
to a *benign universe*
(say, a New England college campus),
act accordingly.
Smile.

GOD AND GOOD

EXIT *dark universes.*

Brighten *your universe.*

JETTISON toxic people from *it.*

*

Assemble, over the decades –
if you can, a small group around you

Each of whom can and will give you
* * * Loyalty, Love & Laughter * * *

[And be sure to do your share 120%]

*

More than 50% of human happiness
derives from a good love partner;

Less than 50% of good love partners
are good marriage partners.

*

Love is great. Love is dangerous.
Love is elusive. Love is attainable.
Love is sublime. Love makes us craze.

*

Love is great. Love is terrible.
Marriage is great. Marriage is terrible.
Children are great. Children are great.

*

Take good people
for granted
– at your own peril

Allow toxic individuals
to remain in your circle
–at your own peril

*

Treat someone
with full respect

– and you have a potential ally

Treat someone
with disrespect

– and you have a guaranteed enemy

Treat someone
with abuse

– and you have a lifelong mortal menace
on your case

GOD AND GOOD

*

A pre–requisite for a good love partner
and/or mate
is the ability
to give love well and
to receive love well

*

Listen and learn like a baby
Float like a butterfly
Then, when you make your move…
Do it with conviction
And daring.
And go for victory.

*

Victory is always better than defeat.
But one can transcend setback,
and ultimately prevail
in even greater and more nuanced victory.
That road has been traveled.

*

Convey your message respectfully and clearly
(and carry thermonuclear warheads)

*

Beware of guys
with no guy–friends,
and
of girls
with no girl–friends

Beware
of guys or gals
with dozens
of *"closest friends"*

*

Surround yourself with
Loyal friends
(preferably from high school)
Loving family
Serious allies
Talented staffers
Proven professionals
Brilliant teachers
Veteran advisors
Guiding parents
Stimulating books and media
–   and ONE good Love
–   (even if necessarily, sequentially)

*

GOD AND GOOD

Viewing all humans
as *gifts from heaven*
will advance you
on the chessboard of life

It will enhance your soul
with bountiful spirit

But, note,
case by case,
they may be more of a gift
to their mom,
than to you

*

Carry many and varied arrows in your quiver.

*

Hug your children –

– and all will be well

when the day is done

*

Seek truth, but accept ambiguity
Seek safety, but accept pain
Seize life, but accept retreat
Plan, but accept uncertainty

Seek security, but accept vulnerability
Seek strength, but travel light.

*

Parlay your major strengths

Enhance your top strengths
– even from a dozen different angles
via a dozen different modalities.

It is your "top strength" which must *lead the
charge.*

*

Attack your major weaknesses
– one or two at a time

Neutralizing a major weakness
will take a minimum of 3 lines of attack –
employed simultaneously over time in a
disciplined manner

…Why so much effort?

If the salient weakness
were so readily amenable to repair,
it would not have evolved as your salient
weakness
in the first place

After resolution, take on the next one or two
salient weaknesses...
will keep you busy...out–of–trouble... :)

Your sub–conscious inner guidance system
will prioritize for your conscious guidance
system...

*

Seek after your potential;
Understand that potential is at the core of the
cosmic dynamic and of personal fulfillment.

Chart–out
your overriding **transcending** goals
(such as spiritual fulfillment, perhaps)
As well as
more tangible **life–achievement** goals
(such as becoming an established professional)

And you will win at the game of LIFE

*

Periodically,
articulate out–loud
and even write–out
your updated top 5 goals;

Your "Inner Potentializer / Tactician"
will 'get the message' with greater clarity

And will constantly be on–the–lookout
for anything–anything,
which advances your objectives

You will then find yourself advancing
to your goals more adroitly

*

Understand that
you are part of an extraordinary,
unfolding cosmic dynamic

Understand that
at birth you are already a profound

Creator–potential

– and are linked to Infinity and eternity
before you and after you

*

Understand that each individual is a universe.
Understand that YOU are a universe.

Respect the greatness of the random human.
Accept the frailty of even superstars.

*

GOD AND GOOD

Money is fuel for your life–engine
But only fuel…

A steady supply and a very considerable amount in
diverse storage depots is a good idea

*

LESS is (sometimes) MORE.
MORE is (sometimes) LESS.

There is never too much wisdom
or too little ego.

*

Do not confuse glory with wisdom.

*

Surrounding yourself with people
who consistently TAKE more than they GIVE,
is obviously sub–optimal

After they have drained you of your *Qi,*
they will simply move on
– to their next victim

*

Err on the side of *more communication,*
and less *small talk.*

*

There is never too much versatility or money.

There is never too little humility or thriftiness.

*

If a million people
have already traveled a particular road,
no need to be overly apprehensive
before taking it.

If a hundred thousand
have already traversed it,
still give it thought
before traveling–forward.
If only a thousand
have taken that route
assess very, very carefully
and with due caution and analysis.

If only a hundred
have ventured there,
be very concerned;
danger may lie ahead.
If only ten
have taken that route,
pause, weigh, analyze, be extra vigilant,
take your time before engaging.

GOD AND GOOD

If absolutely no one else
has gone there before,
ask your Mom.

*

Best
not to keep more money
than you actually need
at the moment in public view –
as many will seek to relieve you of it
or turn it against you.

*

Anchor your life in good deeds.
Fill your heart with good will.
Allow your Soul to have a spiritual dimension

*

Smile at adversity.
Survive the storm.
Tenacious and cool.

*

Maintain that sparkle in your eternal soul;
maintain it at *full–sparkle* :)
Be sure to keep that *pilot–light* burning;

keep that *blue flame* burning
with pure intensity.

*

Follow your star.
– and keep a very vigilant eye on cashflow.

*

Fill your heart with Good Will,
no matter what toxicity you are subjected to

Fill your soul with tranquility,
no matter how severe the storm
And you will reap a thousand victories

*

Love, Gratitude and Potential
are the lifeblood of the cosmos.
Tap into these three,
and you are indomitable.

*

Receive and give Love
when you are fortunate to have the opportunity.

Give gratitude to the Heavens
for all Love and Potential related to your being.

GOD AND GOOD

*

Celebrate each morning

the glory of LIFE
the gift of FREEDOM
the gift of POSSIBILITY

your being part of the RE–BIRTH of the world

a recent personal Victory

and then.......... *Advance–Forward !*
*

Cosmic currents of Potential
reward POSITIVE–energy
and neglect NEUTRAL–energy.
– as these currents
reward dynamic pro–ACTIVE
and neglect static frozen–DEFENSIVE.

*

We may be Stardust,
poetically speaking

But, technically speaking
We are Lovedust

*

Be wary of any and all causes
"larger than yourself"

Only those at the top–of–the–pyramid
emerge NET WINNERS

*

Beware of clergy
– of all faiths –
who
(one way or another)
might **USE** (you);
and then ultimately
(one way or another)
might **ABUSE** (you)

This axiom applies
– *to all faiths*
– *in all eras*

All roads generally lead to their
power aggrandizement – directly or indirectly.

*

Treat all with RESPECT
    Powerful and Weak;
    Rich and Poor;
    Older and Younger

*

GOD AND GOOD

Ten supportive individuals
will not guarantee you
success in life

One parasitic, betraying individual
can undermine
your entire life

*

If one is optimally pressing to optimize
one's potential,

one will tend to feel fulfilled along a key
internal axis

If one *nails an objective,*
but does not re–boot and embark along
the next *potential–quest,*

the human psyche, at its very core,
will not be happy...

*

Fully questing for one's potential
along multiple axes,

will tend to rejuvenate the soul.

Including quest for spiritual *potential
in–the–mix,*

will tend to optimize fulfillment.

*

Do not assume that
academics seek the TRUTH
or that
clergy seek GODLINESS
or that
lawyers seek the LAW
or that
justices seek JUSTICE.

Start with no assumptions.

*

Four components have sustained nations
over the millennia:

Spirituality,

Education,

GOD AND GOOD

Family,

Creative tenacity

*

The ultimate KEY, respectfully, is, as follows:

If we can,
on–the–one–hand,
understand our Infinitude/Divineness…

And yet, simultaneously,
be down–to–earth and grounded,
we then stand to inherit
both heaven and earth

*

Understand your *mortality,*

while remembering simultaneously

that you are a complete and complex

– and somewhat infinite – *universe.*
*

Religions and spiritual movements
which primarily
spiritually empower the masses,
advance humanity

Religions and spiritual movements
which primarily
politically empower
 the movement's hierarchic elite,
inevitably turn out to be
the bane of humanity

*

For any movement to assert that it
spiritually empowers its masses,
while, in the process,

it simultaneously demonizes other groups
(subtly or overtly),

– is a perversion of spirituality
and a cynical manipulation

of its own idealistic adherents

Variations of this nefarious power–gambit
have caused endless horrors
spanning the millennia
to this day

*

GOD AND GOOD

Random acts of kindness
(not that I'm too good at this)
will tend to accrue to your benefit
Random acts of kindness
just may unleash the angelic
(dimension or spirit or power)
within you

*

Almost all revolutions
ultimately morph into engines
for power aggrandizement – personal, political,
territorial, etc.

Therefore,
try to avoid being overly enraptured,
captivated, hypnotized or otherwise
held hostage by the revolution *du jour.*

In fact, best to get out of its way.

*

Add arrows to your quiver,

whenever you have the opportunity.

Use them judiciously, very judiciously.

*

The purpose of each individual
Is to Quest for his/her Potential

*

Each of us has our own unique individual potentialities

– and, indeed, these evolve and morph over time

*

Your unique potentials might be in any realm(s)

examples: spiritual, religious, intellectual, maternal,
paternal, literary, emotional, business, trade, vocation,
finance, corporate, music, art, friendship, science,
engineering, the humanities, clergy, etc.

*

Even simply integrating this core concept –

that your purpose is to quest after your individual
potentials –

into your psyche
will start transforming your life

*

Your psyche will plan, process and think differently
Your mind will gear–up accordingly,

*

Positive advances and increased life–fulfillment
will ensue

short term and long term

*

Try to get-past your parents' assorted misdeeds
against you in your youth
Jettisoning the stuff,
will liberate you to more fully reconnect
with that invaluable and unique love-flow.

(And, relax; 99.9% of parents love their children
– always have, and always will)

*

Who you spend time with,
has *profound, major impact*
on who you become

*

We can shape our destiny

Capitalizing on *opportunity* – small and large –
is often a key determinant

By Individual acts of small grace,
Cumulatively we raise up the entire cosmos,
You are the product of your own.
You are heavily impacted by your mental-image of
yourself.
Consider enhancing-it periodically.

*

We are all Potential – and agents of Potential

Advancing on you trajectory of Potential,
yields true fulfillment.

Grow – or Die

*

GOD AND GOOD

Fame or triumph or applause
are not necessary for 'significance.'
'Significance' casts a wider net.

Enhance someone's 'significance' or 'standing,'
and you will add to your own.
Undermine someone's 'significance' or 'standing,'
and you *play with fire*

*

In life, one needs to potentially fend-off three classes of
'opponents':

    (a) the classic external opponent
    (b) any 'drag' entity still within our personal circle
    (c) the internal 'opponent' – the threads within our
    psyche making victory more difficult.

Note that (a) can be dealt with more adroitly, if (b) and
(c) are dealt with.

*

Understanding a problem,
is half the solution.
'Awareness' – in all its manifold applications –
will empower you every time.

*

There is nothing more powerful
than an idea whose time has come.
The idea just lies there
– awaiting the proper catalysts to give it traction.
Consider being part of that catalyst.

*

Our peer group's expectations of us,
are a key driver of our destiny

*

Protect your core interests.
Contribute beyond your immediate self
– or *ultimately shrivel*

*

Life can be *travail*
and life can also be *adventure*
– depending on which lens you put on

*

Action, will, determination and finesse,
will tend to overcome many barriers

GOD AND GOOD

*

Victory is far better than defeat.
But one can transcend setback,
and ultimately prevail
in even greater and more nuanced victory.

That road has been traveled.

Victory is far better than defeat,
However, no need to broadcast either.
Either (victory or defeat) must be managed adroitly.
Therein lies the legacy.

*

Shed bad people and bad memories

They will both sap your *CHI*.

*

Understand that you are *amazing*
and that your life is uniquely *significant*
You are the *cutting-edge*
of a 1000+ generations of *advance*
Understand that you are integral to the Infinite Divine
and that you are a microcosm Universe

*

and, finally,
understand that
you are thoroughly integral to...

..........................the Divine

– ALL OF US CUMULATIVELY

*

We are all interconnected

– past–present–and–future

*

like one multi–arrayed network of a
billion–trillion
human/spiritual

Personal Creations stretching forward to the farthest
reaches of time

– and it is our awesome and infinite
cumulative CONSCIOUSNESS – WILL – CHI –
"ruach Adoshem" (Spirit–of–the–Divine)

– which drives the eternal cosmos ever–forward...

and *onward !*

"Advance!"

one-word core doctrine,

– Israeli Armored Corps

*

Don't Look Back !

– GOD to LOT's wife (Genesis)

Ultimately, we can transform ourselves
into Temples of the Spirit

To the extent that we do,
we cumulatively transform the entire world

– unknown *Hasidic rebbe*

end of Summa

דוד אריה בן
אברהם יעקב הלוי

GOD AND GOOD

see Appendix   >

Q4P∞™

Quest for Potential

(infinitely recursive)

Appendix Section:

Appendix Section
TABLE OF CONTENTS

Appendix A: Metaphysics Analysis	405
Appendix B: Schematically	409
Appendix C: Extraordinariation	414
Appendix D: Consciousness Connection?	417
Appendix E: Evolution from the Perspective of Summa Metaphysica	420
Appendix F1: Hasidic v. Kabbalistic	422
Appendix F2: The Suffused Divine	426
Appendix G: Push v. Pull	427
Appendix H: "The Spiraling Collective"	428
Appendix I: Balance and Diversity	430
Appendix J: Convergence	431
Appendix K: Cracking the Cosmic Code	433
Appendix L: Life	437
Appendix M: Is Q4P Morally Neutral?	438
Appendix N: Extraordinariation juxtaposed v. *tohu va-vohu*	439
Appendix O: "Secular Divine" v. "Religious Divine"	440
Appendix P: Optimization	441
Appendix Q: Q4P juxtaposed v. Vicissitude	443
Appendix R: More Powerful v. Perfert	444
Appendix S: Boox #1 v. Book #2	445
Appendix T: Following the Analogy	448
Appendix U: By-definition *Telescoping Elasticity*	450

Appendix Section
TABLE OF CONTENTS
continued

Appendix V: Hypothesizing about Cosmic Origins   451

Appendix W: Physics, Metaphysics & Poetry   452

Appendix X: Holographic Universe Theory,   454
    Information and SUMMA

Appendix Y: Counterposing *Summa Metaphysica*   456

Appendix Z1: Survival   458

Appendix Z2: Primordial Realm Hyphotesis   460

Appendix Z3: Launch   462

Appendix Z4: Where is Option B?   464

Appendix Z5: Cosmic Nesting (Iterativeness)   466

Appendix Z6: Modern Evolutionary Synthesis   468

Appendix Z7: *Anima mundi*   469

Appendix Z8: The Soul of the Universe   471

Appendix Z9: Possibility   472

Appendix Z10: "The Free Lunch?"   474

Appendix Z11: Birnbaumian Panentheism   475

Appendix Z12: Cosmic Level: Individual Level   477

Appendix Z13: Major Problems in Science   481

Appendix Z14: "Nothing" by David Birnbaum   483

Appendix Z15: Gnosticism   485

Appendix Z16: Atheist v. Potentialist   487

Appendix Z17: Particle Physics and Q4P$^\infty$ 488

Appendix Z18: A Fix-It "Conceptual Plug"?   491

Appendix Section

TABLE OF CONTENTS

continued

Appendix Z19: Metaphysics and Physics   491

Appendix Z20: Take #2: Where Is The Competing Metaphysics   493

Appendix Z21: The Assertion/Claim   496

Appendix Z22: The Q4P∞ 'Package'   497

Appendix Z23: Explication   498

Appendix Z24: Context   500

Appendix Z25: Where is the Divine?   502

Appendix Z26: String Theory and 'Provability'   504

Appendix Z27: Multiverse Theory   505

Appendix Z28: Theory of Everything (in Physics)   506

Appendix Z29: Occam's Razor   508

Appendix Z30: Schopenhauer v. Birnbaum   509

Appendix Z31: Simple v. Simplistic   511

Appendix Z32: *Aesthetic Elegance*   512

Appendix Z33: The Red Queen Hypothesis   514

Appendix Z34: Punctuated Equilibrium   516

Appendix Z35: The Font/Soul of the Cosmos   519

Appendix Z36: Time   520

Appendix Z37: An Ultra- Dynamic Multi-Dimensional   522
        Organic Entity

AppendixZ38: "The Mind of God"   524

Appendix Z39: Metaphysical Assumptions   526

Appendix Z40: The "Double Play": Push-Pull   528

Appendix Z41: Framing Beliefs   530

Appendix Z42: New Paradigm Imminent   531

Appendix Section

TABLE OF CONTENTS

continued

Appendix Z43: God   534

Appendix Z44: Man: Mortal or Divine   535

Appendix Z45: New Interpretations   537

Appendix Z46: Take #3: Physics & Metaphysics   538

Appendix Z47: "...*beyond science...*"   540

Appendix Z48: "The Same Recipe"   541

Appendix Z49 The Consciousness Continuum   542

Appendix Z50: "Backward Causation"   544

Appendix Z51: Galapagos   545

Appendix Z52: Ecology   546

Appendix Z53: A Compelling Case   548

Appendix Z54: *neo-Survival-of-the-Fittest*   *551*

       or Q4P$^\infty$/Extraordinariation?

Appendix Z55: 1999: Cosmologist Martin Rees   555

Appendix Z56: 2000: Cosmologist Brian Greene   557

Appendix Z57: 2004: Cosmologists Tyson & Goldsmith   558

Appendix Z58: 2006: Cosmologist Leonard Susskind   559

Appendix Z59: 2006: Quantum Computation   560

       Theorist Seth Lloyd

Appendix Z60: 2008: Cosmologist Paul Davies   563

Appendix Z61: 2010: Cosmologists Hawking & Mlodinow   565

Appendix Z62: 2010: Cosmologist Haisch presents   566

       very similar to Summa

Appendix Z63: Quest for Possibility or Quest for Potential?   570

GOD AND GOOD

APPENDIX A:

Metaphysics Analysis

One can never PROVE a metaphysics.

By definition.

Because one would have to stand outside the entire cosmos to view it all –

and simulate Creation itself – to test it all.

*

However one can certainly ASSESS different metaphysics.

Metaphysics is always hypothesis. But, hopefully very, very intelligent hypothesis.

One can, indeed, analyze different metaphysical constructs with a consistent set of questions.

*

Now, some of the questions involved in assessing various metaphysics might be the following: (These questions tend to overlap, but have different thrusts and nuance.)

Is the metaphysics overarching? All-embracing?

Does the metaphysics handle the key questions in philosophy? (re-capped in the INTROS and FOREWORDS of the two books of this series)

Does the metaphysics have a fatal flaw(s); a major gap(s),

– or does it essentially legitimately 'stitch-together' all the key issues

*

To what extent is the metaphysics TETHERED to classic works or spiritual texts?

*

Does the core of the metaphysics RESONATE within us?

*

Is the case made exclusively "in an Ivory Tower" –

– or is the case somewhat brought-down-to-earth, as well?

Is the presentation some sort of miasma (murky, obscuring vapor)

– or is it actually fairly articulate and systematic?

Are the themes, however allegedly profound, articulated in a totally obscure manner –

– or in a generally intelligible manner?

*

Do we grasp the CREATIVE ESSENCE of the presentation?

*

Does the proposed metaphysics gently 'tip-toe around the garden' –

or does it attempt to get to the very core of the cosmic code?

*

Does the proposed metaphysics primarily concern itself with playing with SEMANTICS and DEFINITIONS –

or does it actually provide an overarching INTEGRATED FORMULATION for the cosmic order?

*

A proposed metaphysics must be assessed, as well,
by these not inconsiderable – and, frankly, non-
negotiable, demands, as well:

Does the proposed metaphysics truly embrace all
known dynamics – in all fields?

Does the proposed metaphysics embrace our
experiences and accumulated wisdom over the
centuries?

Does the metaphysics embrace all that we scientifically
believe to have occurred – and the overwhelming great
bulk of what we hypothesize to have occurred – since
the dawn of time?

*

Does the particular proposed metaphysics – about our
most extraordinary universe and profound existence –

run flat and dry

– or does it, on some level,

actually, touch our soul?

* * *

APPENDIX B:

Schematically

(as introduction to this particular appendix, first let us take one more quick look at the Baal Shem Tov's philosophy.....

see lead paragraph

on the Baal Shem Tov's doctrines

(a.k.a. the BESHT's doctrines)

Elements of Besht's doctrines

Jewish Encyclopedia Online, http://www.jewishencyclopedia.com/
view.jsp?artid=18&letter=B (accessed October 5, 2009)

"The foundation-stone of Hasidism as laid by Besht is a strongly marked pantheistic conception of God. He declared the whole universe, mind and matter, to be a manifestation of the Divine Being; that this manifestation is not an emanation from God, as is the conception of the Kabbalah, for nothing can be separated from God: all things are rather forms in which He reveals Himself..."

* * * * * * * *

Now, having the BESHT's doctrine noted above
for easy reference, to schematically outline what is happening
as regards our formulation,

juxtaposed against other formulations

* * * * * * * * *

let

A = God

B = Man

AB = GodMan

* * * * * * * * *

Maimonides:

encapsuled one core proposition:
God created Man (Aristotelian)

A created B

*

Lurianic Kabbalah:

encapsuled in one core proposition:
Man is an emanation from God

(sort of, from WITHIN God);
GOD WITHDRAWS to create Man

(*tzimtzum*)

B comes from WITHIN A

*

Baal Shem Tov:

encapsuled in one core proposition:
All is a Manifestation OF God

(panentheistic)

A and B are part of AB

*

SUMMA / Birnbaum:

encapsuled in one core proposition:
Holy Quest for Potential (to the infinite recursive power)
drives GOD, MAN and the COSMOS ever-forward
towards EXTRAORDINARIATION.

Now, *Summa Metaphysica* lays the FORMULATION
out in

18 multi-faceted propositions:

9 in the first book, *God and Evil*
9 in the second book, *God and Good*

But, let's give you the "Monarch notes'

'test-prep version' here

on *Summa* / Birnbaum

*

Thus, to attempt to outline SUMMA in 6 quick propositions:

1.

QUEST FOR POTENTIAL∞ is on a journey from POSSIBILITY through METAPHYSICAL REALMS through REALITY, then towards PERFECT FULFILLMENT & REALIZATION ('EXTRAORDINARIATION')

(the first part of this proposition has components in-common with RASHI (*'na-asheh adahm b 'zalmenu'*
–
Let us make Man in our Image - Genesis), and with Lurianic Kabbalah (*En Sof...Sefirot*) and Plato's *Forms*... aside from being anchored in '*Eheyeh Asher Eheye*h' – Exodus)

2.

Infinite Potentialities at the end–of–the–rainbow ('EXTRAORDINARIATION'), retroactively ignite Creation – and the Divine 'spark'

3.

We are ALL part of HOLY QUEST FOR POTENTIAL
(this is ~panentheistic, parallel to the BESHT)

4.

We are all part of a grander, evolving COSMIC
Consciousness.

(this has components in common with the BESHT and
with Teilhard, the Jesuit philosophical renegade)

5.

Divine consciousness (the Godhead of the cumulative
consciousness) withdraws to give greater freedom
to MAN
(an anchor of the proposed solution to *theodicy* in Book
#1)

(this has components in common with the Torah's
Hester Panim (Hiding of the Divine Face) and with
Lurianic Kabbalah *tzimtzum*)

6.

ALL (AB) are on an ongoing journey towards
EXTRAORDINARIATION.

(components, almost in common with *'Messianic era'*)

* * *

APPENDIX C:

Extraordinariation

To our readers:

Summa Metaphysica proposes the concept of
Extraordinariation.
This concept is proposed and elaborated upon in
the chapter
Mu: Cosmic Tool Kit- Shelf #2 above
(in the first section of this book, Cosmic Womb
of Potential)

The following is a finalé commentary piece on the
theme.

by DANIEL N. KHALIL:

EXTRAORDINARIATION

To say that the feeling in the listener's soul at the climax
of Beethoven's *Ninth Symphony* is 'perfect' is drastic
and degrading understatement. The meta-emotional
human response to this piece of art (and it is not alone)
is outside of perfection as it is outside of language.
It is transcendent, extra, extraordinary.

It has been said that God is the ultimate artist, creating a world-dynamic with all the idiosyncrasies of complex art. To praise His work as being merely 'perfect' or 'efficient' is to miss its creative essence. It is to embrace the engineer while neglecting the artisan. This is a neglect bolstered by science and mathematics, disciplines whose unique understanding of the universe's exactitude has been used to turn the focus from its delicate elegance. The cold progression of evolution engenders an appreciation for the lion's strength, for the cheetah's speed; the precision of physics provides a window into the flawlessness of our cosmos; but there is more.

Darwinian evolution need not have yielded the frail butterfly, the vulnerable dove; the Earth's orbit need not have yielded the grace of changing seasons, snow-decorated forests. Indeed laws of nature and principles of physics need not have yielded complexity at all. Nevertheless, complexity permeates our world from subatomic particles to cosmic galaxies. It is this complexity that allows for the sophisticated beauty that stands in wait of our perception daily.

Yet the paradox of this complexity surfaces as we probe it more deeply. Structural biologists have shown that fundamental biology depends on predictable chemistry. Quantum mechanics has shown that chemistry, in turn, can be dissected into the physics that underlies it. Einstein showed that even within physics separations are an illusion. His special theory of relativity (1905) revealed that the division between space and time is artificial. His subsequent general theory of relativity (1915) showed the same of the distinction between space-time and matter.

Thus, the broad perspective reveals our world's complexity while the deep, penetrating perspective reveals its unity. Stepping back, we appreciate worldly complexity, stepping close we are astounded by its unity. Such is the paradox. Complexity and unity challenge one another as they each thrust forward expanding their respective scopes simultaneously. New species are discovered as unified theorems are developed. This duality teases us with its plainness: we can only watch, spellbound, as our cosmos' singularity and its nuance develop and unfold, hand-in-hand, before us. Herein lays the irony of our world's progression: a relentless trajectory towards unbounded extraordinariation.

APPENDIX D:

Consciousness Connection?

Consciousness remains a vast unknown.

Above, in the main body of the book, I posit a "cumulative consciousness". And this speculative conjecture is an integral part of my philosophical construct.

Now, we know from Astrophysics that approximately half-a-billion years after the *Big Bang* (with the *Big Bang* currently calculated at 13.7 billion years ago), Supernovas (collapsing hi–mass stars) started 'creating/ manufacturing/cooking' the so–called heavier elements (elements heavier than #26 Iron) in their cores, and then projected them outwards to the far reaches of the universe.

These heavier Elements were, in turn, necessary building–blocks for LIFE.
Meaning, without the DEATH of the supernovas, there would be no LIFE.

Meaning, on some level, from DEATH,
emerges (fuller and fuller) LIFE.
Now, we posit as a consistent theme throughout
SUMMA,
that: the *human parallels the cosmic.*
The question is just exactly how.

So, we see from Astrophysics, that DEATH can
profoundly yield LIFE.
The question is:
Is there a parallel in *human* death?

So, perhaps, perhaps,
(individual) human death enhances the
cumulative cosmic consciousness.

This is fragile and dangerous terrain,
and I simply do not have a good intuitive feel here.
Hence, placement in an Appendix.

However, intriguingly,
Maimonides, Guide to the Perplexed,
from Friedlander's translation,
Part I, 74, 7th argument:

> "*Amr,* and therefore the souls of all the departed
> form only one being as has been explained by
> *Ibn Bekr Ibn Al-zaig,* and others who ventured to
> speak on these profound subjects. In short, such
> intricate disciplines, which our mind can scarcely
> comprehend, cannot furnish any principles for the
> explanation of other subjects."

Somewhat cryptic, for sure, but positing that,
post-Death – *all souls merge into one.*

Now, Souls are certainly not necessarily
Consciousness.

But, then again, maybe they are (very) closely
inter–related...

Thus, perhaps, the Death of an individual, somehow
enhances the cumulative consciousness – on some
level, however profound.

Perhaps, we should respectfully leave this particular
matter (Consciousness) at that (for this treatise)...

Feb 11, 2008

APPENDIX E:

Evolution from the Perspective of Summa Metaphysica

According to my reading of natural evolution, *random genetic mutations* provide a 'menu' for Quest for Potential$^\infty$ to "review" – and then select from – or "lock-in on" – a new 'genetic line' most likely to achieve optimal potential (which includes survival)... and then transpose the genetic change across the entire species, and possibly beyond that.

This "reading of the data" would even harmonize even "punctuated equilibrium" nicely into an integrated theory.

This "reading of the data" – through my lens of "Quest for Potential$^\infty$/Extraordinariation" – would help explain, for instance, why we end up so many thousands of species of glorious flowers, plants, birds and butterflies, for starters.

"Quest for Potential$^\infty$/Extraordinariation" would help explain the ultimate emergence of, say, the poetry of an Alfred Tennyson, the spirituality of a Thomas Merton, the artistry of a Pablo Picasso....

Natural Selection – as classically hitherto understood – clearly plays a very key role in Evolution, but not necessarily the overwhelmingly dispositive role. For, according to our hypothesis, the "Selection" itself has transcendent forces operating upon it.

"Evolution itself, moving upwards coordinately and undeviatingly from the lowest to the highest, demonstrates most clearly a prevision from afar – a preset purpose for all existence. Divine greatness is thereby enhanced and all the goals of faith confirmed, and trust in and service of the Divine is all the more justified – since all strives upwards and man has it in his power to improve and perfect himself and his world, he is manifestly thereby doing the will of his Creator. Spiritual perfection is thus seen to be in the center of all existence." *Rabbi Abraham Kook, Orot Ha-Kodesh* (c.1920)

APPENDIX F1:*

Hasidic v. Kabbalistic

BAAL SHEM TOV (founder of Hasidism)
(b. 1698, Sara, Ukraine; d. 1760, Medzhybizh, Ukraine)
("The Besht")

"The foundation-stone of Hasidism as laid by Besht
is a strongly marked pantheistic conception of God. He
declared the whole universe, mind and matter, to be a
manifestation of the Divine Being; that this manifestation
is not an emanation from God, as is the conception of
the Kabbalah, for nothing can be separated from God: all
things are rather forms in which He reveals Himself..."[a]

[a] *Jewish Encyclopedia Online*, http://www.jewishencyclopedia.com/
view.jsp?artid=18&letter=B (accessed October 5, 2009)

BASIC IDEAS OF HASIDISM
Creator and Universe

"'The hasidic leader R. Menahem Mendel of Lubavich observes (*Derekh Mitzvotekha* (1911), 123) that the disciples of the Ba'al Shem Tov gave the "very profound" turn to the doctrine of the oneness of God so that it means not alone that He is unique, as the medieval thinkers said, but that He is all that is:...there is no other existence whatsoever apart from His existence, blessed be He. This is true unification...just as there was no existence apart from Him before the world was created so it is even now." ...as a corollary of hasidic pantheism (more correctly, panentheism)...'"[b]

(author's note: there are no extant writings of the Besht)

[*b] As noted in Encyclopaedia Judaica on *Baal Shem Tov* {1997} [CD-ROM]

GOD AND GOOD

Author's editorial comment / perspective on the classic and historic 'dispute' between Lurianism and Hasidism on the subject:

As the gemorah might say,
"Eylu v-aylu divre' Elokim Chayim"

i.e. Both (exegesis) positions stand valid
side-by-side eternally

and, indeed, in this case,
both philosophical propositions:

*The Lurianic*** [The universe as EMANATION from God] –*

and the Hasidic position
[The universe as MANIFESTATION of God]

Both tether different (intertwined) aspects of the proposed Quest for Potential$^{\infty}$ paradigm.

*

***Lurianic* is a thrust of Kabbalistic

Meaning, philosophical thrust #1 does not exclude philosophical thrust #2, as the respective theological / philosophical camps supposed; On the contrary, BOTH philosophical thrusts must be true side-by-side in order to explicate and outline – in even the most general terms – the contours of an all-embracing metaphysics.

*

APPENDIX F2:

The Suffused Divine

Rav Chaim of Volozhin[a] (b.1749, Volozhin, Belarus; d. 1821, Volozhin, Belarus) elucidates *Hashem* (the Divine) as filling – and surrounding – all worlds.

> "It says in many places in the Zohar that 'Hashem fills all worlds' and 'surrounds all worlds.' This means that from Hashem's perspective, He fills all worlds, and we, from our Torah-oriented vantage point, see Hashem as surrounding all worlds. The meaning of the concept of 'Hashem filling all worlds' is concealed from us.
>
> The truth is that from Hashem's perspective, even after creating the world, He fills all the worlds and all existence; literally, '*There is nothing else beside Him*' (Devarim 4:35)."

Meaning, as per Summa, the Divine is not "over there" and we are "over here"; Rather, the Divine suffuses all. And, parallel to our metaphysics, wherein Quest for Potential$^\infty$ is the core of the Divine, and the Divine drives the cosmos....

---

[a] Rav Chaim of Volozhin, *Nefesh Hachaim*, The Judaica Press, Inc. Brooklyn, NY, © 2009, p. 112

APPENDIX G:

Push
v.
Push & Pull

Classic Western and Jewish philosophy*
(call them both Model #1) each has −

> the "Concrete subject" −
> *God* −
> "**pushing**" Creation forward −
> *in the moment*.

Whereas my metaphysics
(call it Model #2) has −

> a) Q4P∞/Extraordinariation
> "**pushing**" Creation forward inexorably
>
> as well as
>
> b) the future perfection goal-point −
> *Infinite Divine Potential* −
> "**pulling**" and igniting Creation −
> *from the future*.

Thus, these are 2 very different "models"
− on multiple levels.

* Kabbalistic Jewish philosophy diverges from mainstream Jewish

APPENDIX H:

"The Spiraling Collective"

The outwardly-spiraling COLLECTIVE-vortex-unity potentially incorporates the following interlaced layers, among others

SPIRITUALITY

CONSCIOUSNESS

INTELLIGENCE

LOVE

LIFE-FORCE

ENERGY

EQUATIONS

POTENTIAL

Taking-a-stab at a more schematic representation of
the current state of our little Quest for Potential$^\infty$ dynamic,
we respectfully offer the schematic on the left.

"The Spiraling Collective": an industrious and ultimately
spiritually-driven 'collective,' which has a habit of creating
solar systems and life forms, and is even rumored, via its
GODHEAD, to have parted the Red Sea once, a long time
ago...

– D. Birnbaum

APPENDIX I:

Balance and Diversity

To focus first on our own planet,
balance of life and *diversity of life*
are embedded in the overarching theme of
Quest for Potential∞/Extraordinariation.

.....*which* maneuvers on an ongoing basis
to protect and advance* these two important
"sub-motifs," among others.

balance of life is maintained to protect *survival*

APPENDIX J:

Convergence

All roads lead to the infinite fount of *Quest for Potential*$^\infty$.

Religion, spirituality, the life sciences, physics, chemistry, astronomy et al. all converge on the road to Infinity.

They do not quite **merge**, as the quest for ultimate infinity is elusive, but they do **converge.**

In our quasi–finite milieu they are seemingly separate, – at least without the *Quest for Potential*$^\infty$ overlay onto them.

However, on that ethereal road to the infinite fount of *Quest for Potential*$^\infty$ they converge closer and closer.

Why is that?

Because they were originally tributaries of the "fount" of Quest for Potential$^\infty$/Extraordinariation. Thus, an objective observer looking at their trajectories would track back to their original divergence from the fount.

Thus, they are each truly not "complete" without that "Crown" (of *Quest for Potential$^\infty$*) affixed to them.

And it is at the "Crown–point" that they converge, *de facto* merge, and de facto unify.

***

Key "gaps" and "loose-ends" across the spectrum of fields of human study and inquiry, will tend to "fill-in" relatively seamlessly employing the above.

***

Note that *"Keter"* (Crown) is, as well, an important component in Kabbalah. There is a convergence, to utilize that same term once again here, between my usage of the term Crown and the Kabbalistic explication of *Keter.*

APPENDIX K:

Cracking the Cosmic Code*

Physics attempts to do so.

Secular philosophy attempts to do so.

Religious philosophy attempts to do so.

All hit major "roadblocks."

Why is that?

*or more precisely, unraveling another crucial *layer or two* of the cosmic code

Because, the *code–breaker* is Quest for Potential$^\infty$/
Extraordinariation, (Q4P), which is at the **intersection**
of all three, but not classically ***thoroughly within*** any
of the three.

Do the three indeed intersect?

The mainstream *classic wisdom* would be –
not necessarily.

But the *mainstream classic wisdom* is wrong.

All three intersect at their fount (see exhibit above –
Convergence).

And their *fount* is the crucial intersection.

Only a dynamic with the transcendent - and "intersecting"
– overarching power of Q4P,
could possibly have had the power to ignite a cosmos.

Q4P would be in the realm of Metaphysics. Not quite physics and not quite philosophy of any classic stripe.

Only a theme from within the general genre of Metaphysics could ultimately be able to provide a potentially satisfying *possible* simultaneous answer to hitherto inexplicable conundrums in those 3 classic realms noted above –

> [classic physics]:
> Where did the *first quark* came from?
> Meaning, where did the very smallest sub-atomic particle, whatever that turns out to be, come from?
>
> [classic philosophy]:
> Why there is *any reality* at all?
> Meaning, why is there not simply a state of "nothingness"?

[classic religious philosophy]:
What are the eternal origins of the *infinite ('eternal')
Divine*? Meaning, by what imperative/actualization is
there the Divine which you posit/assert?

However, the introduction of Q4P does, respectfully,
simultaneously and elegantly "solve" all three issues, and
the constellation of related issues in each field.
I have covered these matters – at least on the surface –
over the course of the two volumes of *Summa*.

*

APPENDIX L:

Life

Life would appear to be both –

– an end *in and of itself* of Q4P

as well as

– a *portal* to greater Q4P

These rich and crucial themes need to be developed.

APPENDIX M:

Is Q4P[∞] Morally Neutral?

That does not appear to be the case.

"Giving-ness" is crucial for child-rearing, and child-rearing is crucial for cosmic Q4P. And "giving-ness" is clearly identifiable with "good" (at least by me). Presumably "giving-ness" was crucial to creation itself, but I have not *discerned the play* there.

As readers and writers, our natural inclination might be to associate *greater good* with greater potential. That would be my position.

On net balance the cosmos thus would seem to tilt towards the *positive.*

However, the tilt towards the positive is not necessarily overwhelming – by any means.

Dealing with this question is a very major undertaking. And I'm not so brave.

APPENDIX N:

Extraordinariation juxtaposed v. *tohu va-vohu*

One can hypothesize that Extraordinariation is juxtaposed against *tohu va-vohu* (the empty chaotic nothingness).[a]

To take matters further, one can hypothesize that to keep the cosmos from imploding back into nothingness, Extraordinariation must advance with more dynamism and richness *outward*, than *tohu va-vohu* pulls inward.

This theme can be developed elegantly, and dovetails well with the other components of Q4P, but it remains forever within the realm of hypothesis.

[a] see Genesis 1:2: "And the earth/land was *tohu va-vohu*."

APPENDIX O:

"Secular Divine"
v.
"Religious Divine"

As noted elliptically in the text,
Q4P (Quest for Potential$^\infty$/Extraordinariation)
works as a "Secular Divine" metaphysics and works
well as a "Religious Divine"* metaphysics.

But, either way, we are dealing with an infinitely radiating,
infinitely-grasping consciousness, and infinitely–grasping
power: The Divine.

One cannot posit transcendent, energizing and infinite on
all fronts, and then come back and say that this is not a
"Divine" entity/dynamic/force.

*Godhead included

APPENDIX P:

Optimization

The *signature component* of Q4P
(Quest for Potential$^\infty$/Extraordinariation) is *optimization.*

The component will tend to optimize *anything and everything.*

*

For example, *life on earth* will emerge both on the oxygen-sustained surface, as well as in toxic hydrothermal vents in the depths of the ocean.

Optimization has "worked-out" the solution-path in each case.

But, remember, *optimization* is the *signature component* of Q4P, which in turn is *at the heart of* Infinite Divine Potential.

*

GOD AND GOOD

From Big Bangs to the *evolution of snails, optimization* will
be *hard at work.*

From advancing *human consciousness,* to advancing
peak-experiences, from the spiritual through the sexual,
optimization has a 24/7 "consulting contract."

*

Both the *optimization* components of *(Newtonian) calculus*
and the iterative components of *Mandelbrot fractals*
are the (intertwined) mathematical threads here. They
presumably underpin the mathematical component, which
I hypothesize to be present.

(All) the other fields and extraordinary dimensions to this
optimization component, presumably are intertwined–with,
and wrap-around, the math.

This may prove somewhat hard to clinically prove :)

*

APPENDIX Q:

Q4P∞ juxtaposed v. Vicissitude

Some readers, after concluding reading the Summa set, posed the same question with which I started the series in the first place: If Q4P, why evil? Now, that question was dealt with heavily in Book #1 and dealt with again intermittently over the course of Book #2.

But, let's approach the question from one more angle, a very rough analogy, as we end this series.

The trip from the Old World to the New World involved stormy and quite-lethal voyages across the Atlantic. And even when the New World was reached, there was no shortage of travail. But there was 'advance.'

And we advance–forward.

APPENDIX R:

More Powerful v. Perfect

The proposed Summa metaphysics is not perfect.
Perfection is hard to come by when trying to
get one's arms around the infinite.

However, Summa would respectfully appear to be
quite significantly *more powerful* and *elegant* than the
competing known metaphysics formulations offered to
date (over the past three to five thousand years).

APPENDIX S:

Book #1 *(God and Evil)*
v.
Book #2 *(God and Good)*

Many readers of the *Summa* much prefer Book #1 over Book #2.

Presumably, it is clearer, and its style is more in a classic expository presentation/form. Plus Book #1 actually uses real, normal sentence structures.

Furthermore, Book #1 is *almost* a stand-alone, fairly comprehensible original and hi-energy, complete Metaphysics.

But only '*almost.*'

Whereas Book #1 conceptualized and framed-out the existence of Quest for Potential (enroute to dealing with theodicy, and before I brought Extraordinariation into the equation), Book #2 attempts to *get its arms around* the entire Q4P.

However, the mission of Book #2 is not so simple. How does one use regular language to describe an infinitely expanding (as we speak) Infinitude?

I thought about Book #2 for fourteen years before commencing 5-6 years of writing. And I only even conceived of a *line of approach* 12 years into the fourteen years of mulling-over this little task. So, either I'm slow or the task is challenging, or some combination thereof.

As noted in the introductory section to God and Good, Book #2 is heavily *intuitive* as the major motif, and heavily *intellectual* as the minor motif, whereas Book #1 was the mirror-image in these regards.

To achieve my (ambitious?) goals for Book #2, I needed to not only push my own psyche to its limits, which was frankly painful, but I needed to push your psyches to their respective limits, which I presume may have been somewhat grating, aggravating, frustrating or some combination thereof.

I saw no other route.

And time marches on.

Remember that Book #1 initially encountered very significant resistance when it was published in 1988. No one criticized it; it just wasn't "grasped." Then, about 2-5 years after publication, it achieved 'traction,' for whatever combination of reasons. Note that Book #2 *plays at a totally different level* (higher) than Book #1, which itself was *not shy* in its goals.

— Birnbaum

APPENDIX T:

Following the Analogy

Using one of our basic assumptions, that HUMAN parallels COSMIC, one can conjecture that there is a possibility of perpetual **rebirth** to (at least *portions of*) the cosmos.[*A]

In physics, there is a (cyclic) school of thinking along these lines, as well.[*B]

*

Our Infinite Divinitude ultimately pierces through the possible various cosmic births and deaths. It is this Infinite Divinitude which is necessary for Cosmic birth to begin with. But, as articulated, the primary fount of the Infinitude is its cumulative future potential.

*

Thus, not only does the *human spirit* potentially transcend one's death; it even ultimately potentially transcends the Death and rebirth *ad infinitum* (hopefully), of components of the cosmos itself.

***

[*A] The Midrash/Kabbala talk about cosmic cycles. According to this (hitherto) esoteric school of thought, we may be in the 4th or 5th or 6th cosmic cycle.

[*B] See also encyclopedia entries for Cyclic Model Cosmology:

> \# Paul Steinhardt; Neil Turok 2002
> \# Lauris Baum; Paul Frampton 2007

Note that, respectfully, Summa does not *take a position* on whether or not the cosmos is cyclic.

APPENDIX U:

By-definition *Telescoping Elasticity*

One of the great advantages of Q4P as the proposed core cosmic dynamic is its *by–definition* inherent **telescoping elasticity**. As conceptualized, it can telescope from classic *nothingness* to *infinitude.* We need that crucial "telescoping" aspect built-in to the core of the unitary proposed dynamic.

Meaning, that not only must the dynamic qualify as the core of the evolving Divine Infinitude, it must be unitary, "simple" and have *telescoping elasticity,* as well, among other nice (infinite) aspects delineated over the course of the two-book Summa series.

APPENDIX V:

Hypothesizing about Cosmic Origins

Clearly, this – hypothesizing about cosmic origins – is the most challenging aspect of metaphysics.

Now, while one can write with conviction about the **elegance** of a hypothesis, one cannot truly write with conviction about the **validity** of a cosmological hypothesis.

But the near-certain **validity** *per se*, of a cosmological hypothesis is not truly the conceptualizer's goal.

For, in dealing with the realms of the infinite and cosmic origins, our levels of consciousness to date (and perhaps for a long time to come) may simply be inadequate

A worthwhile goal, however, would be a more **dynamic and elegant** hypothesis than has hitherto been offered. That is what Summa proposes.

We seek to advance forward – another layer or two – towards cracking the cosmic code. We do not presume to articulate the penultimate core.

APPENDIX W:

Physics, Metaphysics & Poetry

a) PHYSICS will not solve PHYSICS without
METAPHYSICS....and
b) METAPHYSICS will not solve METAPHYSICS
without POETRY....

now, re: (a)

Why is that?

PHYSICS operates with a quasi-*dead-spot* on its
cumulative brain that PHYSICS is a stand-alone field....
albeit directly interacting with the hard sciences.
This is wrong.

All fields are interconnected – meaning the hard and soft
sciences – and it will frankly require integrating multiple
fields to penetrate truly deeply into the
cosmic code.

now, re: (b)

Why is that?

Metaphysics operates with a quasi-*dead-spot* on its own cumulative brain that METAPHYSICS is a stand-alone field...albeit directly interacting with the hard sciences. This is wrong.

The concepts necessary to get us to the core of cosmic code are too abstract for METAPHYSICS alone (whether from 5,000 years ago or contemporary). [Among other thinkers, the legendary theologian Rav Kook (b. 1865), Chief Rabbi of Palestine from 1921-1935, understood and followed-through on this.]
POETRY, while still hampered by the limitations of the human word and human consciousness, nevertheless affords us the opportunity of potentially thrusting closer to the core of **cosmic mystery**...

Of course, once one enters the world of POETRY, one enters another netherworld....

Sort of, *damned if you do; damned if you don't*

But, nevertheless, poetry ultimately *has a place* in the arsenal of the metaphysician....

APPENDIX X:

Holographic Universe Theory, Information and SUMMA

In God and Evil (1988) I hypothesize *"bootstrap creation"* to deal with the classic philosophical/metaphysical/ cosmology conundrum of *creation ex nihilo* i.e. – How is the cosmos seemingly created out of nothing?

God and Evil proposes an analogy to a *leveraged buyout* in finance. Basically, in a *leveraged buyout* one can potentially buy a company primarily by (sort of) guaranteeing the seller the company's anticipated future earnings stream to (allegedly) cover the (periodic multi-year) payments. [Often the Buyer is the CEO or another *prime protagonist* related to the business entity.]

Summa proposes that *future potentials* (in parallel to future earnings) **ignited the cosmos** (in parallel to the **buy** of a *leveraged buyout*). This is a core theme which courses through this two-volume metaphysics series.

However, among other potential underlying vulnerability points to this hypothesis is the question –
How does the "present" (at Creation) know the (infinite) future (potentialities)?

Conveniently for me, along emerges Holographic Theory [see Wikipedia entry] into mainstream physics over the past twenty+ years (c. 1990–2010 and now advancing-forward).

Now, Holographic Theory increasingly has no shortage of explicators and variations on its core themes. However a common denominator of the various hypotheses under this (Holographic) umbrella would be that *INFORMATION* is
(a) (somehow) stored on the space-time boundary, and that
(b) this information may interact internally in a modality that defies the classic linear *arrow of time*.

Now, once the internal interaction of information can possibly interact outside the boundaries of the classic linear *arrow of time*, "a bootstrap universe" cosmological hypothesis has a further (albeit certainly not necessarily sufficient) – and key – physical sciences toehold.

APPENDIX Y:

Counterposing
Summa Metaphysica (1988, 2005)
with
Spinoza (d. 1677)

There are many intersection points, but the two treatises are radically different, if not diametrically opposite at the core:

Spinoza posits a coldly impersonal core unifying dynamic; I posit a fiery all–pervading advancing dynamic and consciousness.

Spinoza holds GOOD and EVIL to be relative concepts;
I hold them to be objective and distinct.

Spinoza discerns no ultimate purpose to the cosmos; I do – Quest for Infinite Potential/Extraordinariation.

Spinoza does not grant Man any special place whatsoever in the universe; Summa does.

Spinoza posits a thoroughgoing *deterministic* universe
(i.e. that absolutely everything that happens, occurs
through the operation of *necessity*).

I certainly do not.

Randomness, Emotion, and (total) Free Will are key
components in my Metaphysics. Ultimately, Quest for
Potential$^\infty$/Extraordinariation layered-over Randomness,
Emotion and Free Will – is *iterative* as its key component,
and not overarchingly *deterministic*.

*

Both works do have in common, however, an emphasis on
an interlocking cosmic *lattice-work.*

APPENDIX Z1:

Survival

How does "survival" fit into the Quest for Potential$^\infty$/ Extraordinariation paradigm?

Clearly "survival" is necessary. Obviously. But it is far from sufficient. Thus, *necessary, but not sufficient.*

"Survival," in my paradigm, does not occupy the overwhelming paramount position ascribed to it by many *"survival of the fittest"* 19th and 20th century Darwinists. If it did, we would see far more species of slugs, and radically fewer species of butterflies.

At the same time, over the eons the relative priority of *survival* to *extraordinariation* may have intermittently shifted:

More species with high probability survival in-place
> *more emphasis on extraordinariation*, etc.

More species in a precarious survival situation
> *more emphasis on survival*.

Clearly, to *stay in the game*, survival is necessary.
But we hypothesize that overall, the *macro–signature theme* of our cosmos is "extraordinariation." In any event, while this area, like most areas involving the cosmos is nuanced and textured, the key thrust (*extraordinariation*) is clear.

APPENDIX Z2:

Primordial Realm Hypothesis

At the 'beginning' there **was not** "nothing."

At the "beginning" there **was**
"layer upon layer of pure possibility"
– whatever that precisely means.

Call it "*metaphysical possibility*."

Call it "*the plentitude of possibility*."

No matter what the precise jargon, it was "possibility."

'Possibility' then somehow morphs to
(its "first cousin")
Quest for Potential$^\infty$/Extraordinariation.

Precisely how? I do not know.

Why do I call the two "first cousins"?

Because they are very closely related and inter-related.

One is somehow embedded within the other.

Precisely how? I do not know.

Only 'possibility' can *bona fide* be hypothesized by the metaphysician to have been eternal.

It is **the sole** term/theme/concept which works. Period.

It is simple – and it rings true. To me.

A theologian can now peg-off the above and hypothesize –
      a) that God is the embodiment of "possibility"
      or
      b) that God is the embodiment of "potential."
      or
      c) that God is the embodiment of
          "extraordinariation"
      or
      d) that God is the embodiment
          of "possibility/potential/extraordinariation."

The last one (d) would be my personal, private view.

But as a (putative) metaphysician, I would just keep it simple:
    At the "beginning" – there was "possibility"

APPENDIX Z3:

Launch

Obviously we have no clue as to the sequence leading up to "launch" – or the Big Bang.

However, we are not shy to speculate.

Possibility > Embryonic Q4P$^\infty$ > Enhanced Q4P$^\infty$ (incorporating now, Formal Logic + Mathematics + Physics + Chemistry) > "the conference" > the Big Bang

"the conference"?

At some point the above-noted sciences – and they are ultimately actually one integrated field – are developed in metaphysical realms, but have no universe (reality) within which to *play-out* their full inherent *fullness/greatness* (meaning, full potential).

Pre-Big Bang, they would not have the capability of *full consciousness, love and parenting,* among other dynamics.

Again, they are not in a position to *play-out their (fuller/fullest) potential.*

Hence, "the conference"

It was a long conference.

But at some point, there was the inevitable resolution of the optimal path (to reach the next level of fullest potential) and the subsequent "decision" to "launch" (our cosmos).

(Q4P$^\infty$ = Quest for Potential/Extraordinariation)

APPENDIX Z4:

Where is Option B?

Summa proposes a unified metaphysics....
call it Option A

But, where is the competing Option B?

Obviously, we have questions with regards Option A.

But, with Option A, we do seem to have an elegant, overarching, seemingly seamless, powerful, crisp metaphysics which seems to elegantly finesse an almost endless series of issues – cosmology, cosmogony, theodicy, theology, evolutionary biology, teleology – and *on and on*....

Option A happens to nicely dovetail as well with components of the Torah and with key components of Lurianic Kabbalah – aside from being universalistic and humanistic and empowering – to all.

So, therefore the next obvious step might be to stack our Option A against Option B.

But, **what is** Option B? And, **where is** Option B?

Which is the *salient* – contender, challenger, old champion?

You might say that there are 100+ contenders?
And that they are too numerous to count?

OK, but which is *the salient contender?*

No salient contender?

That is the point.

While Summa makes numerous assertions, they all dovetail nicely into the Potential framework – its unifying 'spinal column' – and the overall construct is philosophically elegant.

It is not clear which other metaphysics challenges it.

APPENDIX Z5:

Cosmic Nesting (Iterativeness)

Q4P$^\infty$

– is hypothesized in Summa Metaphysica to exist
and to nest:

Q4P (Q4P (Q4P

(In formal mathematical terms:
infinite self-similar progression-regression
is suggested)

Mandelbrot Fractiles nest:

The *geometry* of [Mandelbrot set] *fractiles*
[developed by Polish/French/American Jewish
émigré mathematician Benoit Bernard Mandelbrot
heavily c. 1970-1982 during his thirty-five year
(1958-1993) tenure at IBM]
deals with the creation of *ever-repeating*,
"self-similar patterns" nested within each other.

Nature nests:

> the pattern on twigs on a branch resembles
> the pattern of limbs branching off the trunk
>
> the pattern of a major river looks like the pattern of
> its smaller tributaries
>
> the fractile pattern of the bronchus of the human
> lung, keeps repeating in the smaller and smaller
> bronchioles
>
> Natural water frost crystal growth shows fractile
> branching

Generations nest:

> Son of the son of the son of the son, etc....

Consciousness, Anger, Love and Sexual Arousal

> (among other dynamics)
> all possibly have *nesting* dimensions
>
> meaning, layer upon nuanced-layer ratchets-up the
> particular dynamic.

APPENDIX Z6:

Modern Evolutionary Synthesis*a

The modern evolutionary synthesis is a union of ideas from several biological specialties which provides a widely accepted account of evolution. It is also referred to as the *new synthesis*, the *modern synthesis*, the *evolutionary synthesis*, *millennium synthesis* and the *neo-darwinian synthesis*.

Some key points are –

• Evolution is gradual: small genetic changes regulated by natural selection accumulate over long periods.

• Natural selection*b is by far the main mechanism of change; even slight advantages are important when continued.

*a *Wikipedia Online*, http://en.wikipedia.org/wiki/Modern_evolutionary_synthesis (accessed February 6, 2012)

*b No scientific community consensus as of May 2012 as regards the precise modality of selection

---

from the author -

What is the actual modality of Natural Selection?

Is it perhaps Quest for Potential$^\infty$ continuously super-selecting from a plethora of mutations served-up by nature ongoing over the millennia?

APPENDIX Z7:

Anima mundi

The world soul (Greek: ψυχή κόσμου, Latin: *Anima mundi*) has been a component of several systems of thought. Its proponents claim that it permeates the cosmos and animates all matter, just as the soul animates the human body. The idea originated with Plato and was an important component of most Neoplatonic systems:

> Therefore, we may consequently state that: this world is indeed a living being endowed with a soul and intelligence... a single visible living entity containing all other living entities, which by their nature are all related.[1]

The Stoics believed it to be the only vital force in the universe. It also features in systems of eastern philosophy in the Brahman-Atman of Hinduism, and in the School of Yin-Yang, Taoism, and Neo-Confucianism as *qi*.

[1] Plato, Timaeus, 29/30; 4th century BCE

Wikipedia Online, http://en.wikipedia.org/wiki/Anima_mundi (accessed February 1, 2011)

APPENDIX Z8:

The Soul of the Universe

One can hypothesize that –

the *soul of a child* has a 1:1 correspondence
with the *soul of the universe*

As a child's spirit bursts with love and potential and hope,
so does the spirit of the universe.

As a child *embodies* all of our cumulative aspirations
and hopes, so does the universe *encompass* all of our
aspirations and hopes.

And as a *child* is but *one* (*nested*) *link* in the ever-
morphing and advancing interlinked chain of Quest for
Potential, so does a s*napshot of the universe* at any
moment in time, represent but one (*nested*) *link*....

APPENDIX Z9:

Possibility

Perhaps, our particular universe came into being because it was the most *extraordinary potential* POSSIBLE universe – and the cosmos optimizes.

APPENDIX Z10:

"The Free Lunch?"

The estimable physicist/cosmologist Stephen Hawking posits[*a] that "there is no God." His (alleged) truism is that "there is, indeed, a *free lunch*." What Hawking means and articulates is that the entire universe more-or-less spontaneously popped out of nothingness.

Hawking's reasoning, as he explicitly articulates it, is that – (A) since when one factors-in newly-hypothesized dark energy[*b] (c.1998), positive and negative energy mathematically balances-out the universe, then (B) one can (allegedly) consequently conclude that there is no God (necessary for Creation).

However, the Hawking logic is fatally flawed, as is more or less obvious.

For (A) can be true, without (B) being true.
Meaning, (B) does not necessarily flow from (A).

Summa Metaphysica (first volume 1988) along with many predecessor metaphysics formulations, some pre-dating it by thousands of years, hypothesizes[*c] a net-zero-balanced universe.[d] Some, if not the overwhelming majority, of these "net-zero" metaphysics, along with Summa Metaphysica, embrace a transcendent force and/or a Divine in the creation equation. Even if *we* are cumulatively hypothesized as being integral to the Divine, as per Summa.

With due respect to Hawking, not even a rock, let alone a universe, spontaneously pops-out of nothingness.

Respectfully, giggling five years old girls frolicking at the seashore on a balmy June day, tip-toeing through the foamy surf where ocean wavelets lap onto the beach, did not simply pop out of nothingness.

Respectfully.

***

[a] Summer 2011, see Hawking interview/feature on Wormhole Series on the Science Channel. See his inter-related book The Grand Design by Stephen Hawking and Leonard Mlodinow, Bantam Books, a division of Random House, NY 2010

[b] a hypothesis which started emerging in the contemporary scientific community in the past 40 years, but mainly started gaining traction since ~1998, when scientist Michael Turner (University of Chicago) coined the term.

[c] see Summa Metaphysica: Volume I: God & Evil 1988: Unified Formulation

[d] i.e. positive and negative energy balance-out the universe

APPENDIX Z11:

Birnbaumian Panentheism

Quest for Potential∞ is at the core of the Infinite Divine.

The Infinite Divine is synonymous with the unfolding cosmic order.

<u>Panentheism in Judaism*</u>

   "While mainstream Rabbinic Judaism is classically monotheistic and follows in the footsteps of the Aristotelian theologian Maimonides, the panentheistic conception of God can be found in certain Jewish mystical currents. A leading scholar of the Kabbalah, Moshe Idel ("Hasidism: Between Ecstacy and Magic," SUNY, 1995, pp. 17–18), ascribes this doctrine to the kabbalistic system of Rabbi Moses Cordovero (1522–1570) and in the eighteenth century, Rabbi Israel ben Eliezer, the Baal Shem Tov, founder of the Hasidic movement, as well as his contemporary, Rabbi Menahem Mendel, the Maggid of Bar. There is some debate as to whether Lurianic Kabbalah, with its doctrine of *tzimtzum*, can be regarded as panentheistic. According to Hasidism, the Infinite *Ein Sof* is incorporeal (has no body) and is both transcendent and immanent...."

*Wikipedia online, http://en.wikipedia.org/wiki/Panentheism#Panentheism_in_Judaism (accessed September 20, 2011)

APPENDIX Z12:

Cosmic Level: Individual Level

Current scientific guestimates
figure 100 billion+

galaxies in the observable universe

and

then, the same number, a 100 billion

stars in the Milky Way Galaxy

and then, a third layer –

the same 100 billion

(10^{11})

neurons in the human brain

GOD AND GOOD

Now,
the 100 billion neurons in the brain

in turn yield 100 trillion (10^{14}) synapses

    which generate thought, creativity, emotion etc.

Thus,
the cosmos (Q4P$^\infty$) presumably calculates that
    100 billion (or thereabouts)
is the efficient
    CRITICAL MASS number
    to seek/pursue/extend/force-multiply
    Q4P$^\infty$/EXTRAORDINARIATION !

on multiple levels
 cosmic > individual

as it thunders-on towards Infinitude....

and Extraordinariaton.

APPENDIX Z13:

Major Problems in Science
[Selected Quotes from
*ON BEING**ᵃ*
by Dr. Peter Atkins**ᵇ]

"The first great question of being is one that has probably entertained us all at one time or another: where did it, the universe, all come from? How did it begin?..." (p. 1)

"There are, in fact, three related profound questions to address in the context of creation. One is the mechanism of the coming into being of the universe: what actually happened at the beginning? Another is whether there is any meaning to the question of what preceded the universe and had, in some sense, the potential to become a universe. Here we are confronted by the linguistically and conceptually engaging question of whether absolutely nothing can have potency to become something. The third is whether an agent was needed to trigger the process of cosmogenesis, the process of turning that nothing into what is to all appearances something, or can nothing turn itself into something on its own? All three questions sound as though they might fall within the range of science to answer. A fourth question, why there is a universe, is rather different, but still apparently very interesting...." (p. 2)

"As a result of their intrinsic caution, almost every scientist is wisely unwilling to express a view about the events accompanying the inception of the universe. Quite honestly, they haven't a clue...." (p. 5)

"The task before science in this connection will be to show how something can come from nothing without intervention. No one has the slightest idea whether that can happen and, if so, how it can come about...." (p. 11)

"The unfolding of absolutely nothing—what out of reverence for the absence of anything, including empty space, we are calling Nothing—into something is a problem of the profoundest difficulty and currently far beyond the reach of science. It is, however, a target at which science must aim even though to some, even to scientists of a pessimistic or perhaps just realistic bent, it would seem to be for ever out of science's reach...." (p. 12)

"Presumably before the creation, when there was Nothing, there was no charge; so the coming into being of the universe was accompanied by the separation of 'no charge' into opposites. Charge was not created at the creation: electrical Nothing separated into equal and opposite charges...." (pp. 13-14)

"I promised to return to the question of *why* there is
a universe. What is its purpose? Something so big,
complex, and all embracing some hold, must be there
for a reason…." (p. 18)

"…science is a ceaseless probing with a view to
overturning authority….science, though delighted
by the glorious complexity of the world, seeks the
simplicity that lies beneath it….science is extraordinarily
difficult, as it seeks covert mechanism….science is
ever thrusting forward, wriggling into new modes of
understanding,…science gives an opportunity for
humanity to achieve the aspirations it already has and
opens its eyes to new ones…." (pp. 26-27)

"A scientist, the arch-descendent of Occam, looks first
for the simplest explanation, then builds elaborations
only if the explanation's barren, rocky simplicity proves
inadequate…." (p. 33)

"One problem with evolution is how it began.
Competition between primitive organisms is all very
well, the triumph of one message over another,
but how did matter step across the national bridge
from the inorganic to the organic in the first place?
…It would be much more satisfying—satisfying of
curiosity, intellectually satisfying, and possibly spiritually
satisfying—if we could find a physical process by which
that gap was bridged, presumably without the apparent
intervention of an agent…." (pp. 38-39)

"…Scientists are still puzzled about how this complexity [of life] emerged under the impact, presumably, of natural selection, and it remains a problem of evolution. That is not to say that there are not many ideas about how it came about. Just as for the origin of life itself, which is still a real puzzle, evolutionary biologists are not without ideas, but have not yet identified which, if any, is valid…." (pp. 60-61)

[a] Peter Atkins, *On Being* (Oxford, England: Oxford University Press, 2011), pp.1-2, 5, 11-14, 18, 26-27, 33, 38-39, 60-61.

---

[b] Scientist Peter Atkins is the author of almost 70 books, including *Galileo's Finger: The Ten Great Ideas of Science, Four Laws That Drive the Universe,* and the world-renowned textbook *Physical Chemistry*. A Fellow of Lincoln College, University of Oxford, he has been a visiting professor in France, Israel, New Zealand, and China, and continues to lecture widely throughout the world.

APPENDIX Z14:

"Nothing"

It would be incorrect, of course, to imply or infer that *Summa* maintains that NOTHING preceded all. That position, respectfully, would, by definition, be a metaphysical 'dead end.'

The 'starting point' of the cosmos is not NOTHING.

Rather, *Summa* proposes that 'Possibility' was/is eternal. And 'Possibility' is clearly a far more complex and a far richer concept than 'Nothing.'

While, one can posit that by definition 'Possibility' is eternal, one can also posit that by definition 'Nothing' is just that – nothing. And no entity or agent or force can turn *nothing* into *something*. By definition.

Now, 'Possibility' may, indeed have dimensions/facets of which we are either unaware, or cannot fully grasp.

'Possibility/Potential' in turn, may have had the ability to traverse – or impel the traversing – from the metaphysical to reality as we know it.

'Possibility/Potential' may have had the power, ultimately, to divide '0'* (hypothesized core "zero-point/integer") into positives and negatives, as discussed in the text. And, herein, in my estimation, is most probably the crux of the genesis of our little universe.

> "Cosmologists sometimes claim that the universe can arise 'from nothing.' But this is loose language. Even if shrunk to a point or a quantum state, our universe is latent with particles and forces: it has far more content and structure than what a philosopher calls 'nothing.'"
> (Martin Rees, Our Cosmic Habitat, p. 142)

*technical note:
maybe we should treat the Hebrew word *ayin* as "0"

APPENDIX Z15:

Gnosticism
(selected WIKI excerpts)*

"Gnosticism (from gnostikos, "learned", from Greek: γνῶσις *gnōsis*, knowledge) is a modern scholarly term for a set of religious beliefs and spiritual practices found among some of the early Christian sects called "gnostic" ("learned") by Irenaeus and other early Christian heresiologists. The term also has reference to parallels and possible pre-Christian influences of the Christian gnostics.

Gnosticism was primarily defined in Christian context, or as 'the acute Hellenization of Christianity' per Adolf von Harnack (1885), until Moritz Friedländer (1898) advocated Hellenistic Jewish origins, and Wilhelm Bousset (1907) advocated Persian origins...."

Common characteristics

"….The Christian sects first called "gnostic" a branch of Christianity, however Joseph Jacobs and Ludwig Blau (Jewish Encyclopedia, 1911) note that much of the terminology employed is Jewish and note that this "proves at least that the principal elements of gnosticism were derived from Jewish speculation,…."

Monad (apophatic theology)

"In many Gnostic systems (and heresiologies), God is known as the Monad, the One, The Absolute, Aion teleos (The Perfect Æon), Bythos (Depth or Profundity, Βυθος), Proarkhe (Before the Beginning, προαρχη), and E Arkhe (The Beginning, η αρχη). God is the high source of the pleroma, the region of light. The various emanations of God are called æons.

Within certain variations of Gnosticism, especially those inspired by Monoimus, the Monad was the highest God which created lesser gods, or elements (similar to æons). According to Hippolytus, this view was inspired by the Pythagoreans, who called the first thing that came into existence the Monad, which begat the dyad, which begat the numbers, which begat the point, begetting lines, etc…."

[*]*Wikipedia Online*, http://en.wikipedia.org/wiki/Gnosticism (accessesd February 26, 2012)

APPENDIX Z16:

Atheist v. Potentialist
Atkins* v. Birnbaum

consonant with Summa:

"simplicity"

"...The only clue we have at the outset is that the final answer will almost certainly be one of extreme simplicity, for only the perfectly simple can come into existence.... what we perceive of as complexity may be the outcome of chains of simplicity." (p. 7)[*a]

"...Somehow matter must have been created out of something resembling nothing...." (p. 11)[*a]

Intersecting with Summa:

"Mega-organism"

"…our own nominally civilized, cultivated, intelligent, and reflective level of life emerged when organisms stumbled on a way of passing on intricate, unpredictable information to others around them and following them. It did so by inventing language and effectively binding together all human organisms, past, present, and future into a single mega-organism of potentially boundlesss achievement." (p.33)[*b]

polar opposite to Summa:

"collapse into chaos"

"Aspirations... feed on (purposeless) decay"

"....All change, I shall argue, arises from an underlying collapse into chaos. We shall see that what may appear to us to be motive and purpose, is in fact ultimately motiveless, purposeless decay. Aspirations and their achievement, feed on [purposeless] decay." (p. 21)[*a]

[*a] Peter Atkins, *Creation Revisited, The Origin of Space, Time and the Universe* (London, England: Penguin Books, 1992)
[*b] Peter Atkins, *Galileo's Finger, The Ten Great Ideas of Sciences*, (Oxford, England: Oxford University Press, 2003)

APPENDIX Z17:

Particle Physics and Q4P$^\infty$

Interacting with a layer of Q4P$^\infty$?

Higgs mechanism*

"In particle physics, the Higgs mechanism is the process that gives mass to elementary particles. The particles gain mass by interacting with the Higgs field that permeates all space...."

*Wikipedia Online, http://en.wikipedia.org/wiki/Higgs_mechanism (accessed March 5, 2012)

APPENDIX Z18:

A Fix-It "Conceptual Plug"?

The Summa series started out with God and Evil (1988). In that work it was demonstrated how Q4P$^\infty$ potentially might not just solve the classic philosophical-religious conundrum of Theodicy, but would seem to simultaneously solve as well several other key philosophical issues in metaphysics.

As pointed-out in this volume, God and Good, many/most/all major fields – not just Metaphysics – would seem to have gaping holes in them. The appendix relating to noted scientist Atkins, for instance, highlights via excerpts from his works – gaping holes in the physical sciences.

This 'gaping-hole' issue ranges through Astrophysics, Biology, Anthropology, Philosophy, Theology, Cosmology, Life Sciences and on-and-on.

The key fields – and probably all related fields – have major gaps.

Now, adroitly plugging Q4P$^\infty$/Extraordinariation into the respective gaps, seems to potentially close-the-gaps. (Is that the world's most grandiose assertion or what?)

Thus, we have an intriguing potential *simultaneous* solution on a very grand scale.

Are we *catching your attention* yet?

Several examples:

Evolutionary Biology: What drives Evolution?

Physiology: What drives Consciousness?

Astrophysics: What ignited/drove the Big Bang, in particular?

Cosmology: What ignited creation and maintains the Cosmos more generally?

Metaphysics: What is the *purpose* of Man, the cosmos?

Astronomy: Why is the cosmic order so *wondrous*?

Life Sciences: What drives Life? What is Life?

GOD AND GOOD

What makes Life so tenacious?

Anthropology: what drives the 'Ascent of Man'?

Love Science: What drives Love?

and, of course, our initial inquiry into the Theodicy question-

Religious Philosophy: Theodicy question – If there is a God who is all-powerful and merciful, why is there gross evil?

APPENDIX Z19:

The Data

Comporting to the data v. Data proving the hypothesis

Metaphysicians doing metaphysics seek an all-embracing hypothesis, at-a-minimum comporting to the data. Metaphysicians seek 'aesthetic elegance.'

Physicists doing physics want *testability*. They want data proving the hypothesis. To them, a successful experiment is by definition elegant. To them, Grand Theory metaphysics is not Center Stage – as by definition it cannot be proven.

Now, Summa poses an intriguing issue for physics.

Because, on the one hand, (infinite) Summa cannot necessarily be proven in the classic sense, which physics would prefer. Eve though it is always hard to prove the infinite and/or timeless.

But, on the other hand,

    (a) Summa fills-in crucial and key gaps in physics

        and

    (b) No data or knowledge accumulated in the past 5,000+ years at all contradicts Summa.

No other metaphysics can make these claims.

Thus, the fully synchronous data underpins Summa, while Summa underpins physics and astrophysics et al.

APPENDIX Z20:

Take #2: Where Is The Competing Metaphysics?*

The Bard Symposium '*take*'

The three basic groups of academics represented at the April 2012 international academic conference at Bard College (NY) on *Summa Metaphysica* were:
A) Religious philosophers
B) Secular Philosophers/Metaphysicians
C) Scientists

Conference co-Chair Gary Hagberg** posed the (above-noted) question, (see title above) to the assemblage of academics:

answers

(A)
Group A academics leaned-towards the proposition that each of their respective religions could potentially embrace *Summa* as an elegant dovetailing *add-on* to their respective belief systems.

(B)
Group B academics leaned-towards the proposition that Neoplatonism as a whole was the closest (albeit indirectly) competing neo-metaphysics. However, Neoplatonism is more a *modality* of looking at problems, rather than a particular specific all-embracing intellectual or metaphysical structure. Indeed, we all operate on a Neoplatonism platform. Meaning, that there was, indeed, no salient viable directly competing metaphysics.

[However, respectfully, Aristotelianism and its Jewish offshoot, Maimonidean philosophy are important historical systems, still embraced by many, which do *so-to-speak* on significant levels compete with *Summa*. Daniel Khalil directly and articulately deals with – and exposes the *fatal metaphysical gap* in – Aristotle and Maimonides in his Foreword to Summa II: God and Good.]

(C)
Group C academics went along with Oxford scientist and Conference *presenter* Peter Atkins' "interesting" mini-metaphysics that "*purposeless decay*" was the allegedly more powerful and competing metaphysics. Atkins repeatedly articulates this theme in his published works.

When challenged as to whether he preferred to view himself as the product of Birnbaumian Quest for Potential$^\infty$/Extraordinariation or of Atkinsonian *purposeless decay*, Atkins responded with the latter, to the dismay of the assemblage.

In Summation

re: the proposed "Purposeless decay" metaphysics:
Thus, the prime direct challenge to the Potential/
Extraordinariation metaphysics, is, according to at least
one segment of the Conference, only "purposeless
decay." Frankly, hard-to-believe that this pessimistic
quick-fix – which has no formal structure and no
answers to many key questions – is even qualified to
challenge. Aside from the fact that the 'visceral appeal'
of "*purposeless decay*" is not, shall we say, stellar.
As well, it has neither a "starting point" nor significant
"integration" beyond a few specific physics issues.

re: the Aristotelian metaphysisc:
As noted above, Khalil deals with the fatal gap in
Aristotelian or neo-Aristotelian systems.***

Conclusion:
Thus, with no readily available seriously challenging
metaphysics, we would need to juxtapose Summa
against putative competing systems as they are
potentially offered-up.

* see also "Appendix Z4: Where is Option B?"

** Chairman, Dept. of Philosophy, Bard College

*** For the record, Orthodox Jewish scientist and academic Khalil
does not challenge the religious doctrines of Orthodox Jewish
Maimonides. Nor does Khalil truly need to do so in order to challenge
the metaphysics of Maimonides. [Please note that Khalil and I are in-
sync on both fronts here.]

APPENDIX Z21:

The Assertion/Claim

The assertion/claim herein is that *Summa* is the optimal *working hypothesis* for a unified and integrated metaphysics. Of course, like all hypotheses, it should be probed, challenged and debated.

While it is certainly true that Summa frontally challenges the heavily-entrenched academic *status quo*, perhaps *Summa's* hypothesis is actually *right*.

Perhaps that* is possibly sufficient reason for establishment academia to very seriously debate and consider it, even if the academic establishment is simultaneously threatened by it.

*being right

APPENDIX Z22:

The Q4P$^\infty$ 'Package'

...Includes but is not limited to the components

Recursive / Looping upon itself / Self-Referencing / Iterative / Self-Sustaining*a

As argued, "Possibility" is the sole "dynamic" which can arguably have been eternal. This is "self-evident." Then hypothesizing that Q4P$^\infty$ evolved from "Possibility" is, respectfully, not a major *conceptual leap*.

Q4P$^\infty$ is a rare "conceptualized dynamic" which could be hypothesized to have taken the (budding) cosmic order from the metaphysical to the physical.

It is this *sui generis* inter-related *bundle of attributes**b – and related – which decisively *arm the Q4P$^\infty$ candidacy* as the *prime protagonist* in the cosmic drama.

---

*a Self-sustaing relates, as well, to the "leveraged buyout" aspect delineated in the text: *Potentials down-the-road* ignite the present (Genesis Point). But note that these same *potentials-down-the-road* also help *sustain and nourish* the ongoing drama.

*b It is the architectural/conceptual 'elegance' of 'the package' which so-to-speak 'gives it a chance.'

APPENDIX Z23:

Explication

Q4P$^\infty$ is perhaps also explicated as –

The cosmic Supra-Instinct & Essence.

The underling cosmic Progenitor & Dynamic.

The cosmic Common-Denominator & Imperative.

The font, essence and drive of the cosmos.

The [Divine] *Qi* of the Cosmos.

The (elusive) [Chinese] Tao – the "source of everything."*a

The (elusive) [Jewish] Lurianic Kabballah mystical *En Sof*.*b

The Infinite and dynamic Divine.

The Biblical *Eheyeh asher Eheyeh*.*c

Simultaneously, the *Macro* and *Micro* essence of the cosmic order.

The Holy Grail of the cosmos….

The *mysterium tremendum*

**while at the same time,
encompassing the entire dynamic cosmic order**

*[a] Never explicated by obscure Taoism (Daoism), even though everyone is referred to the collected works of Laozi (and Zhuangzi) which, in turn, never explicate the Tao except very elliptically and very obscurely/ambiguously. [Note that Taoism is a philosophy or religious tradition which emphasizes living in harmony with the aforementioned (obscure) Tao.]

*[b] The "*No End*": Dealt with extensively in Summa I: God and Evil

*[c] "I WILL BE THAT WHICH I WILL BE" – The self-proclaimed Identity of the God of Israel to Moses at the 'Burning Bush' episode – when God reveals Himself to Moses.

APPENDIX Z24:

Context

Heretofore, we essentially generally operated without overall context. Most fields of knowledge have floated essentially on their own (or linked to close fields) in an ineffable and greatly inexplicable cosmos. Not explicated-by or tethered-to an all-enveloping metaphysics. *Summa*, however, offers a powerful all-embracing context and integrated thesis.

While the author and many academic luminaries believe *Summa* to be *on-the-mark*, it may or may not be. But, certain aspects regarding *Summa* are hard to dispute:

It seems to be elegant, powerful, overarching, integrated and holistic.

Its core thesis has remained unchallenged.

It alone among known metaphysical schemas systematically and conceptually seems to truly unify Science, Spirituality, Philosophy and Religion.

And, finally, *Summa* is essentially "the only game in town." There is simply no known *bona fide* directly competing, éven somewhat compelling (overarching and well-integrated) metaphysics known to us.*

* Respectfully, classic religious philosophies are not counted here as competing metaphysics. Respectfully, their systems tend to include as integral to their core paradigms, a particular ineffable and inexplicable deity or divine. Ditto for (obscure) Taoism. Rather, religious philosophies can and should consider Summa as a potential add-on or wrap-around schema.

The alleged competitor to Summa – Neoplatonism's ancient offshoot schema Aristotelianism – is, respectfully, simply too simplistic, too assumption-laden, too incomplete and, respectfully, more accurately in the realm of religious philosophy. As noted [see Khalil "Foreword"]: Aristotelianism has a gaping-hole in it.

As well, Aristotelianism is often dead-wrong. For instance, it postulates that the Sun rotates around the Earth.

APPENDIX Z25:

Where is the Divine?

Metaphysical challenge:
Choose from these *multiple* choice options:

a) Nowhere

b) Up there / Separate from us

c) Here

d) Here, and it encompasses all / We are part of It
   – and integral to It.

Summa rejects (a) and (b), agrees with (c) but embraces (d).

The author is dubious that any metaphysics, which
embraces (a) or (b) can present a viable integrated,
holistic and fully-satisfying option. Summa believes that
the metaphysical debate needs to take place within the
embrace of (c) or (d).

Atheism embraces (a)

Note that Aristotelianism (Aristotle was the student of Plato, who in turn was the student of Socrates) and classic mainstream Western (religious) thought classically both embrace (b).

Taoism and much Eastern philosophical/religious thought embrace (c) or (d).

"We are made of light, and we are all part of God's mind. Most importantly, we are the universe itself having the experience of knowing that." (Fred Alan Wolf, *Time Loops and Space Twists*, p. 232)

APPENDIX Z26:

String Theory and 'Provability'

String Theory is a contender for the "theory of everything in physics."

After 40 years of intense effort (and failure) by String Theory advocates to make predictions which can definitively be tested by experiment, String Theory is nevertheless essentially accepted by its many and often quite-eminent scientific community proponents because of it's elegance, its conceptual aesthetic appeal, and its relative power *vis à vis* other contending theories. As well, there is the hope of its advocates that in the future there may be some measurable consequences. On net balance to date, it is a noble effort by many hundreds of scientists to transcend mortal and current scientific limitations.

Thus, in Physics, which demands as an almost inviolable *sine qua non* (essential condition) testability, **provability** and ultimately proof, in this instance an untested and unproven theory is nevertheless held in the highest possible (international) esteem.

Note that Metaphysics, which more often than not probes the infinite, the transcendent, and universal cosmic axioms, does not require scientific proof *per se*. It inviolably requires, however, the absence of *contradiction* with physics and science, as a whole.

APPENDIX Z27:

Multiverse Theory

Multiverse is a theory in physics. It is not a classic metaphysics overarching the gamut of fields of knowledge.

So, for instance, as regards the classic question as to where our universe came from, if one proposes as an answer that it is part of – or a "daughter of" – a multiverse cosmic order, one still needs to address where the "mother universe(s)" came from.

APPENDIX Z28:

Theory of Everything* (in Physics)

"A **theory of everything (TOE)** or **final theory** is a putative theory of theoretical physics that fully explains and links together all known physical phenomena, and predicts the outcome of *any* experiment that could be carried out *in principle*.

Many candidate theories of everything (in physics) have been proposed by theoretical physicists during the twentieth century, but none have been confirmed experimentally. The primary problem in producing a TOE is that general relativity and quantum mechanics are hard to unify. This is one of the unsolved problems in physics....

While loop quantum gravity [theory] attempts to unify quantum field theory and general relativity/gravitation, string theory and its successor M-theory, remain the only prominent candidates as a theory of everything."

*Wikipedia Online, http://en.wikipedia.org/wiki/Theory_of_everything (accessed April 25, 2012)

---

from the author –

Summa, of course, fully embraces physics, and believes that Q4P$^\infty$ is by definition fully synchronous with physics.

Metaphysics is about painting a "bold brush stroke" super-macro overarching conceptual Theory of Everything (meaning, a "real deal" Theory of Truly Everything). The correct [overarching] metaphysics theory would embrace within its fold the correct [overarching] physics theory. The author respectfully believes that ultimately physics will be compelled to *make its way* to Q4P$^\infty$ in order to *cross the final theoretical bridge* in its quest for a Theory of Everything (in Physics), including Big Bang Theory.

Note that as a reference to their work, metaphysicians avoid using that (TOE) terminology or a more precise phrase for metaphysics like "Macro Theory of Everything," because the terminology projects/resonates as being too presumptuous. But *conceptual macro brush strokes* is essentially what metaphysics is ultimately all about. Macro Everything. That is what metaphysicians are paid to do.

APPENDIX Z29:

Occam's Razor

"**Occam's razor** (also written as **Ockham's razor**, Latin *lex parsimoniae*) is the law of parsimony, economy or succinctness. It is a principle urging one to select among competing hypotheses that which makes the fewest assumptions and thereby offers the simplest explanation of the effect."*

Summa offers a so-to-speak 'simple', but purportedly sophisticated and powerful proposition:

**Quest for Potential$^\infty$ ignited,
drives and indeed, is, the cosmos.**

Occam might smile.

Wikipedia Online, http://en.wikipedia.org/wiki/Occam's_razor (accessed April 25, 2012)

APPENDIX Z30:

Schopenhauer v. Birnbaum

*from Wikipedia**

"**Arthur Schopenhauer** (22 February 1788 – 21 September 1860) was a German philosopher known for his pessimism and philosophical clarity. At age 25, he published his doctoral dissertation, *On the Fourfold Root of the Principle of Sufficient Reason*, which examined the four separate manifestations of reason in the phenomenal world.

Schopenhauer's most influential work, *The World as Will and Representation*, claimed that the world is fundamentally what humans recognize in themselves as their will. His analysis of will led him to the conclusion that emotional, physical, and sexual desires can never be fully satisfied. The corollary of this is an ultimately painful human condition. Consequently, he considered that a lifestyle of negating desires, similar to the ascetic teachings of Vedanta, Buddhism and the Church Fathers of early Christianity, was the only way to attain liberation.

Schopenhauer's metaphysical analysis of will, his views on human motivation and desire, and his aphoristic writing style influenced many well-known thinkers, including Friedrich Nietzsche, Richard Wagner, Ludwig Wittgenstein, Erwin Schrödinger, Albert Einstein, Sigmund Freud, Otto Rank, Carl Jung, Joseph Campbell, Leo Tolstoy, Thomas Mann, and Jorge Luis Borges...."

So Schopenhauer's *The World as Will and Representation* posits that the world is fundamentally 'will'; and 'pessimist-school' Schopenhauer comes to the conclusion that *negating* 'will' is the *'route to liberation.'*

Birnbaum's *Summa Metaohysica* posits that the world is essentially 'potential'; and, to continue counterposing Schpenhauer, 'optimist-school' Birnbaum comes to the (quick) conclusion that *proactive* 'Quest for Potential' is the true *'route to liberation.'*

Wikipedia Online, http://en.wikipedia.org/wiki/Arthur_Schopenhauer (accessed May 21, 2012)

APPENDIX Z31:

Simple v. Simplistic

Metaphysicians and scientists like their theories *simple yet sophisticated*. Thus, Einstein's iconic Theory of Relativity, $E=MC^2$ is simple, but highly sophisticated.

Many theories and laws of physics follow this general paradigm: *Simple, yet sophisticated*.

Now in our little realm of metaphysics, we posit that $Q4P^\infty$ is *simple, yet sophisticated*.

$Q4P^\infty$ enthusiasts would argue that (linear) Aristotelianism (i.e. Eternal God deployed primal matter and created the Earth) is simply *simplistic**.

> "Everything should be made
> as simple as possible,
> but no simpler"
>
> — Albert Einstein
> (c. 1933)

*or in any event, more in the realm of theology

APPENDIX Z32:

Aesthetic Elegance

At the April 2012 Bard College international academic symposium on Summa Metaphysica, (Grinnell College Associate Professor of Philosophy and symposium panelist) Tammy Nyden repeatedly made-the-case that Summa's *aesthetic elegance* intrigued her and resonated.

After multi-day discussion/debate at Annandale-on-Hudson, Upstate, NY as to the *sine qua non* (~the necessary aspect) of a powerful metaphysics, the consensus emerged that since metaphysics (by its infinite nature and ambition) does not lend itself to formal scientific proof, its *aesthetic elegance* indeed emerges as perhaps its key defining aspect.*

Of course, *aesthetic elegance*, seemingly subjective, in reality embraces many clinical components. Presumably the metaphysics under examination at-a-minimum *passes muster vis à vis* the litmus test checklist proposed at the very beginning of the appendix section in Appendix A: Metaphysics Analysis.

Now, the human psyche is awesomely complex. But it ultimately often seeks to boil-down a litmus test checklist to just one concept. *Aesthetic elegance* presents itself as a viable candidate in metaphysics.

* Incorporated into qualification for *aesthetic elegance* would necessarily be the requirement that the metaphysics comports with 'actual knowledge' i.e. the hard and soft sciences

APPENDIX Z33:

The Red Queen Hypothesis

Classic application to evolution:

from Wikipedia[*a]

"The **Red Queen's Hypothesis**, also referred to as **Red Queen, Red Queen's race** or **Red Queen Effect**, is an evolutionary hypothesis. The term is taken from the Red Queen's race in Lewis Carroll's *Through the Looking-Glass* and involves the Red Queen and Alice constantly running, yet remaining in the same place.

"Well, in our country," said Alice, still panting a little, "you'd generally get to somewhere else — if you run very fast for a long time, as we've been doing."

"A slow sort of country!" said the Queen. "Now, here, you see, it takes all the running you can do, to keep in the same place. If you want to get somewhere else, you must run at least twice as fast as that!"

The Red Queen Principle can be stated thus:

In reference to an evolutionary system, continuing adaptation [and successive procreation] is needed in order for a species to maintain its relative fitness amongst the systems being co-evolved with.[b]...."

BIRNBAUMIAN application to the cosmic order:

Successive evolutionary and cosmic advance – on myriad levels – is necessary for the cosmos not to devolve into entropy.[c]

A parallel to this might be the dynamic of skimming a rock along the surface of a pond. The rock must be projected within a given angle tolerance and within a given speed and acceleration tolerance, in order not to fall into the water.

To "defy gravity," the skimming rock must advance. Likewise, the cosmic order: To defy entropy, it must advance... playing-out cosmic potential and advancing-towards Extraordinariation.

[a] *Wikipedia online*, http://en.wikipedia.org/wiki/Red_Queen's_Hypothesis#cite_note-1 (accessed June 4, 2012)

[b] http://pespmc1.vub.ac.be/REDQUEEN.html

[c] Birnbaumian corollary to the Second Law of Thermodynamics

APPENDIX Z34:

Punctuated equilibrium*

from Wikipedia

"**Punctuated equilibrium** (also called **punctuated equilibria**) is a theory in evolutionary biology which proposes that most species will exhibit little net evolutionary change for most of their geological history, remaining in an extended state called *stasis*. When significant evolutionary change occurs, the theory proposes that it is generally restricted to rare and geologically rapid events...."

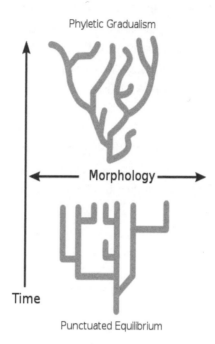

Punctuated equilibrium, consists of morphological stability and rare bursts of evolutionary change

---

from the author –

Clearly, Punctuated Equilibrium works far better with Q4P$^\infty$ in the equation, i.e. with Q4P$^\infty$ driving and igniting the leaps-forward. What other hypothesized dynamic is punctuating the equilibrium?

Indeed, when now lining-up all the areas – even just those

alone which have been articulated in Summa – where Q4P$^\infty$ provides a significantly more elegant conceptual framework than any sans-Q4P$^\infty$ hypotheses, it would seem that a somewhat compelling case has been made. Especially since there is no known competing, compelling alternative.

Respectfully, Summa *de facto* stands alone. It may turn out to be wrong, but it would currently seem to be the overwhelmingly and distinctively aesthetically elegant metaphysics.

Perhaps mainstream academic scientific and philosophical thought should endeavor to transcend its inertia. Perhaps academia will now undergo its own Punctuated Equilibrium...and go with a winning new paradigm ;) as its working hypothesis, as opposed to its current (somewhat pathetics) modus operandi: of operating without any real conceptual context.

Wikipedia Online, http://en.wikipedia.org/wiki/Punctuated_equilibrium (accessed June 4, 2012)

APPENDIX Z35:

The Font/Soul of the Cosmos

Ninety five percent of all religious and spiritual belief systems *de facto* vector towards this issue.

This question/quest for the Font/Soul of the cosmos is the Holy Grail of –
>   Religious, Spiritual, Philosophical and Metaphysical
>   inquiry

*

Summa attempts/proposes a 'silver bullet' – $Q4P^\infty$ – to pierce through to the core of the cosmic
>   origins/essence/engine/drive/purpose.

The Summa hypothesis is no doubt quite-powerful and quite-elegant.

There is no competing compelling metaphysics.

The only question is whether Summa is indeed essentially correct.

APPENDIX Z36:

Time

To whatever extent, over the next decades and centuries, physics ascertains potential non-linear dimensions of time, Summa advances.

As readers of Summa know, the thesis hypothesizes that as a key component thereof, the plethora of potentials down-the-road were instrumental in igniting the 'genesis point.'

So this key component mandates some non-linear dimensions or pathways in time. In other words, some link between the future and the past.

So, for instance,

As holographic theories gain in traction, Summa advances.

If 'black holes' turn out to impact time any-which-way, Summa advances.

If the 'speed of light' barrier protects the linearity of time in particular, Summa advances.

If it turns out that time can indeed be compressed or expanded, Summa advances.

If it turns out that, on some level, the future co-exists simultaneously with the present or that the present somehow exists within the future (or vice versa), Summa advances.

The manifold mysteries of time are inextricably linked to the mysteries of creation.

"Time travel and causal loops are not merely the stuff of science fiction. The theory of relativity, which permits time to be warped by motion and gravitation, predicts circumstances in which physical objects, including observers, can loop back into the past. An explicit model of a universe that permits time travel was found by Kurt Gödel in 1948 using Einstein's general theory of relativity"... (Paul Davies, *The Goldilocks Enigma*, p. 252)

APPENDIX Z37:

An Ultra- Dynamic Multi- Dimensional Organic Entity

The cosmos: Interactive, integrated, expanding, evolving, fluid, processing, information-transferring, energy-distributing, life-generating/affirming/sustaining/ reproducing, pulsating on more than 100 rhythms, in possible perpetual motion, expanding/morphing/ transforming for at least 14 billion years, our cosmos is not as simply "mechanistic" as the common wisdom would have it. One can make a strong case that it is a "living", "breathing" and "sentient" super-entity/dynamic, as well as a supra-entity/dynamic.

– With a defining name – Q4P$^\infty$ (aka the aforementioned biblical *Eheyeh Asher Eheyeh*) – The Infinite Divine.

It is possible that various frequencies/components/flavors of human emotion/creativity/artistry/literary prowess/ consciousness/spirituality/intellectuality/sensuality add to the extraordinariation of Q4P$^\infty$. It is possible that these are optimal axes for Q4P$^\infty$ to project onward for enhanced advancement/expansion/flowering of succeeding generations of these elements.

Of course, if humans radioactivate the planet, that particular thrust might not be helpful to assorted cosmic advance.

from a secular / scientific / mechanistic perspective -

"All interactions between particles in the universe...convey not only energy but also information in other words, particles not only collide, they compute. What is the entire universe computing, ultimately? Its own dynamical evolution... As the computation proceeds, reality unfolds."

- from the back-cover of *Programming the Universe* by Seth Lloyd, Professor, Mechanical Engineering, MIT (now, Oct 2012). Seth Lloyd is, as well, Director, MIT Center for Extreme Quantum Information, Cambridge, Massachusetts

APPENDIX Z38:

"The Mind of God"

Stephen Hawking –
(1988)

"If we do discover a complete theory…then we shall all, philosophers, scientists, and just ordinary people, be able to take part in the discussion of the question of why it is that we and the universe exist. If we find the answer to that, it would be the ultimate triumph of human reason—for then we would know the mind of God…."

– A Brief History of Time[*1]

Paul Davies –
(1992)

"I belong to the group of scientists who
do not subscribe to a conventional religion
but nevertheless deny that the universe is
purposeless accident. Through my scientific
work I have come to believe more and more
strongly that the physical universe is put
together with an ingenuity so astonishing
that I cannot accept it merely as a brute fact.
There must, it seems to me, be a deeper
level of explanation...."

– *The Mind of God*[2]

[1] Stephen Hawking, *A Brief History of Time*. New York: Random House, 1988. (p. 193)
[2] Paul Davies, *The Mind of God*, New York: Simon & Schuster, 1992. (p.16)

APPENDIX Z39:

Metaphysical Assumptions

incorrect: Time is linear

correct: Time is non-linear

incorrect: "Originally" there was NOTHING

correct: Eternally there was Possibility

incorrect: We are *finite* beings

correct: We are *finite+* beings

incorrect: God is "there" and we are "here"

correct: There is no divide in the Divine

incorrect: We are no longer able to "connect" with the
           Divine

correct: As we are integral to the Infinite Divine,
         by definition we eternally organically connect

incorrect: Physics is a secular science, inherently
           antithetical to an Infinite Divine

correct: All scientific Investigation is an examination of
         components of the Infinite Divine.
         There is no divide between scientific and spiritual
         investigation.

incorrect: The Infinite Divine can be delineated

correct: As the Infinite Divine is an ever-morphing and
         evolving supra-Entity, best to focus on attempting
         to delineate "the core attribute(s) of the Infinite
         Divine"
         [Summa proposes that this core is: $Q4P^{\infty}$]

APPENDIX Z40:

The "Double Play": Push-Pull

Summa has proposed two separate dynamics as having ignited Creation and the *cosmic advance* as we know it.

(1) The splitting of the Zero-Point

(2) The "leveraged buyout" of future potentials

To clarify, the hypothesis holds them as simultaneous 'igniters.'

Simultaneous *in-tandem* 'agents of creation.'
The ultimate "Double Play."

*

Taking this to yet another level,
in parallel to our
Potential v. Fulfillment discussion earlier,

one can speculate that –

(1) is symbolically proto-male – PUSH

while

(2) is symbolically proto-female – PULL

*

APPENDIX Z41:

Framing Beliefs

"There are many other unprovable framing beliefs, and they have perplexed philosophers since humans first thought systematically about such things. Is there really a world out there, or are there only our sense impressions? Are there other minds? Do we have free will? Has the universe existed for billions of years, or did it come into existence five minutes ago, together with false memories and evidence? These are staple topics of any introductory course of philosophy. Framing beliefs – that there is an external world, and other minds, and free will – lie beyond the scope of proof. Nonetheless, they are what give meaning to the chaos of experience.*"

---

from the author -

I am proposing the Summa hypothesis/theory/paradigm – Q4P$^\infty$ / Extraordinariation – as a "Framing Belief"

* Jonathan Sacks, *The Great Partnership*, New York: Random House, Inc. 2011, p.33

APPENDIX Z42:

New Paradigm Imminent***

"As we were leaving, a stranger came up to me, gentle and unassuming, and said, 'I've just written a book that I think you might find interesting. If I may, I'll send it to you.' I thanked him and some days later the book arrived. It was called *Just Six Numbers* [© *2001*], and with a shock of recognition I realized who the stranger was: Sir Martin, now Lord, Rees, Astronomer Royal, Master of Trinity College, Cambridge and President of the Royal Society, the world's oldest and most famous scientific association. Sir Martin was, in other words, Britain's most distinguished scientist.

The thesis of the book was that there are six mathematical constants that determine the physical shape of the universe. Had any one of them been even slightly different, the universe as we know it would not exist. Nor would life. It was my first glimpse into the new cosmology and the string of recent discoveries of how improbable our existence actually is. James Le Fanu, in his 2009 book *Why Us?*, adds to this a slew of new findings in neuroscience and genetics to suggest that we are on the brink of a paradigm shift that will overturn the scientific materialism of the past two centuries.

The new paradigm must also lead to a renewed interest in and sympathy for religion in its broadcast sense, as a means of expressing wonder at the *'mysterium tremendum et fascinans'* of the natural world. It is not the least of the ironies of the New Genetics and the Decade of the Brain that they have vindicated the two main impetuses to religious belief – the non-material reality of the human soul and the beauty and diversity of the living world – while confounding the principle tenets of materialism: that Darwin's 'reason for everything' explains the natural world and our origins, and that life can be 'reduced' to the chemical genes, the mind to the physical brain. (James Le Fanu, *Why Us?*, p.258)

There may be, in other words, a new synthesis in the making. It will be very unlike the Greek thought-world of the medieval scholastics with its emphasis on changelessness and harmony. Instead it will speak about the emergence of order, the distribution of intelligence and information processing, the nature of self-organizing complexity, the way individuals display a collective intelligence that is a property of groups, not just the individuals that comprise them, the dynamic of evolving systems and what leads some to equilibrium, others to chaos. Out of this will emerge new metaphors of nature and humanity, flourishing and completeness."*

*** Jonathan Sacks, *The Great Partnership*, New York: Random House, Inc. 2011, pp.75-76

---

from the author –

As noted in the 2001 Sir Martin Rees book *Just Six Numbers*, there are at least 6 cosmological constants, (and, actually maybe a dozen+) which, if adjusted by even 1 decimal point would preclude the cosmos having life, among other things, as we know it.

Thus, "life" – and existence – exists at the "knife-edge" of the precision of these constants.

By-and-large the scientific community and the theological community is
not-quite-sure exactly how to understand this "synchronicity."

However, from Summa's perspective the resolution is clear. Obvious. The cosmic order orients itself – and its crucial/integral cosmological constants – to advance inter-related goals of life, potential and extraordinariation.

APPENDIX Z43:

God***

"God is the distant voice we hear and seek to amplify in our systems of meaning, each particular to a culture, a civilization, a faith. God is the One within the many; the unity at the core of our diversity; the call that leads us to journey beyond the self and its strivings, to enter into otherness and be enlarged by it, to seek to be a vehicle through which blessing flows outwards to the world, to give thanks for the miracle of being and the radiance that shines wherever two lives touch in affirmation, forgiveness and love."*

*** Jonathan Sacks, *The Great Partnership*, New York: Random House, Inc. 2011, p.94

APPENDIX Z44:

Man: Mortal or Divine***

"When I behold Your Heavens, the work of Your fingers,
The moon and stars that You set in place,
What is man that You are mindful of him,
Mortal man that You take note of him?
Yet You have made him little less than the angels
And adorned him with glory and majesty."

Psalm 8:3-5
(c. 1000 BCE)

"Pico della Mirandola (1463-94) was one of the moving spirits of the Italian Renaissance. Born into an aristocratic family, he was a child prodigy, mastering Latin and Greek at an early age and winning the title of papal protonotary when we was only ten. Initially intending a career in the Church, he went to the University of Bologna to study law, but widened his interests to include philosophy, which he pursued at the universities of Ferrara and Padua.

In 1486 he completed his monumental 900 Theses, *Conclusiones philosophicae, cabalasticae et theologicae*, on the entire range of human knowledge. To accompany them he wrote his *Oration* on the *Dignity of Man*, widely regarded as a manifesto of the Renaissance. In it he argued that the human person was the centerpiece of creation, the one being other than God himself who had no fixed nature. Endowed with freedom, he could rise higher than the angels or fall lower than the animals. This is how he imagines God addressing the first human:

> Adam, we give you no fixed place to live, no form that is peculiar to you, nor any function that is yours alone… All other things have a limited and fixed nature prescribed and bounded by our laws. You, with no limit or no bound, may choose for yourself the limits and bounds of your nature. We have placed you at the world's center so that you may survey everything else in the world. We have made you neither of heavenly nor of Earthly stuff, neither mortal nor immortal, so that with free choice and dignity, you may fashion yourself into whatever form you choose. To you is granted the power of degrading yourself into the lower forms of life, the beasts, and to you is granted the power, contained in your intellect and judgment, to be reborn into the higher forms, the divine."*

*Oration on the Dignity of Man (1486), the text available at: http://public.wsu.edu/~brians/world_civ/worldcivreader/world_civ_reader_1/pico.html#2. See Ernst Cassirer, Paul Oskar Kristeller and John Herman Randall, Jr, *The Rennaissane Philosophy of Man*, Chicago, University of Chicago Press, 1948; M.V. Dougherty (ed.), *Pico della Mirandola: New Essays*, Cambridge University Press, 2008.

APPENDIX Z45:

New Interpretations***

"I end with a fascinating comment by the nineteenth-century Jewish mystic Rabbi Zadok haCohen of Lublin (1823-1900).

> 'Every day there are new interpretations of Torah, because every day, continually, God renews the work of creation.' Since the world was created according to the Torah...presumably, the renewal of the world comes about through new aspects of Torah. That is why after the blessing [in the morning prayers] 'creator of the heavenly lights' which speaks about the daily renewal of creation, the sages instituted a second blessing which is a form of blessing over the Torah...in which we ask to know the new interpretations of Torah which come about through the new aspects of creation....'

> *Rabbi Zadock haCohen, Tzidkat ha-Tzaddik, 92*
> (c. 1870)

According to Rabbi Zadok, since the God of creation is the God of revelation, and since the Torah is itself a commentary on the natural world, every new scientific discovery generates new religious insight. By daily renewing creation, God is daily renewing, our insight into his creative will."

*** Jonathan Sacks, *The Great Partnership*, New York: Random House, Inc. 2011, pp.111-112

APPENDIX Z46:

Take #3: Physics & Metaphysics

In secular society, and even in religious society, our natural inclination is to keep a close eye on Physics for its most up-to-date "wisdom" re: Cosmology (the origin and dynamics of the cosmos). After all, Physics best understands the equations and their import, does it not?

The 'problem' is, however, that according to Summa, "Creation" / the "Big Bang" / the Emergence of our Universe, was an epic attempt to break-free of the sterile universe of the equations, to "transcend" the equations.

The "Cosmological Breakthrough" was an attempt to move the cosmic order into Reality – a world of texture and emotion, of love and sunsets, of giggles and relationships. It was an attempt at maximizing the Potential/Extraordinariation of the cosmic order.

Thus, classic physics more logically plays the role of "Expert Witness" in verifying the plausibility of a particular Metaphysical construct, but does not by any means hold the flag of the Must-Go-To place to find an explicator for the "breakthrough."

We seek "aesthetic elegance" in hypothesizing "the key to the cosmic code." We seek "the common cosmic denominator. We seek the "key to the kingdom." The "unity key." We, respectfully, do not seek yet another complex equation.

APPENDIX Z47:

"...beyond science..."

"The preeminent mystery is why anything exists at all. What breathes life into the equations of physics, and actualized them in a real cosmos? Such questions lie beyond science, however: they are the province of philosophers and theologians"***....

---

from the author –

Martin Rees is Royal Society Research Professor at Cambridge University, Astronomer Royal of Great Britain and conceptual theorist. He was the recipient of the 2001 Peter Gruber Foundation Cosmology Prize.

*** Cosmologist Martin Rees, *Our Cosmic Habitat*. New Jersey: Princeton University Press. 2001. p. xi

APPENDIX Z48:

"The Same Recipe"***

on-point: Q4P / Cosmic Traction

"A universe hospitable to life—what we might call a biophilic universe—has to be very special in many ways. The prerequisites for any life—long-live stable stars, a periodic table of atoms with complex chemistry, and so on—are sensitive to physical laws and could not have emerged from a Big Bang with a recipe that was even slightly different. Many recipes would lead to stillborn universes with no atoms, no chemistry, and no planets; or to universes too short lived or too empty to allow anything to evolve beyond sterile uniformity. This distinctive and special-seeming recipe seems to me a fundamental mystery that should not be brushed aside merely as a brute fact.'" (p. xvi)

on-point: Q4P / Extraordinariation

"Likewise, we should surely probe deeper, and ask why a unique recipe for the physical world should permit consequences as interesting as those we see around us."…(p. 163)

*** Cosmologist Martin Rees, *Our Cosmic Habitat*. New Jersey: Princeton University Press. 2001. pp xvi, 163

APPENDIX Z49:

The Consciousness Continuum

Where does it begin? Where is it at?

What is it? Why is it? "Who" is it?

Across how many dimensions of time and space does it span?

To what extent is it shared? partitioned-off?

To what extent is it stored eternally? In-time and out-of-time?

If we are separate from the Divine, to what extent does the Divine read our individual consciousnesses?

If we are, a' la Summa, extensions of the Divine, where does my consciousness end – and yours start?

If there is a Godhead, was there indeed a contraction of Divine consciousness – a *Hester Panim* – spanning the Holocaust time frame, among other time frames?

Is ascending consciousness a gateway to *Summa's* fuller Extraordinariation?

To what extent, is an emerging consciousness a goal of Creation?

But, did it not require an extraordinary consciousness to effect Creation in the first place?

Did the Cosmic Consciousness indeed anticipate and foresee the plethora of (neo-infinite) potentials down-the-road, as per Summa, and then 'bootstrap-leverage' those potentials into the "pull-aspect of Creation."

Did the Cosmic Consciousness indeed grasp the neo-infinite potential inherent in "splitting 0", as per Summa, and then have the savvy to do just that in the "push-aspect of Creation"?

Does the Cosmic Consciousness – to this very day – optimize evolution and in-parallel attempt to *"balance-out"* the forces of Nature?

My "TAKE"

I believe that we (humans+) are the *'forward wave'* of consciousness.

And, I believe that our cumulative consciousness – integrated with the entire extended Divine consciousness – will plot the next level of Extraordinariation and Consciousness.

APPENDIX Z50:

"Backward Causation"

(meaning, the FUTURE impacting the PAST)

[support for the "bootstrap" component of Summa's metaphysics]

"Quantum Mechanics Could Permit
a Subtle Form of Teleology"

"Crazy though the idea may seem at first, there is in face no fundamental impediment to a mechanism that allows later events to influence earlier events. In fact, there are some famous theories of physics that explicitly involve *backward causation* – future events having causative power over past events. Wheeler proposed one such theory with his then student Richard Feynman in the mid-1940s. In the Wheeler-Feynman theory of electrodynamics, electromagnetic interactions can travel both forward and backward in time. There is no experimental evidence in favor of the theory, I hasten to add. Something similar was proposed for gravitation by Hoyle and Narlikat, and for quantum cosmology by Gell-Mann and Hartle and by Hawking. Again, observation and experiment are silent on these ideas, but the theories are certainly not 'antiscientific,' and variants of them are still being investigated today."*...

* Cosmologist Paul Davies, *The Goldilocks Enigma*. United Kingdom: Little, First Mariner Books edition. 2008. pp. 242-243

APPENDIX Z51:

Galapagos

I, as well, traveled to the Galapagos Islands. Not on the HMS Beagle (c. 1835), but via HMS Boeing (December 2006), 171 years later.

My reaction – after surveying the incredible giant Tortoises, the exotic fierce-looking but harmless iguana, and the surreal pastel-blue footed seabirds (the 'Blue-footed booby') – was that Mr. Darwin, for all his greatness, had missed "the main event."

One does not need Galapagos to discern the core themes of Natural Selection. One might very well, however, employ Galapagos, to discern Quest for Potential$^\infty$ / Extraordinariation.

Isolated from the South American mainland, (500 miles west of Ecuador), the sundry Galapagos species had their own survival/extraordinariation evolutionary calculus. The threats were quite different and the resources/ environment were quite different. In sum total, it was a unique, stand-alone environment within-which to evolve. Differently. With a little Extraordinariaton thrown-in.

APPENDIX Z52:

Ecology
[by Dr. Andrei Alyokhin]*

The very basic laws of ecology describing the growth and regulation of populations of living organisms appear to fit the metaphysical model of the cosmic Quest for Potential$^\infty$ proposed by David Birnbaum. Obviously, ecology is only one of many subdisciplines within the rather broad science of biology, and biology is only one of many natural sciences (albeit a very important one). Therefore, this observation alone does not serve as an immediate and decisive proof that the Quest is indeed the major driving force behind each and every natural process.

Nevertheless, it is truly fascinating that an established scientific theory based on experimental evidence and mathematic models is in such a strong agreement with a philosophical theory of Conceptual Theorist Birnbaum, and developed independently of any formal natural history research. This is unlikely to happen by chance alone. Therefore, it is reasonable to propose the Quest for Potential$^\infty$ as a *working hypothesis* for explaining the impetus behind the cosmic dynamic.

Testing this hypothesis would involve a critical review of other scientific theories explaining particular phenomena in chemistry, physics, sociology, etc. for their agreement with Birnbaum's proposed Overarching Theory of Everything.** Ultimately, this may yield a unified view of the Universe, which would be a major leap in fulfilling our potentiality as conscious beings.

– *Dr. Andrei Alyokhin
Associate Professor
School of Biology and Ecology
University of Maine
Orono, ME

** Birnbaum is reluctant to use the grandiose term himself, but clearly this is precisely his goal.

APPENDIX Z53:

A Compelling Case

One cannot expect to clinically prove a dynamic Framing Belief* of the Cosmic Order – of the overarching/infinite magnitude of Quest for Potential∞.

But ideally one could provide a rather compelling *circumstantial/supporting/empirical* case.

Perhaps we have done so.

Supreme Court Justice Louis Brandeis said that ideally when solid *circumstantial evidence* is presented in court, it would be like a *spider's web* – so strong that nothing could hope to escape. According to my consulting litigators, in an ideal legal cobweb, all the inferences and implications are internally consistent – like the fabric of the web.

Ideally, a powerful case would clearly trump competing scenarios.

Perhaps we have done so here.

There is no (repeat: no) *contradictory* evidence to Summa's hypothesis. Not one iota of contradictory information. After

5,000+ years of accumulated data and wisdom – across a myriad of fields.

Over a 40+ year period – I have quite-carefully reviewed field-after-field – to reality-check Summa. Does Summa – overlaid over the particular field – enhance the field – or contradict the field?

In each and every case, overlaying Summa either has a neutral effect or, more often, enhances the field. Often, Summa radically enhances the field. There are no exceptions. Meaning, there are no instances where Summa detracts from the field.

Thus, on weighing all the evidence, the probability that Summa is essentially on-the-mark, is quite high. And the possibility that it is totally off-base, is quite remote.

Moreover, there is massive and compelling affirming evidence – from multiple directions, avenues and fields – and from careful, direct and empirical observation – to buttress Summa's hypothesis. One has only to objectively weigh the hypothesis.

In addition, as explicated, there is de facto no competing metaphysics.

So I have presented.

There are no eyewitnesses coming forward from the Creation-point. With regards the Creation point, Summa has made-a-case for circumstantial and deductive (and spiritually consonant) evidence.

And contemporaneously, we are all, indeed, very direct eyewitnesses. And we can all carefully evaluate the contemporary situation – across the panoply of fields – and in our own lives – through a Summa lens.

Very straightforward: Does it work?

* see Exhibit Z41 several exhibits prior

APPENDIX Z54:

neo-Survival-of-the-Fittest or Q4P[∞]/Extraordinariation?

Approximately 67 million years ago, a sleek, red-crowned flying dinosaur existed, with a wingspan of ~35 feet, and a flying range of possibly ~9 days at-a-clip at 15,000 feet at 80 mph for 10,000+ miles.

Here are Wikipedia excerpts –

Quetzalcoatlus

Quetzalcoatlus (/ketsəlkou'ætləs/) was a pterodactyloid pterosaur known from the Late Cretaceous of North America (Maastrichtian stage, about 68–65.5 million years ago), and one of the largest known flying animals of all time....

> ### Scientific classification
>
> Kingdom: Animalia
> Phylum: Chordata
> Order: Pterosauria
> Suborder: Pterodactyloidea
> Family: Azhdarchidae
> Genus: **Quetzalcoatlus**
> Species: *Q. northropi*

More recent estimates based on greater knowledge of azhdarchid proportions place its wingspan at 10–11 meters (33–36 ft)....

The nature of flight in Quetzalcoatlus and other giant azhdarchids was poorly understood until serious biomechanical studies were conducted in the 21st century....

After factoring wingspan, body weight, and aerodynamics, a sophisticated computer program led the two researchers to conclude that *Q. northropi* was capable of flight "up to 80 miles an hour for 7 to 10 days at altitudes of 15,000 feet". Mike Habib further suggested a maximum flight range of 8,000 to 12,000 miles for *Q. northropi*....

[Note that the entire circumference of the Earth is 25,000 miles.]

* Quetzalcoatlus belongs to the order Pterosauria which were flying reptiles. They existed [144.5 million years] from the late Triassic to the end of the Cretaceous Period (210 to 65.5 million years ago).

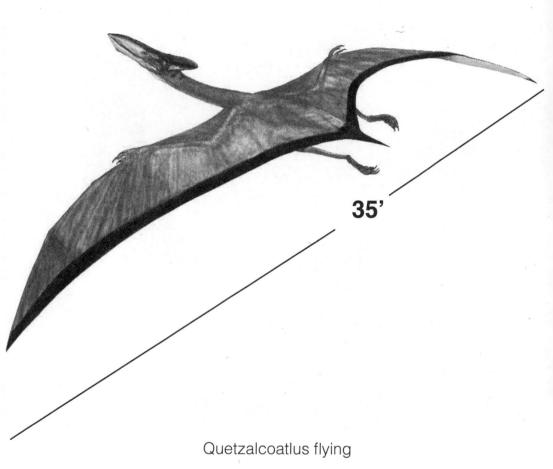

35'

Quetzalcoatlus flying

Quetzalcoatlus on land, feeding

Wikipedia Online, http://en.wikipedia.org/wiki/Quetzalcoatlus (accessed November 4, 2012)

APPENDIX Z55:

1999: Cosmologist Martin Rees

Noted astrophysicist and cosmologist Martin Rees (b. 1942, England, and President of the Royal Society 2005-2010) noted the following in the finale of his 1999 work "Just Six Numbers":***

> "But it remains a fundamental challenge to understand the very beginning – this must await a 'final' theory.... Such a theory would signal the end of an intellectual quest that started with Newton, and continued through Maxwell, Einstein and their successors. It would deepen our understanding of space, time, and the basic forces....

This goal may be unattainable. There could be no 'final' theory; or, if there is, it could be beyond our mental powers to grasp it. But even if this goal is reached, that would not be the end of challenging science. As well as being a 'fundamental' science, cosmology is also the grandest of the environmental sciences. It aims to understand

how a simple 'fireball' evolved into the complex
cosmic habitat we find around us – how, here on
Earth, and perhaps in many biospheres elsewhere,
creatures evolved that are able to reflect on how
they emerged."*

---

from the author –

Every once-in-a-while, Sir Martin, a sort-of 'simple
concept' makes-an-appearance on the world stage
– a 'simple concept' which simultaneously apparently
'solves' an array of formidable, inter-related, and hitherto
seemingly intractable issues.

*** Martin Rees, *Just Six Numbers*. Great Britain: Weindenfeld & Nicolson, 1999. pp. 176-177

APPENDIX Z56:

2000: Cosmologist Brian Greene***

"The search for the fundamental laws of the universe is a distinctly human drama, one that has stretched the mind and enriched the spirit… We are all, each in our own way, seekers of the truth and we each long for an answer to why we are here. As we collectively scale the mountain of explanation, each generation stands firmly on the shoulders of the previous, bravely reaching for the peak. Whether any of our descendants will ever take in the view from the summit and gaze out on the vast and elegant universe with a perspective of infinite clarity, we cannot predict. But as each generation climbs a little higher, we realize Jacob Bronowski's pronouncement that 'in every age there is a turning point, a new way of seeing and asserting the coherence of the world [(Jacob Bronowski, *The Ascent of Man*, p. 20]. And as our generation marvels at our new view of the universe—our new way of asserting the world's coherence—we are fulfilling our part, contributing our rung to the human ladder reaching for the stars."

*** Brian Greene, *The Elegant Universe*. New York: First Vintage Books edition, 2000. p. 387

APPENDIX Z57:

2004: Cosmologists Tyson & Goldsmith***

"Every once in a while, however, a significantly new take on an important theory emerges…. The greatest moments in scientific history have arisen, and will always arise, when a new explanation, perhaps coupled with new observational results, produces a seismic shift in our conclusions about the workings of nature….

Baruch Spinoza, the philosopher who created the strongest bridge between the natural and supernatural, rejected any distinction between nature *and* God, insisting instead that the cosmos is simultaneously nature and God… Let us then proceed with our adventurous quest for cosmic origins, acting much like detectives who deduce the facts of the crime from the evidence left behind."

*** Neil DeGrasse Tyson and Donald Goldsmith. *Origins*. New York: W. W. Norton & Company, Inc. 2004. pp 19-21

APPENDIX Z58:

2006: Cosmologist Leonard Susskind***

"For my own tastes, elegance and simplicity can sometimes be found in principles that don't at all lend themselves to equations. I know of no equations that are more elegant than the two principles that underpin Darwin's theory: random mutation and competition. This book is about an organizing principle that is also powerful and simple....

And what about the biggest questions of all: who or what made the universe and for what reason? Is there a purpose to it all? I don't pretend to know the answers...

...The ultimate existential question, 'Why is there Something rather than Nothing?' has no more or less of an answer than before anyone had ever heard of String Theory."...

*** Leonard Susskind, *The Cosmic Landscape*. New York: Little, Brown and Company. 2006. pp 379-380

APPENDIX Z59:

2006: Quantum Computation Theorist Seth Lloyd***

The universe is a quantum computer

"The universe computes its own behavior.* As soon as the universe began, it began computing. At first the patterns it produced were simple, comprising elementary particles and establishing the fundamental laws of physics. In time, as it processed more and more information, the universe spun out ever more intricate and complex patterns, including galaxies, stars, and planets. Life, language, human beings, society, culture—all owe their existence to the intrinsic ability of matter and energy to process information." (p. 3)

Why is the cosmos so complex?

"The computational capability of the universe explains one of the great mysteries of nature: how complex systems such as living creatures can arise from fundamentally simple physical laws.... The digital revolution under way today is merely the latest in a long line of information-processing revolutions stretching back through the development of language, the evolution of sex, and the creation of life, to the beginning of the universe itself. Each revolution has laid the groundwork for the next, and all information-processing revolutions since the Big Bang stem from the intrinsic information-processing ability of the universe. The computational universe *necessarily* generates complexity. Life, sex, the brain, and human civilization did not come about by mere accident." (pp. 3, 5)

---

from the author –

Lloyd and his key scientific compatriots are now holed-up at MIT's new Center for Extreme Quantum Information Theory (established in 2007) of which Lloyd is the Director [google MIT xQIT]. Lloyds hypothesis converges with mine. The universe does 'compute itself,' and complexity 'is no accident.'

Now, to a proficient cutting-edge secular MIT scientist observing a slice of the universe at-work, the universe might appear as a quantum computer. What the scientist is observing, however (according to our hypothesis) is the quantum aspect of Infinite Divine Extraordinariation at-work.

From my perspective, the MIT group is pretty adroitly

dealing with a very key conceptual slice of the (multi-billion-year) unfolding of the cosmic drama. Thus this 'Quantum Information' group would have a potentially significant interest and "stake" in Summa. And, Summa, in turn, has an extremely significant "stake" in this group.

Of course, on some level we 'talk past each other.' They speak mechanisms; we speak metaphysics. But, on another crucial level – i.e. the entire Universe as ~self-generating and ~complexifying – we crucially intersect. The MIT center potentially buttresses a very major swath of Summa – from the pinnacle of contemporary cutting-edge academic hard sciences.

***

* Lloyd's ~mechanistic terminology posits "a computer which computes"; I might rather say "an Infinite Divine which 'creates' or 'iterates.'" Note that Seth Lloyd is currently (October, 2012) a Professor of Mechanical Engineering at MIT, and has self-described himself as a 'quantum mechanic.' Notwithstanding the probability that Lloyd is more multi-dimensional than he professes, his background context is relevant here.

Note as well that Lloyd's group is a small cadre of iconoclastic top-flight scientists/engineers/mathematicians representing mainly themselves (and not the scientific community at-large), albeit with the *imprimatur* of MIT for their esoteric and mind-stretching research.

*** Seth Lloyd, *Programming the Universe*. New York: Vintage Books, 2006. pp. 3 and 5

APPENDIX Z60:

2008: Cosmologist Paul Davies***

"...Somehow the universe has engineered, not just its own awareness, but also its own *comprehension*. Mindless, blundering atoms have conspired to make not just life, not just mind, but understanding.... Could it just be a fluke? Might the fact that the deepest level of reality has connected to a quirky natural phenomenon we call 'the human mind' represent nothing but a bizarre and temporary aberration in an absurd and pointless universe? Or is there an even deeper subplot at work?".... (p. 5)

"In some manner...life, mind, and physical law are part of a common scheme, mutually supporting. Somehow, the universe has engineered its own self-awareness."... (p. 231)

*** Paul Davies, *The Goldilocks Enigma*. United Kingdom: Little, First Mariner Books edition. 2008. pp. 5 and 231

from the author –

Paul Davies (b. 1946) is possibly my favorite cosmologist.
I have read several of his works since the early 1980s.
Australian Davies, currently at the University of Arizona,
who has a Templeton Prize under his belt, among other
academic trophies, is also a favorite cosmologist of the
academic ruling elite in cosmology.

Reading the above quotes, one can sense Davies's
frustration. The holy grail of cosmology – the cosmic
common denominator/motivating engine lurks just outside
his quite-formidable intellectual grasp. But, as readers of
Summa surely grasp, all that Davies needs to do to nail-
down ultimate victory after his ~25 books on cosmology
and related, is to simply plug-in metaphysical Summa into
his sophisticated astrophysicist matrix.

In contemporary times, theologians and physicists both
vector towards the Goldilocks Enigma.

To theologians, it is an indicator of a "Guiding Hand"
To physicists, it is a conundrum.

Actually, the Goldilocks Enigma is a key – and almost
incontrovertible-support for Q4P$^\infty$. It is Q4P$^\infty$ which so-to-
speak "sets the dial" in each case.

And Q4P$^\infty$ of course "sets-the-dial" to optimize potential
Extraordinariation – which includes Life.

APPENDIX Z61:

2010: Cosmologists Hawking and Mlodinow***

"We each exist for but a short time, and in that time explore but a small part of the whole universe. But humans are a curious species. We wonder, we seek answers. Living in this vast world that is by turns kind and cruel, and gazing at the immense heavens above, people have always asked a multitude of questions: How can we understand the world in which we find ourselves? How does the universe behave? What is the nature of reality? Where did all this come from? Did the universe need a creator? Most of us do not spend most of our time worrying about these questions, but almost all of us worry about them some of the time.

Traditionally these are questions for philosophy, but philosophy is dead. Philosophy has not kept up with modern developments in science, particularly physics. Scientists have become the bearers of the torch of discovery in our quest for knowledge."*

*** Stephen Hawking and Leonard Mlodinow, *The Grand Design*. New York: Bantam Books. 2010. p. 5

APPENDIX Z62:

2010: Cosmologist Haisch*** Clones Summa I (copyrighted & published 1988)

"The purpose I propose that life has is a grand one, and even, I think, a logical one. We are the means whereby God experiences his own potential, and this is why the Universe has some of the amazing properties conducive to life that it has…." (p. 20)

"The purpose of life is to let God make his own potential real. And of course this cannot be limited to human experience. God in this view seeks the experience of all living things on this planet and wherever else life might exist and whatever else it might be like…." (pp. 20-21)

"Back to the question of evil. If we are to believe in a God, we would surely like for him or her to be benevolent and merciful in addition to all-knowing and all-powerful, omniscient and omnipotent. How could he or she tolerate the cruelty that some inflict on others (including on animals) and still merit our respect as a kind and loving God?

What I am proposing—and it is no original idea of

mine—is that God chooses to deliberately stay off the playing field in order to let freedom of choice create the new and original experiences that the Universe affords and that God seeks through us...." (p. 23)

"The idea of an infinite conscious intelligence with infinite potential, whose ideas become the laws of physics of our Universe and others, makes sense to me. The consciousness providing purpose can be called God, who transforms potential into experience and gives our universe a purpose...." (p. 85)

"...God desires to experience his potential.... Because we are the incarnations of God in the physical realm, God experiences the richness of his potential through us...." (p. 86)

"The Godhead has infinite potential, infinite power, infinite ability...but that is all sterile perfection. In *The God Theory* the Godhead chooses to convert potential into experience...." (p. 122)

"...God's consciousness wishes to know itself by expressing itself. God wishes to make his potential real...." (p. 126)

"I believe that we live in a purpose-guided Universe governed by the laws of science. There is no conflict between a Universe of matter and forces and a Universe of purpose, because the purpose is what went into the laws. In order for God to let himself experience a part of his potential, he imagines into existence just the right characteristics that a Universe needed to have in order for life to originate and then to evolve into complex beings, such as you and I. His consciousness caused this and it is his consciousness that we share and that is our essence. But the arena in which all this takes place is fully governed by the laws of nature including Darwinian evolution. Hence there is ample reason to believe in Einstein, Darwin, and God." (p. 206)

---

from the author –

This appendix was added-on by myself in September, 2012, seven years after Summa II was originally first copyrighted and posted online (2005), four years after it (Summa II) was available on Amazon, and twenty-four years after Summa I was published by KTAV – and reviewed and distributed globally.

Note that all the extracts from the Haisch book are almost verbatim reprints of key and highlighted sections of Summa Metaphysica I's featured centerpiece Unified Formulation (reprinted in Summa II).

Summa I (1988) introduces onto the world scene, among other concepts, respectfully, my original concept of Quest for Potential$^\infty$ as well as the inter-related Potential∞ as the core of the Divine.

Note as well that Summa I (God and Evil) maneuvers with the concept of Divine Contraction of Divine Consciousness in Summa I's book-spanning Theodicy presentation. (Former seminary student) Haisch's presentation (2010) of this theme in his above-noted *The Purpose Guided Universe* is almost a verbatim extract from Summa I.

Finally, Haisch's centerpiece theme – the actual title of his book – *The Purpose-Guided Universe* – of Potential fulfillment being the purpose of Creation, is straight out of Summa I.

Thus, note that Haisch's key and central ideas (2006 and 2010) very directly, to put it mildly, precisely parallel or restate – ideas proffered in Summa I (1988) and Summa II (2005).

Note, however, that in the 'history of ideas' it is not unusual for (alleged) 'conceptual breakthrough' ideas to 'bubble up' simultaneously in two unrelated quarters. Of course, in his case there are multiple identical concepts bubbling-up here simultaneously – and therein lies the issue.

Now, *vis à vis* my parochial interests, I am fine with several almost-identical concepts to my own being proffered-forth by a fine astrophysicist. It should be noted, however, that Summa I enjoyed considerable global traction for over 18 years (both online and hard copy) before Haisch's works on cosmology (2006 and 2010). One may, of course, give San Francisco-based Haisch the benefit-of-the-doubt and deem him innocent of conscious wrongdoing.

Vis à vis the global community's interests, I am of course glad that the concepts are being given traction – from whatever serious corner. May this trend continue in its intended spirit of Good Will to all mankind.

*** Bernard Haisch, *The Purpose-Guided Universe*. Franklin, New Jersey: New Page Books. 2010. pp. 20, 21, 23, 86, 122, 126, 206.

APPENDIX Z63:

Quest for Possibility or Quest for Potential?

Summa delineates Potential as a morphing of primeval Possibility. In Summas's schema, Possibility indeed preceded Potential on the embryonic Cosmic Stage. But Summa is excruciatingly careful not to position Quest for Possibility as the key, overarching cosmic dynamic.

Why not? What is the difference?

Possibility *per se* is too unfocused. It is too '*scatter*.' Potential – as employed herein – and indeed in the popular parlance – is radically more focused than Possibility. Simply defined, Potential might be Highly-Focused Possibility.

scatter: Quest for Possibility
more focused: Quest for Potential

So, for example, the young man's Potential might be to become a fine architect and a great father. His Possibilities might include thousands of other…possibilities, such as, say, 'knows how to make cool hotel reservations.' Nice,

but not 'focused/prioritized.'
Part-of-the-package, but not of great cosmic interest.

The next questions might be – Who defines 'focused/
prioritized'? – and Does the focus/prioritization change/
morph over time? These are fair sub-questions, and (if I
am lucky) will hopefully engage graduate students over
the next several thousand years.

But, back to the main axes of discussion: What, indeed,
are the main focused/prioritized Cosmic Possibilities?
i.e. the main Cosmic objective Potentials? We have
addressed this question multiple-times over the span of
Summa, and have attempted not to overdose you with
the same answer, which runs roughly –

Potential$^\infty$: Possible focused/prioritized set:
Quest for Spirituality, Beauty, Integrity, Intellectuality, Life,
Love, Harmony and Compassion.

Potential$^\infty$: Possible Wrap-around Sets:
There are, as well, possible wrap-around sets of
Potentials which enhance the focused/primary set (just-
noted above).

These might include –
a Family-cluster: family/parenting/fidelity/sexuality
or perhaps, an inter-related
Education-cluster: education/learning/teaching
or perhaps other clusters like,
a Value-cluster: Mercy, Nobility, Honor, Valor
or, perhaps others

[Note that many distinguished scientists – presumably in the set of those who have not read Summa – posit that there is, indeed, an overarching Cosmic goal, and that this imperative is Complexity. We have touched on this supposition in the text. Respectfully, this (Complexification) theory is a non-starter. Complexity gets us nowhere. It so happens, however, that in some situations Complexity (e.g. humans, galaxies) is a route to Potential/ Extraordinariation.]

The Cosmos is a focused player. It keeps-its-options-open, but is ultimately (eternally) focused.

573   APPENDIX

GOD AND GOOD

*

end of Appendix section

*

GOD AND GOOD

Author's Finale Midrash

GOD AND GOOD

The Sixth Day of Creation

It was already dark...the first 5 days of Creation had been 'completed'...it was 'late Thursday evening' – on the celestial calendar.

Mankind's creation was slated to commence just after Sundown – on the Sixth Day of Creation.

As fate would have it, Sundown that evening was the finale of Yom Kippur in that epoch in the Realm of the Divine. The Finale service of Yom Kippur – the Holiest day of the calendar – was unfolding.

The Creation of Mankind.

The Divine/Eheyeh – was stoic. The Metaphysical Council had re-confirmed to Him that there was simply no way to create all-good Man. Rather, Man had to have two possible 'faces' – Good and Evil – in order for his Creation to proceed. Insisting on an All-good Man would simply mean No Man.

Indeed, except for one angel, the Angels of Potential had wanted just that, no man. Too much suffering awaited. Too much hurt...too much pain...de-humanization. But the Divine/Eheyah was adamant. Life on every level was to be created – including the centerpiece of creation – Mankind. Quest for Divine Potential∞ – including, but not limited-to Life & Love & Liberty & Beauty & Humanism & Spirituality – would be given a reality-landscape on which to unfold – fully.

The Angels were in near-revolt.
Too much suffering was *in the cards*.
Only the Buddhist/Taoist angels stayed-the-hand of the

rumbling *hell-bent-on-revolt* Jewish angel contingent. The Christian angels started to assess just how many hospitals would need be built over the millennia to handle "the victims" of the imminent Creation of Mankind. Let alone, victims of 'Natural causes.'

The Finale Yom Kippur service proceeded.

The 'window' was closing for the Divine/Eheyeh to *make his move*. The 'event' needed to take place just after Sundown. And 'the Gates' were closing....

The Divine/Eheyeh tracked forward in time. He traversed forward through the millennia – including through the quite-genocidal 20th Century.... He touched the still-alive and dying in Babi Yar's death pits....he knelt in humility and flowing tears in Auschwitz's diabolical gas chambers....the zyklon B pellets doing their ominous and murderous work around Him.... mothers screaming babes-in-arms....a Divine odyssey of 20th Century atrocities-to-come.... Armenian targets.... Greek targets.... Assyrian... Dursim Kurds....Romani....The Soviet Gulag.... Don Cossack.... Holodomor...atrocities across Central America...Asia...Cambodia...Rwanda...Darfur... East Timorese...Falun...and others...the atrocities, the screaming, the humiliation, the blood, the vomit, the stench...the feces-smeared living dead...the tortured and the dying....

Shaken, the Divine/Eheyeh retreated back-in-time to the Finale Service of Yom Kippur in the Celestial Realms.... Fourteen billion years ago by our reckoning.

The Angel of Righteousness and the Angel of Victory – who were designated to herald the coming of Man –

stood *front & center* on the central platform of the Celestial Temple.

On His mark (meaning, on the command of the Divine/ Eheyeh) the Angel of Victory would give-the-signal to the Angel of Righteousness.

Silent, only the Angel Who Buries the Dead stood by the side of the Divine/Eheyeh.

The Divine/Eheyeh asked the Angel Who Buries the Dead whether it was now time to proceed.

The Angel Who Buries the Dead, who was fasting, indicated in the affirmative.

The Divine noticed some sort of tattoo on the forearm of the Angel.

Upon closer examination it was a series of blue numbers.

The Divine/Eheyeh shuddered.

As He had planned all along, He now recited the Prayer of Atonement. Once for all-time.

He asked forgiveness from the *victims-to-come* and from all the concentric circles around them – which, of course included all humanity – of all time.

The Divine/Eheyeh then nodded to the Angel of Victory.

The Angel of Victory gave the signal to the Angel of Righteousness.

The Angel of Righteousness put the *Shofar* (Ram's Horn) to his lips.

"Forward" uttered the Angel of Victory.

The piecing sound then rang forth from the *Shofar*.

***

technical notes:

The *Torah* (Bible) does not clarify when on the Sixth Day Mankind was created, nor whether it was a discrete pinpoint event on that 'Day.' Rather, the Torah just delineates – "on the Sixth Day."

The Finale Service of Yom Kippur is *Neilah* (the "Closing of the Gates")

The 'directive' to the Shofar blower is properly – *T'qiah* (Gedolah) – the name of a type of bass 'musical sound/pattern' – to be achieved.

In contemporary times, Yom Kippur – technically 25 hours long – would properly be over when the equivalent time for 3 stars to be out – is reached (~sundown or 5-15 minutes thereafter)

GOD AND GOOD

from

Kohelet

Ecclesiastes (Chapter 3)

(English)

3 A season is set for everything, a time for every experience under heaven:[a]

[2]A time for [b]being born[b] and a time for dying,

A time for planting and a time for uprooting the planted;

[3]A time for [c]slaying and a time for healing,[c]

A time for tearing down and a time for building up;

[4]A time for weeping and a time for laughing,

A time for wailing and a time for dancing;

[5]A time for throwing stones and a time for gathering stones,

A time for embracing and a time for shunning embraces;

[6]A time for seeking and a time for losing,

A time for keeping and a time for discarding;

[7]A time for ripping and a time for sewing,

A time for silence and a time for speaking;

[8]A time for loving and a time for hating;

A time for war and a time for peace.

Kohelet (Chapter 3)

(Hebrew)

ג לַכֹּל זְמָן וְעֵת לְכָל־חֵפֶץ תַּחַת
הַשָּׁמָיִם: ס *

2 עֵת לָלֶדֶת וְעֵת לָמוּת

עֵת לָטַעַת וְעֵת לַעֲקוֹר נָטוּעַ:

3 עֵת לַהֲרוֹג וְעֵת לִרְפּוֹא

עֵת לִפְרוֹץ וְעֵת לִבְנוֹת:

4 עֵת לִבְכּוֹת וְעֵת לִשְׂחוֹק

עֵת סְפוֹד וְעֵת רְקוֹד:

5 עֵת לְהַשְׁלִיךְ אֲבָנִים וְעֵת כְּנוֹס אֲבָנִים

עֵת לַחֲבוֹק וְעֵת לִרְחֹק מֵחַבֵּק:

6 עֵת לְבַקֵּשׁ וְעֵת לְאַבֵּד

עֵת לִשְׁמוֹר וְעֵת לְהַשְׁלִיךְ:

7 עֵת לִקְרוֹעַ וְעֵת לִתְפּוֹר

עֵת לַחֲשׁוֹת וְעֵת לְדַבֵּר:

8 עֵת לֶאֱהֹב וְעֵת לִשְׂנֹא

עֵת מִלְחָמָה וְעֵת שָׁלוֹם: ס

source: JPS Hebrew–English *Tanach* (pp 1765 and 1768–9)

GOD AND GOOD

Competing Cosmological Theories

Competing Cosmological Theories

A comparison of two proposed
unified cosmological theories

*

**Barrow/Tipler's
SACP Theory
[Strong Anthropic Cosmological Principle]**
(1986)

v.

**Birnbaum's
Q4P Theory
[Quest for Infinite Potential∞/Extraordinariation]**
(volume I 1988;
(volume II 2008)

1-Sentence Encapsulizations **

Barrow/Tipler's **Anthropic**:

> "We had to end up with the current universe,
> because this is the only universe which humans
> could observe"

Birnbaum's **Q4P**

> "***Quest for Potential*$^\infty$** is the original pulse of –
> and continues to be the primary engine of –
> the Divine and the Cosmos"

** for expanded elaboration on each,

see respectively,

Anthropic Wikipedia via search engines

Quest for Potential$^\infty$ via www.SummaM.org

based upon a
Scientific Essay
by
Steven Gross

Jerusalem
January, 2010

SACP v. Q4P

It is assumed that the reader has a nodding acquaintance with the Strong Anthropic Cosmological principle (SACP) (see the book by Barrow and Tipler or Wikipedia) and with Birnbaum's Quest for Potential$^\infty$ (Q4P). Further, I assume that the reader is willing to accept both the SACP and Q4P at least as working hypotheses.

The SACP is an expression of Q4P restricted to a physical plane. {Meaning, SACP may be construed as a potential offshoot of Q4P, but we must understand that SACP is restricted to physicality, as opposed to spirituality, morality and other aspects of the potential gamut of life.)

One (not the only) way Q4P may potentially express itself is to create a universe in which the SACP is an operating principle/force/power.

The SACP explains many puzzling features of our universe and is a physical idea with predictive power. The alternative physical theories posit 10^500 universes (multiverse) (see book by Susskind or Wikipedia) to explain the same features, or simply ignore those features saying that question is 'not a scientific one.'

The SACP becomes a powerful way to express/ implement/develop Q4P, but only on a limited, physical battlefield. The SACP is thus only a physical expression of the Q4P, albeit a powerful one.

SACP does not at all extend to the moral/spiritual levels. It does not explain joy, tragedy, love, irony, pathos etc. In other words, it does not explain the gamut of the human psyche, including the emotional and the aesthetic, among other aspects.

Potential conceptual and logical weaknesses in SACP are well known. See encyclopedia articles.

But, the key issue, as juxtaposed against Q4P in particular, may be that SACP does not answer the quint-essential *big question*, "WHY":
    Why there is anything at all?

SACP tries to explain why there is life, and our particular form of life, once you posit a universe. But, why is there a universe?

This same seeming insurmountable hurdle will be faced by proponents of multiple universe theory, when their "*m*–theory" is juxtaposed against Birnbaum's more nimble and more all-embracing "potential" paradigm.

What is the origin of that which you posit to be *bedrock/eternal/infinite*?

This is not a side question; it is a core question.

Q4P addresses the 'eternal origins' question in its own core Unified Formulation (*Summa Metaphysica*, Volume I, Part II). Q4P frontally and comprehensively integrates carefully conceived responses to all of the issues noted above.

Q4P handles the gamut of emotional, spiritual, moral and aesthetic issues, as well. It develops an expository sampling of 120 Potentials, proffered as 120 Angels.

Q4P as a potential wrap-around SACP, indeed solves – and fills-in – a lot of problems/gaps for SACP. The converse is not true. SACP certainly does not add–to the intellectual rigor or spectrum of Q4P.

Note that like other pre-1988 attempts at unified paradigms, the conceptualizes of SACP (in 1986) did not have an option of reviewing Birnbaum's Q4P (1988; 2008) before presenting their respective hypotheses. Indeed, as Q4P's author operates well outside the scientific community, there is limited dissemination to-date of his paradigm, which is currently more disseminated within the metaphysics/philosophy community. Part of the issue is that Birnbaum positions his paradigm as an overarching solution to key issues across a panoply of fields, ranging from theology to the hard sciences.

Birnbaum has articulated consistently that the solution to key roadblocks in Cosmology and Physics will only be found in creative metaphysics, as per his own paradigm. And Birnbaum is confident that all roads ultimately lead to Summa.

***

Q4P∞™

Quest for Potential
(infinitely recursive)

INDEX
of
Sculpted Terms

INDEX
of
Sculpted Terms *

Bootstrapping (creation): BETA: Cosmic TOOL KIT-Shelf #1; MU: Cosmic "Tool Kit" Extraordinariation Shelf #2; Infinitely-Coiled Spirality; Cosmic "Leveraged Buyout" ("Bootstrapping"), Extraordinariation; Road Map

Cherry-Picked Evolution: MU: Cosmic "Tool Kit" Extraordinariation Shelf #2

Cosmic "Tool Kit": MU: Cosmic "Tool Kit" Extraordinariation Shelf #2

Cosmic 'Leveraged Buyout' ("Bootstrapping"): BETA: Cosmic TOOL KIT-Shelf #1

Cosmic Tango: God's 120 Guardian Angels (Guardian Angel of Sexuality)

Cosmic Womb of Potential: IOTA: Reprise; Appendix C (Extraordinariation)

Cosmic-Tapestry-Weaving: BETA: Cosmic TOOL KIT-Shelf #1

Cumulative / Massed-Array Design: MU: Cosmic "Tool Kit" Extraordinariation Shelf #2

Holy Quest of Potential: Introduction: The Metaphysical Gates of the Forest

Inexorable Life-Questing: BETA: Cosmic TOOL KIT-Shelf #1

Infinite Divine Extraordinariation: Introduction: The Metaphysical Gates of the Forest; Encapsulization; BETA: Cosmic TOOL KIT-Shelf #1; GAMMA: Lead-in; DELTA: Embryonic Design; EPSILON: Noted & Observations; Principia Metaphysica Outline; ETA: Some reflections...insights; KAPPA: The building blocksof the cosmos; LAMBDA: A fresh look at some of our concepts; MU: Cosmic "Tool Kit" Extraordinariation Shelf #2

Infinite Recursiveness: BETA: Cosmic TOOL KIT-Shelf #1

Infinitely-Coiled Spirality: BETA: Cosmic TOOL KIT-Shelf #1

Interlocking Divine Infinitude Quest: BETA: Cosmic TOOL KIT-Shelf #1

Metaphysical Correspondence: BETA: Cosmic TOOL KIT-Shelf #1

Mitosis of "0": ZETA: "Principia Metaphysica

Optimizing Complexification / Contourization: MU: Cosmic "Tool Kit" Extraordinariation Shelf #2

Organic Super-Equation: MU: Cosmic "Tool Kit" Extraordinariation Shelf #2

Physical Leveraged Buyout: MU: Cosmic "Tool Kit" Extraordinariation Shelf #2

Quest for Infinite Divine Extraordinariation: BETA: Cosmic TOOL KIT-Shelf #1

Recursivity is Regnant: DELTA: Embryonic Design

Simultaneous Push / Pull Tension: BETA: Cosmic TOOL KIT-Shelf #1

Spiraling Supra-Dynamics: THETA: The two key (spiraling) SUPRA-DYNAMICS

Template Fidelity: MU: Cosmic "Tool Kit" Extraordinariation Shelf #2

The Potential$^\infty$ Point: Introduction: The Metaphysical Gates of the Forest; BETA: Cosmic TOOL KIT-Shelf #1; DELTA: Embryonic Design; EPSILON: Notes & Observations; LAMBDA: A fresh look atsome of our concepts

The Spiraling Collective: Appendix H

Vacuum-Busting: BETA: Cosmic TOOL KIT-Shelf #1

"One has to prove that God always existed;
But, one does not need to prove
that *possibility* always existed"

– Cousin Sherrie Miller
JERUSALEM

Road Map
for
Summa

(presented initially at end of Summa I)

GOD AND GOOD

Summa Metaphysica

The Potential$^\infty$ Point:
Road Map

Summary/Overview
of the hypothesized
metaphysical underpinnings
of the embryonic journey
of the *Infinite Divine*

GOD AND GOOD

employing just one concept

Quest for Potential$^\infty$/Extraordinariation

Summa Metaphysica
proposes a **simultaneous solution** to –

Cosmogony

Theogony

Theodicy

Road Map

Possibility, is, by definition, *eternal*

*

One cannot really challenge the eternality of *Possibility…*

…. the only concept whose eternality is basically unassailable….

Thus, *Possibility* – in one form or another – is a very prime candidate for the prime engine which pulls *Reality* from out of the *Void*

*

But how is there seemingly *creation ex nihilo* – creation seemingly out-of-nothingness?

*

Possibility per se does not necessarily have the power to pull *Reality* from out of the *Void*

However, a variation on *Possibility* – **Quest for Potential$^{\infty}$** to the infinite power – just might have the power to do just that…

*

How?

The combined power of all potentials *down-the-road*
might be an imperative strong enough....
to cumulatively retroactively *ignite the cosmos*...

Meaning, at Creation the *future* ignites the *present*.

This is our crucial pivot, among several key pivots...

Summma Metaphysica calls this *"bootstrapping
creation"*...

[pre-Creation, TIME can more readily be hypothesized to have
(more) elasticity and/or multi-directionality]

*

Since there is a cosmos, which apparently was *de facto*
'ignited,' at least once, we hypothesize that
Quest for Potential$^\infty$ was the spark...

*

But how might this *ignition* have taken place?

*

Possibility had nowhere to go within the Void...

We hypothesize that *Possibility* coiled within itself.....

morphing to its dynamic offspring *Quest for
Potential*$^\infty$....

Then, Quest for Potential$^\infty$ coiled within itself by a factor of, say, a 'zillion trillion' to the infinite power....

For eons upon eons…

Aching, yearning for expression, realization.........

[investigate *'Mandelbrot Fractals'* in mathematics]

*

The quintessential **irresistible force** –
Quest for Potential$^\infty$

Desperately probing for an opening through *the* quintessential **Immovable object** – *The Void*

*

Trying to discern a path into *Reality*

*

A cosmic impasse

.........a seemingly eternal impasse…

*

Like a coiled-spring vainly attempting to expand infinite-fold within an infinitely small 'space'

An infinitely-expanding metaphysical entity

trapped within a non-existent physical space

*

(infinite) Expansion, with nowhere to go
without Reality…

The *ultimate yearning*….

*

Quest for Potential$^\infty$ eventually fine-tuning its game…

Ultimately achieving 'radar lock' on the *optimal route*
towards *Extraordinariation*

[investigate *'the Calculus'* in mathematics re: optimization]

*

*Quest for Potential$^\infty$/Extraordinariation now
advancing'* towards critical mass…

*

After an eternity of loneliness, the Void *"could not 'take
it' anymore"*…

*

Potential Extraordinariation beckoned…..

*

Potential Extraordinariation teased…

GOD AND GOOD

Potential Extraordinariation seduced

*

Potential Extraordinariation pulsated….

*

Then, potential *Extraordinariation* within potential *Extraordinariation* now infinitely iterating… *achieves critical mass…..*

*

The cosmic-balance is tipped ….The Void *gasps and yields* its hitherto eternal imperviousness

*

……and the heavens exploded forth –

the Potential$^\infty$ Point*

***

end of *Road Map*

* *the Genesis Point*

the Eheyeh-asher-Eheyeh Point …..

that is,
the I-WILL-BE-THAT-WHICH-I-WILL-BE Point

cont'd

***

The paradigm simultaneously also impels a parallel
'reworking' of –
     Intelligent Design
     Anthropology
     Darwinism
     'Man's place in the cosmos' *question*
     'Purpose of Man' *question*

and, of course,
     Cosmology
     Philosophy
     Biology
     et al.

not to mention, all-embracing
     Metaphysics
which impelled us here in the first place

cont'd

We respectfully posit that the implications of the Summa hypothesis span all of humanity's mainstream fields of study, whether the *hard sciences* or the *soft sciences*, as all fields, according to this hypothesis, ultimately track back to the *Singularity* and to the *Big Bang*...the *Genesis* point...what I would have named the ***Potential$^{\infty}$ Point***.

Q4P∞™

Quest for Potential
(infinitely recursive)

Reprint

of

Summa Metaphysica

18 Axioms

<u>Unified Formulation</u>   *(from Summa I)*
9 propositions
100 - 900 series

<u>Principia Metaphysica</u>   *(from Summa II)*
9 propositions
1100 - 1900 series

GOD AND GOOD

(from Summa I: God and Evil)

99.00   THE UNIFIED FORMULATION:
           OUTLINE SUMMARY

THE UNIFIED FORMULATION

100

100.00   Holy potential is at the epicenter of the Divine.

200

200.00   Holy quest for potential is the underlying core
           dynamic of the cosmic order.

300

300.10   Two possible but mutually exclusive sets of
           dynamics were open to man (at Eden).

300.20   The two dynamics are:

"Tree of Life/Bliss"	*"Tree of Knowledge/Potential"*
1. A "gilded cage" existence	A life of challenge, freedom, privacy, and responsibility
2. Intellectual satedness	Pursuit of knowledge
3. Limited growth potential	Infinite growth potential
4. Dependence	Independence
5. Eternal Life	Mortality
6. "Leashed" "natural evil"	"Unleashed" "natural evil"
7. Bliss	Pain and joy
8. Limited potential for "moral good," "moral evil"	Higher potential for "moral good," "moral evil"
9. Lesser dignity	Higher dignity

300.30   In a world predicated on potential, man inexorably took the route of "Tree of Knowledge/Potential."

300.40   "Natural evil" and "moral evil" would consequently forevermore plague and challenge man.

400

400.10   Evil is the implicit flip-side, or converse, of good. Evil is anti-polar to good.

400.20   With the creation of potential for good, which is required for man to be able to reach his spiritual potential, potential for evil indirectly, but nevertheless, inexorably, came into existence as a consequence.

400.30   To destroy evil would, at the least, destroy good.

400.40   While an omnipotent Deity may have an impact on nature, even an omnipotent Deity does not violate universal laws and dynamics implicit in the universal Deity's essence, as violating them could unravel the cosmos.

500

500.10   Main is finite+ seeking to approach Infinity.

500.20   The purpose of man is to quest for his potentialities—spiritual, intellectual, and all other.

500.30   The closer man approaches the achievement of his spiritual and other potentialities, the closer he comes to fulfilling the primal quests of creation.

500.40   Man, (infinite) God, and the universe are all questing for their potentialities.

600

600.00   Man is innately free and striving for fuller freedom.

700

700.10   In order for man to reach his full potential, he must operate from a base of freedom. (This is a law of the universe in concert with balance of dynamics of Tree of Knowledge chosen at Eden.)

700.20   The greater the freedom component of man's base, the greater his ultimate potential (inherent in Tree of Knowledge chosen at Eden).

800

800.10   Man is ascendant—at least in knowledge.

800.20   As mankind and Judaism ascend in knowledge (and possibly in consciousness) on the road to fulfilling a primal drive of creation, there is an implicit demand for fuller freedom. (This is implicit in our paradigm of the Tree of Knowledge.)

800.30   A demand for fuller freedom (as a consequence of an ascent in knowledge) has embodied within it a demand for greater privacy, responsibility, and selfhood—so that man can more ably quest for his potential.

900

900.10   As mankind ascends in knowledge, implicitly demanding more freedom, there is a proportional contraction (*tsimtsum*) of Divine here-and-now consciousness. This is a primary form of *Hester Panim* which yields man ever greater freedom, privacy, responsibility, and selfhood with concomitant potential.

900.20   As the contraction of real-time Divine consciousness continues, (as mankind ascends in knowledge and freedom) there is a commensurate lower incidence and level of direct particular Providence—for the sake of the general Providence of allowing mankind to quest for its full potentialities.

900.30   Quest for potential is an overarching and inviolate holy cosmic dynamic. A violation of quest for potential would be a violation of a core Divine dynamic—which was integral to creation itself, integral to the Divine essence, and integral to the potential of the cosmic order.

end of Unified Formulation

continue on

for Principia Metaphysica Outline

(from Summa II: God and Good)

Principia Metaphysica Outline:

1100 Series

Possibility.
(by definition)

Then,

Embryonic Quest for a POTENTIAL

1200 Series

1225

"Quest for Quest for INFINITE DIVINE
EXTRAORDINARIATION"
emerges as the primary engine of the cosmos

1250

The principles of the hard and soft sciences
sought their full potentials of ACTUALIZATION,
FULL EXPRESSION, LIFE, LOVE, CONSCIOUSNESS
and ultimately, of INFINITY

1300 Series

"Quest for INFINITE DIVINE EXTRAORDINARIATION"
emerges as the evolved overarching drive
of the cosmos

1400 Series

1405

The Infinite Divine Extraordinariation...
at the end-of-the-rainbow – as first, IGNITION,
and then, as GOAL

1410

Quest for Potential$^\infty$ pervades the cosmos

The cosmos IS integrated into Quest for Potential$^\infty$;

1414

This **core** cosmic dynamic is ETERNAL, ENDURING
and TRANSCENDING

1416

Q4P$^\infty$ feeds upon Itself

1417

It unites – and, indeed, is comprised of – all life:
past, present and future

1418

At the vanguard, possibly, is a Godhead

1419

Our individual, extraordinary core Potential
flows within this Eternal and Infinite stream

1420

The Infinite Divine Extraordinariation…
at the end-of-the-rainbow – as first, IGNITION, and
then,
as GOAL – exerted PULL, while full-spectrum
Quest for Potential∞ exerts DRIVE – and PUSH
(note parallel to CHILDBIRTH)

1500 Series

1505

Quest for Potential∞ is, in turn,
composed of two Supra–Dynamics:
Quest-for-ADVANCEMENT/fulfillment and
Quest-for-FULFILLMENT/advancement

1507

These Supra-Dynamics are intertwined with each other
in an Eternal cosmic (double-helix) dance,
and in-tandem cascadingly advance,
playing-out their potential Infinitude

1510

The complementary Supra–Dynamics –
are juxtaposed against each other

in a dynamic and eternal hi-tension
cosmic "tango"

1515

Juxtaposed centrifugal[1] – centripetal[2] forces
perpetually replenishing and stimulating each other…
producing, in turn,
Quest for Additional Possibilities

1520

The panoply of ACTION & ADVANCE
is complemented by the complementary spectrum of
EMOTION & FULFILLMENT & CONSCIOUSNESS

1530

Quest for ADVANCEMENT probes outward
Quest for FULFILLMENT vortexes inward

NOTES by KHALIL

---

[1] Centrifugal: The personal quest for potential$^\infty$ is centrifugal in that it releases energy outwardly. Energy is projected into the cosmic collective and all existence is energized and thus propelled forward.

[2] Centripetal: The personal quest for fulfillment is centripetal in that it releases energy inwardly. Quest for fulfillment relates to constant personal needs and desires. It thus provides an ongoing reflective motivation that is readily translated into the grander quest for potential$^\infty$

1540

Quest for Potential$^\infty$
finds its ultimate CATALYST – and MOTIVATOR…
in its contending sub-strands
Quest-for-ADVANCEMENT and
Quest-for-FULFILLMENT

1550

Quest-for-ADVANCEMENT
and Quest-for-FULFILLMENT
are drawn inexorably towards each other,
…"as the moth to the flame"
– while they simultaneously seek to play-out their
autonomous potential

1560

Through an Asian prism,

Quest-for-ADVANCEMENT is *Yang*
Quest-for-FULFILLMENT is *Ying*

balancing out the cosmos

complementary
opposite
countervailing
~opposing, but mutually enriching

*

Through a Jewish prism,

"ezer k'negdo"
(Genesis / Bereshith 2:18)

~complementary, juxtaposed
and counterbalanced sexes

1570

Through a KABBALISTIC prism,

Quest-for-ADVANCEMENT/fulfillment
is majority MASCULINE energy,
minority FEMININE energy

Quest-for-FULFILLMENT/advancement
is majority FEMININE energy,
minority MASCULINE energy

Both are inextricably intertwined,
inextricably interchanging

Cosmic lovers
in an eternal dynamic tension

1580

The dynamic tension between
Quest-for-ADVANCEMENT and Quest-for-
FULFILLMENT
can be presumed to have escalated
for infinite eons pre–reality
to that famous explosive point
which actualized the COSMOS

1590

The reality–void hitherto had not found
either ACTUALIZATION or a mode of expression of
FULFILLMENT, EMOTION, CONSCIOUSNESS

1600 Series

1610

"The void could not 'take it' anymore"
–Solomon Birnbaum 2004

1615

"Voids abhor voids"
–D. Birnbaum

1620

The reality–void sought
EMOTIONAL RELEASE and REALIZATION,
SPIRITUAL FULFILLMENT,
INTELLECTUAL ATTAINMENT,
HIGHER LEVEL (actually INFINITE) CONSCIOUSNESS,
PURE GOOD-ness / GIVING-ness,
and full–spectrum ACTUALIZATION

1640

at "Creation,"

NOTHING

separates (MITOSIS of "0") into
(steadily expanding)

"actualized POTENTIAL"
and its complement,
(a steadily diminishing)
"VOID"

1645

POTENTIAL energy
>
KINETIC energy

1650

"actualized POTENTIAL"
(an ever–expanding–cosmos...
expanding on multiple levels)
increasingly gobbles–up
physical and emotional
and intellectual and spiritual, etc.
TURF
formerly occupied by VOID

<u>1700 Series</u>

1725

At the end–of–the–rainbow,
Infinite Divine Extraordinariation
(perhaps most importantly - the infinitude of
Consciousness and Givingness)

[this is the spiritual SINGULARITY]

retroactively ignites the
Emptiness
["*tohu va-vohu*"]
at the Creation-point

1750

ONLY infinite and unbounded POTENTIAL
as a goal, as a theoretical 'end–point,'
could and would have the power to ignite a Cosmos

1800 Series

1825

and what actualizes the putative Divine?

The DIVINE is–in–the–process of infinite
SELF–EVOLVEMENT
ongoing for billions of eons
...traversing from metaphysical realms
to ever–fuller and richer
PHYSICAL ACTUALIZATION
...as it courses towards
the "very–end–of–the–rainbow"

*

almost 'by definition' POTENTIAL always existed

*

It is merely potential, possibility

initially

*

By definition, It (potential possibility) is the ONLY
dynamic which can possibly be eternal.

*

We are all part of the Embryonic Divine

*

"Science cannot solve the ultimate mystery of nature. And that is because, in the last analysis, we ourselves are part of nature and therefore part of the mystery that we are trying to solve." *Max Planck* (c.1932)

1835

Thus, if Possibility/Potential is infinite,
and Possibility/Potential is the core of the Divine,
the Divine is Infinite +

1850

Potential/Possibility may have more facets and
dimensions to it
– Divine or otherwise – than we were alerted to in
contemporary culture,
but by definition only potential/possibility is eternal.

<u>1900 Series</u>

The DIVINE – as opposed to the Embryonic Divine –
is simultaneously EVERYTHING + A GOAL
to be approached in ever–greater–and–greater
fullness and richness and consciousness

end of Principia Metaphysica

GOD AND GOOD

*

end of

Summma Metaphysica

series

*

(*but, the protégé also rises…*)

note to readers:

the Quest for Potential$^\infty$ concept
was introduced in 1986 via Birnbaum copyright
and then onto the global scene in 1988
via the KTAV Publishing First Printing
and the associated reviews.
The initial website (1989) was
www.GodAndEvil.com

God and Evil, in turn,
has been assigned as a Course Text
at dozens of universities globally

GOD & EVIL

Course Text
(partial list)

Bard College
Annandale-on-Hudson, New York

Bar Ilan University
Ramat-Gan, Israel

Brandeis University
Waltham, Massachusetts

Gresham College
London, United Kingdom

Harding University
Memphis, Tennessee

Hartford Seminary
Hartford, Connecticut

Hebrew Union College
Cincinnati, Ohio

Course Text
continued

Hebrew University
Jerusalem, Israel

Jewish Theological Seminary
New York, New York

Union Theological Seminary
New York, New York

Regis University
Denver, Colorado

Stetson University
Deland, Florida

University of California, Los Angeles (UCLA)
Modern Religion Jewish Thought
Los Angeles, California

Yeshiva University
New York, New York

Harvard Matrix

MILLENNIUM COLLECTION

independent of harvard university

Harvard Matrix DAVID BIRNBAUM

NEW PARADIGM

MULTI-MEDIA

PLATFORM, UNIVERSE, LENS, EXTRA-DIMENSION, THINK TANK, PUBLISHING HOUSE

21st CENTURY CUTTING-EDGE ICONIC CONSTRUCTS

HARVARD MATRIX™

MANHATTAN

WITH CREDIT TO
KTAV PUBLISHING

CLICK▶

MILLENNIUM
COLLECTION

HARVARD MATRIX

NEW PARADIGM CONSTRUCTS

100+
dynamic & cutting-edge
jewish renaissance authors

SENIOR EDITORS
Martin S. Cohen　　**Benjamin Blech**

HarvardMatrix.com

publishers of *Summa Metaphysica*

[30+ clickable sites]

MILLENNIUM
COLLECTION

David Birnbaum
Editor-in-Chief

MesorahMatrix

ReferenceMatrix

PublisherMatrix

★ Harvard Matrix DAVID BIRNBAUM

MANHATTAN

MESORAH MATRIX

Mesorah1000.com

Sanctification1000.com

Tikkun1000.com

Modeh1000.com

Birkat1000.com

MANHATTAN

REFERENCEMATRIX

Manhattan1000.com

AmazonX1000.com

eReader1000.com

Collection1000.com

YouTubeX1000.com

Contact1000.com

MANHATTAN

PUBLISHERMATRIX

● philosophy ————————
Philosophy1000.com
Bard1000.com

● history ————————
Civilization1000.com
Crucifixion1000.com
GTSx1000.com

● commentary ————————
Observer1000.com

● ancillary / graphic metaphysics—
Q4P1000.com
Womb1000.com
ToolKit1000.com
Potential1000.com
Extraordinariation1000.com

● summa spinoffs————————
CosmicWomb1000.com
Angels1000.com
LostManual1000.com

David Birnbaum

books by
BIRNBAUM

Metaphysics

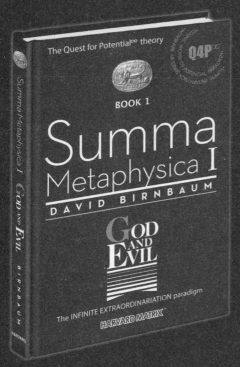
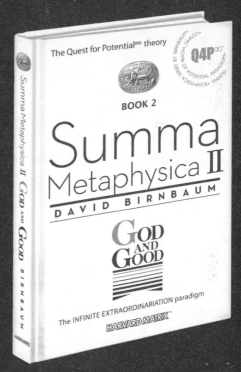

www.MetaphysicsA.com

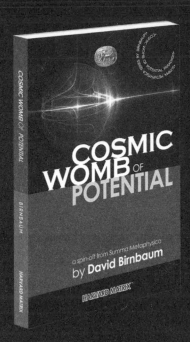

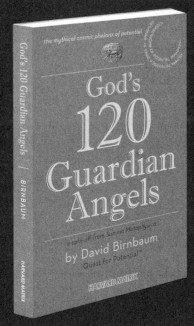

www.SummaSpinoffs.com

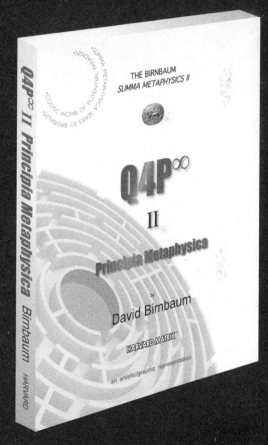

THE BIRNBAUM
SUMMA METAPHYSICS I

Q4P$^\infty$

I

Unified Formulation

by

David Birnbaum

HARVARD MATRIX

an artistic/graphic representation

THE BIRNBAUM
SUMMA METAPHYSICS II

Q4P$^\infty$

II

Principia Metaphysica

by

David Birnbaum

HARVARD MATRIX

an artistic/graphic representation

an artistic/graphic representation

www.MetaphysicsB.com

Metaphysics

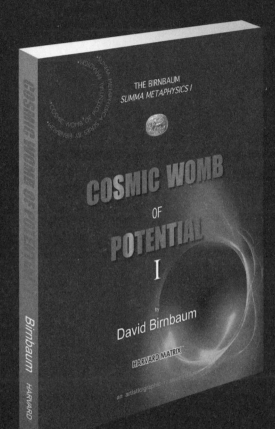

an artistic/graphic representation

www.MetaphysicsB.com

COSMIC
ARCHITECHTURE I

COSMIC
TOOL KIT

SHELF #1

by
David Birnbaum

HARVARD MATRIX

COSMIC
ARCHITECHTURE II

COSMIC
TOOL KIT

SHELF #2

by
David Birnbaum

HARVARD MATRIX

an artistic/graphic representation

www.MetaphysicsC.com

Metaphysics

an artistic/graphic representation

www.MetaphysicsC.com

History-related

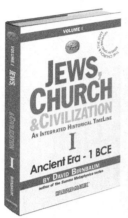 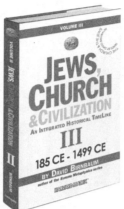  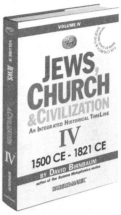

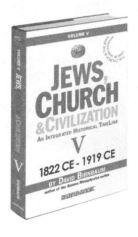 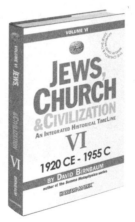 

www.BirnbaumHistory.com

History-related

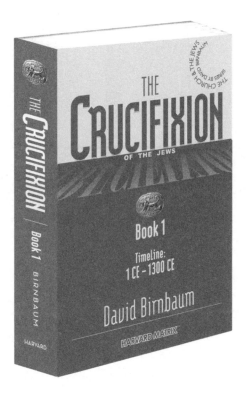
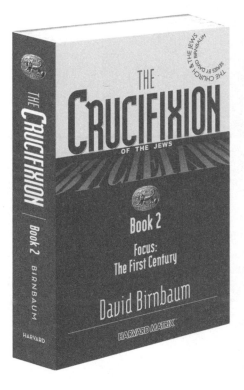

www.TheCrucifixion.org

MANHATTAN

WITH CREDIT TO
KTAV PUBLISHING

HarvardMatrix@gmail.com

www.HarvardMatrix.com

independent of harvard university

Birnbaum's

Q4P∞™

Quest for Potential
(infinitely recursive)

Q4P (Q4P (Q4P ...

Quest for Potential

within

Quest for Potential

within

Quest for Potential

ad infinitum

"A Major Work in the Philosophy of Religion"*

"...there is no comparable volume offering such a comprehensive, authoritative and intelligible discussion of the problem...a remarkable effort to offer a fresh approach..."
>   Paul Mendez-Flohr
>   Professor of Philosophy, Hebrew University,
>   Jerusalem Editor, *Contemporary Jewish Religious Thought*

"...an original, and, in this reader's opinion, a very promising point of view...the author gathers a philosophically coherent and, in the end, highly modern insight... a unified metaphysics..."
>   Louis Dupré
>   Professor of Religious Studies, Yale University

"...a major work in the Philosophy of Religion...
a masterful achievement...a novel and satisfying approach...
a major intellectual achievement."
>   *Canon William Johnson
>   Professor of Philosophy, Brandeis University

cont'd

"...a major contribution to the Jewish conversations through the ages, on theodicy, and the problem of evil generally."
    Dr. Norman Lamm
    President, Yeshiva University

"...a framework for a renewed exploration into the most agonizing aspects of the meaning of religious belief... It is an impressive attempt to focus intellectually on the Holocaust without diminishing the primal outcry of pain."
    Rabbi Nachum Rabinovitch
    Rosh Yeshiva Birkat Moshe, Israel,
    Former Dean, Jews College, London

"David Birnbaum brings the rich resources of the Jewish tradition to bear on the universal problem of theodicy. The result is a new synthesis... I can certainly recommend it as a fascinating contribution to the philosophy of religion which merits the attention of Christians and Jews alike."
    John J. Collins
    Professor of Theology, University of Notre Dame
    Editor, *Journal of Biblical Literature*

cont'd

[continued]

"*God and Evil* represents a bold attempt to formulate an ingenious theory, which, drawing upon creative reinterpretations of classical Jewish doctrine, places the Free Will Defense within a broader metaphysical framework..."
Rabbi Walter S. Wurzburger
Professor of Philosophy, Yeshiva University
Editor, *Tradition*

"All who read this book will find much instruction, insight, and material for reflection...I find the overall thesis of the book touching and inspiring..."
Rabbi Irving Greenberg
President, The National Jewish Center for Learning and Scholarship (CLAL)

"A major work...a great intellectual and spiritual effort"
Joseph Dan
Professor of Kabbalah, Hebrew University

***

***

"*the best book in print on the subject.*"
—HERITAGE JOURNAL

"*Author and scholar David Birnbaum wrestles with the age–old problem of the existence of evil... a compelling, stimulating and creative contribution...*"
—JUDAICA BOOK NEWS

"*Birnbaum's God and Evil is an extremely significant volume which grapples forthrightly and originally with the problem... well–organized... clearly written... persuasive... Birnbaum comes as close as possible to solving the awesome dilemma of evil in a world created by a just God.*"
—JEWISH WORLD

"*Birnbaum wrestles with the problem of evil from a Jewish perspective, but provides fresh insights for Christians as well. This is a good book, written in faith, and with honesty and passion...*"
—THEOLOGICAL STUDIES
Georgetown University

"*Wiesel and Birnbaum share a deep respect for, and loyalty to, their ancestral faith. Yet the contrast between their approaches is ultimately perhaps as instructive as the approaches themselves. Birnbaum's approach is essentially that of the intellectual, philosopher, and theologian...*"
—CANADIAN CATHOLIC REVIEW

"*a bold and highly original synthesis...audacious yet sensitive, traditional and yet highly innovative...yet within the parameters of an authentically Jewish halakhic point of view...an intellectual odyssey*"
—JEWISH REVIEW

***

SUMMA Conference

Bard 2012

International Academic Conference

Metaphysics

16-19 April, 2012

Program

Dr. Bruce Chilton, Chairman
Dr. Gary Hagberg, co-Chairman

Bard

A PLACE TO THINK

The Quest for Potential∞ theory

Q4P∞

BOOK 1

Summa
Metaphysica I
DAVID BIRNBAUM

GOD AND EVIL

The INFINITE EXTRAORDINARIATION paradigm

HARVARD MATRIX

Bard
A PLACE TO THINK

Bard
A PLACE TO THINK

BARD COLLEGE

International Academic Conference

on

Summa Metaphysica

by

David Birnbaum

April 16 - 19, 2012

HarvardMatrix@gmail.com

www.SummaM.org

www.DBacademic.com

www.BARD.edu

✦ Harvard Matrix DAVID BIRNBAUM ✦

International week-long Academic Conference

SUMMA
Conference

Bard 2012

on David Birnbaum's
Summa Metaphysica work

Leon Botstein

President, Bard College

Conference Opening
April 16, 2012

Bruce Chilton

Chairman

Garry Hagberg

Co-Chairman

Bard
A PLACE TO THINK

Jacob Neusner
Professor of the History and Theology of Judaism
Bard Scholar-in-Residence
2-day "JUST WARS" conference to follow 4/23-24

International week-long Academic Conference

on **David Birnbaum's Summa Metaphysica work**

Bruce Chilton
Chairman

Bruce Chilton is a scholar of early Christianity and Judaism, now Bernard Iddings Bell Professor of Religion at Bard College, and formerly Lillian Claus Professor of New Testament at Yale University. He holds a degree in New Testament from Cambridge University (St. John's College). He has previously held academic positions at the Universities of Cambridge, Sheffield, and Münster.

He wrote the first critical commentary on the Aramaic version of Isaiah (The Isaiah Targum, 1987), as well as academic studies that analyze Jesus in his Judaic context (A Galilean Rabbi and His Bible, 1984; The Temple of Jesus, 1992; Pure Kingdom, 1996), and explain the Bible critically (Redeeming Time: The Wisdom of Ancient Jewish and Christian Festal Calendars, 2002; The Cambridge Companion to the Bible, 2007).

He founded two academic periodicals, Journal for the Study of the New Testament and The Bulletin for Biblical Research. He has also been active in the ministry of the Anglican Church, and is Rector of the Church of St. John the Evangelist in Barrytown, New York.

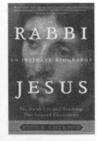

His popular books have been widely reviewed. Rabbi Jesus: An Intimate Biography showed Jesus' development through the environments hat proved formative influences on him. Those environments, illuminated by archaeology and by historical sources, include: (1) rural Jewish Galilee, (2) the movement of John the Baptist, (3) the towns Jesus encountered as a rabbi, (4) the political strategy of Herod Antipas, and (5) deep controversy concerning the Temple in Jerusalem.

Bard
'A PLACE TO THINK

Harvard Matrix DAVID BIRNBAUM

Leon Botstein
President, Bard College

(born in Switzerland)

- is an American conductor and the President of Bard College (since 1975). Botstein is the music director and principal conductor of the American Symphony Orchestra and conductor laureate of the Jerusalem Symphony Orchestra, where he served as music director and principal conductor from 2003-2010. He is also the founder and co-Artistic Director of the Bard Music Festival. He is a member of the Board of Directors of The After-School Corporation, a nonprofit organization dedicated to expanding educational opportunities for all students. He also serves as the Board Chairman of the Central European University. Botstein became the youngest college president in U.S. history at age 23, serving from 1970 to 1975 at the now-defunct Franconia College.

Bard
A PLACE TO THINK

International week-long Academic Conference

on **David Birnbaum's Summa Metaphysica work**

Garry L. Hagberg
Co-Chairman

- is an author, professor, philosopher, and jazz musician. He currently holds a chair in philosophy at the University of East Anglia.

Hagberg became a professor of philosophphyhy at Bard College in 1990, and subsequently the James H. Ottaway Jr. Professor of Philosophy and Aesthetics. The chair was endowed during his time at Bard. He has been the recipient of many fellowships and grants from Dartmouth College; Cambridge University Library; Institute for the Theory and Criticism of the Visual Arts; British Library, London; St. John's College, and Cambridge University.

Bard
A PLACE TO THINK

Harvard Matrix DAVID BIRNBAUM

Bernhard Lang | University of Paderborn

- a German Catholic theologian.

Long since 1985 professor of the Old Testament at the University of Paderborn. He became Doctor of Divinity in 1975 at the University of Tübingen. In 1977, he habilitated at the University of Freiburg im Breisgau. From 1977 to 1982 he was professor in Tübingen and from 1982 to 1985 Professor at the University of Mainz. Since 1985 he is professor at the University of Paderborn. Visiting professor in 1982 were long in Philadelphia, in 1991 at the Ecole des Hautes Etudes en Sciences Sociales in Paris, 1992/1993 at the Sorbonne, 1999/2000 at the University of St. Andrews. Since 2008 he is Honorary Doctor of the University of Aarhus in Denmark.

Lawrence H. Schiffman | Yeshiva University

Rabbi Dr. Schiffman was appointed as the Vice-Provost of Undergraduate Education at Yeshiva University and Professor of Jewish Studies in early 2011.

He had been the Chair of New York University's Skirball Department of Hebrew and Judaic Studies and serves as the Ethel and Irvin A. Edelman Professor in Hebrew and Judaic Studies at New York University (NYU). He is a specialist in the Dead Sea Scrolls, Judaism in Late Antiquity, the history of Jewish law, and Talmudic literature. He received his B.A., M.A., and Ph.D. degrees from the Department of Near Eastern and Judaic Studies at Brandeis University.

Gheorghe Popa
Alexandru Ioan Cuza University

- a Vice-Rector for research of "Alexandru Ioan Cuza" University, Iasi, Romania.

Coordinator, on behalf of the "Alexandru Ioan Cuza" University of Iasi, of the European research network PECO - 08469 for the years 1993 - 1995, entitled "Fundamental studies of discharge in view of their technological applications". Romanian coordinator of the Programme COPERNICUS - ERB 3512 PL 561 (COP 1561) for the period 1995 – 1998. Responsible from Romanian side within the "Brancusi" program of cooperation between "Al.I.Cuza" University of Iasi, Romania and University Paris – sud, Orsay, France (2003-2004 and 2007-2008)

John Mark Reynolds
Biola University

- is the founder and director of the Torrey Honors Institute, a great books program at Biola. His academic areas of specialty are ancient philosophy and epistemology, however he also lectures frequently on philosophy of science, cultural apologetics, home-schooling and cultural trends. He regularly appears on talk radio shows, such as the Hugh Hewitt show, and blogs regularly for Washington Post's "On Faith" column and Scriptoriumdaily.com.

Marcelo Gleiser

Dartmouth College

(born in Rio de Janeiro) is a Brazilian physicist and astronomer.

Marcelo Gleiser is the Appleton Professor of Natural Philosophy and Professor of Physics and Astronomy at Dartmouth College. He graduated from the Catholic University of Rio de Janeiro and obtained his Ph.D. from King's College London in 1986. After postdoctoral appointments at Fermilab and The Kavli Institute for Theoretical Physics in Santa Barbara, he joined the faculty at Dartmouth College in 1991. In 1994, he received the Presidential Faculty Fellows Award (PFF) from the White House and NSF. He is a Fellow of the American Physical Society. Author of over 100 peer-reviewed articles, Gleiser is a world-renowned cosmologist. His research focuses on the physics of the early universe, the emergence of complexity and the origin of life. Gleiser is also the author of three books exploring the religious and cultural roots of science. His latest, A Tear at the Edge of Creation: A radical new vision for life in an imperfect universe (Free Press 2010) was published in 12 languages. He is also a frequent presence in science documentaries in the US and abroad and the co-founder of the National Public Radio blog 13.7 on science and culture.

Peter William Atkins
University of Oxford

- is a British chemist and former Professor of Chemistry at the University of Oxford and a Fellow of Lincoln College. He is a prolific writer of popular chemistry textbooks, including Physical Chemistry, Inorganic Chemistry, and Molecular Quantum Mechanics. Atkins is also the author of a number of science books for the general public, including Atkins' Molecules and Galileo's Finger: The Ten Great Ideas of Science.

He was a member of the Council of the Royal Institution and the Royal Society of Chemistry. He was the founding chairman of IUPAC Committee on Chemistry Education, and is a trustee of a variety of charities.

Atkins has lectured in quantum mechanics, quantum chemistry, and thermodynamics courses (up to graduate level) at the University of Oxford. He is a patron of the Oxford University Scientific Society.

Donald Goldsmith
PBS television

- was the science editor and co-writer of the PBS television series The Astronomers and the co-writer of NOVA's Is Anybody Out There? with Lily Tomlin. He has written and edited 15 books on astronomy, including The Runaway Universe, Worlds Unnumbered, Supernova!, and The Hunt for Life on Mars. Donald Goldsmith received his Ph.D. in astronomy from the University of California, Berkeley, and has taught astronomy courses there and at other institutions, including Stanford University, Cornell University, and the University of California at Santa Cruz. He has received the lifetime achievement award in popularizing astronomy from the American Astronomical Society, the science writing award from the American Institute of Physics, and the Dorothea Klumpke-Roberts award for increasing public awareness of astronomy from the Astronomical Society of the Pacific.

Tammy Nyden
Grinnell College

Areas of Special Competence:
> Metaphysics and epistemology in the history of science and philosophy, especially in the 17th century. The Dutch Enlightenment, especially Spinoza and the reception of Cartesianism. The History and Philosophy of Science

Other Academic Interests:
> Asian Philosophies (particularly Buddhist and Daoist Philosophies and interactions between 17th century European and Chinese philosophical traditions)

Education / Degrees:
- Ph.D. in Philosophy, Claremont Graduate University, 2003
- M.A. in Philosophy, Baylor University, 1995
- B.A. in Philosophy, University of Nevada, Las Vegas, 1993

Bernhard Lang

University of Paderborn

Larry Schiffman

Yeshiva University

Gheorghe Popa

Alexandru Ioan Cuza
University

John Reynolds

Biola University

Marcelo Gleiser

Dartmouth College

Peter William Atkins

University of Oxford

Donald Goldsmith

PBS television

Tammy Nyden

Grinnell College

www.YouTubeX1000.com

Harvard Matrix DAVID BIRNBAUM

UNIVERSITÄT PADERBORN
Die Universität der Informationsgesellschaft

UNIVERSITATEA
ALEXANDRU IOAN CUZA

PUBLIC
BROADCASTING
SERVICE

YESHIVA UNIVERSITY

DARTMOUTH

VOX CLAMANTIS IN DESERTO

1769

UNIVERSITY OF
OXFORD

BIOLA
UNIVERSITY

GRINNELL COLLEGE

www.Philosophy1000.com

>> MESORAH MATRIX: Participants to-date November, 2012

Rabbi Benjamin Blech, Rabbi Martin S. Cohen, Chief Rabbi Dr. Jonathan Sacks, Dr. Michelle Sarna, Rabbi Saul Berman, Rabbi Yitzchak Blau, Dr. Judith Bleich, Rabbi Chaim Brovender, Rabbi Reuven P. Bulka, Prof. Elisheva Carlebach, Rabbi Shalom Carmy, Rabbi Alfred Cohen, Rabbi David C. Flatto, Rabbi Barry Freundel, Mrs. Rachel Friedman, Rabbi Menachem Genack, Rabbi Hillel Goldberg, Rabbi Nathaniel Helfgot, Rabbanit Chana Henkin, Rabbi Simcha Krauss, Dr. James Kugel, Rabbi Dr. David Mescheloff, Rabbi Aaron Rakeffet-Rothkoff, Rabbi Shlomo Riskin, Dr. Tamar Ross, Rabbi Sol Roth, Dr. Lawrence Schiffman, Dr. David Shatz, Rabbi Shubert Spero, Dr. Suzanne Last Stone, Rabbi Joel B. Wolowelsky, Dr. Avivah Zornberg, Rabbi Amitai Adler, Rabbi Dr. Brad Artson, Rabbi Dr. Michael J. Broyde, Rabbi Yehonatan Chipman, Rabbi Dr. Eliezer Diamond, Rabbi Dr. Elliot N. Dorff, Rabbi Dr. S. Tamar Kamionkowski, Rabbi Dr. Miriyam Glazer, Rabbi Jill Jacobs, Rabbi Rivon Krygier, Rabbi Dr. Gail Labovitz, Rabbi Asher Lopatin, Rabbi Jonathan Slater, Rabbi Jonathan Wittenberg, Rabbi Noam Zion, Rabbi Ira Stone, Prof. Michael Graetz, Rabbi Lawrence Hoffman, Prof. Dan Greyber

LIGHTS OF CREATION & TRANSCENDENCE / Mesorah Matrix Series
David Birnbaum

MESORAH MATRIX

10 - BOOK SERIES
100+ Essayists

Sanctification

Tikkun Olam

Modeh Ani

Birkat Kohanim

Betrothal / Ha-rei Ath

The Kaddish

Havdalah

Eheyeh asher Eheyeh

Search for Meaning

V'Shamru

THE SPARK OF THE INFINITE DIVINE

MANHATTAN

Benjamin Blech
Yeshiva University,
"Understanding
Judaism"

Martin S. Cohen
Editor, Conserva-
tiveJudaism,
JTS

Michelle Sarna
The Tikvah Center,
Educational Allliance

Jonathan Sacks
United Hebrew
Congregations

James Kugel
Institute for the
History of the
Jewish Bible

Shalom Carmy
Yeshiva University,
Tradition Magazine

Elisheva Carlebach
Columbia University,
Graduate Center,
CUNY

Marcelo Gleiser
Dartmouth College,
science blog 13.7

HarvardMatrix@gmail.com

www.HarvardMatrix.com

Emanuel Feldman
Tradition Magazine,
Ariel Chumash

Menachem
Genack
Orthodox Union,
Norpac

Shlomo Riskin
Ohr Torah Stone
Colleges,
Efrat

Suzanne Stone
Yeshiva University,
Center for Jewish
Law

Bruce Chilton
Bard College,
Yale University

Lawrence
Schiffman
Yeshiva University

Peter Atkins
University of Oxford,
Lincoln College

Saul Berman
Encyclopedia
Judaica,
Edah

LIGHTS OF CREATION & TRANSCENDENCE
David Birnbaum / Mesorah Matrix Series

www.Judaism1000.com

HARVARD MATRIX™

MANHATTAN

HarvardMatrix@gmail.com

www.HarvardMatrix.com

Mesorah Matrix [Mesorah1000.com] is a major – and potentially *landmark* – intellectual-spiritual-philosophical endeavor. The plan well-underway is to publish 10 separate books – each on a very focused Jewish theme – under the Mesorah Matrix umbrella. By the end of 2013, over 100 leading authors/essayists globally will be involved in the decade-spanning project.

The focused-purpose and raison d'etre of the series is to more fully draw-out the *spiritual* and *transcendent* embedded within Judaism. These are sometimes referred-to as *Elyonoth* or 'Higher-Sphere' themes. The intent of the quite-unique 10-volume series is to be 'transformational'.

There will be a total of 5-7 renowned independent editors, each responsible for 1-3 themes/books. Each book, in turn, will have 10-15 separate essays – each by a separate essayist/author. The publisher is seeking vibrant and erudite pieces for this major endeavor – from Judaism's elite across the global spectrum.

The Editor-in-Chief of the over-all series is David Birnbaum of Manhattan, author of the Summa Metaphysica philosophy series (independent of Mesorah Matrix). [see www.Philosophy1000.com]

The highly anticipated
Masorah Matrix Series

has four books underway so far:

Sanctification
co-edited by
Rabbi Benjamin Blech

Tikkun Olam
co-edited by
Rabbi Martin S. Cohen

Modeh Ani
co-edited by
Dr. Michelle Sarna

Birkat Kohanim
co-edited by
Rabbi Martin S. Cohen

Benjamin Blech*

- born in Zurich in 1933, is an Orthodox rabbi who now lives in New York City.

Rabbi Blech has been a Professor of Talmud at Yeshiva University since 1966, and was the Rabbi of Young Israel of Oceanside for 37 years. In addition to his work in the rabbinate, Rabbi Blech has written many books on Judaism and the Jewish people and speaks on Jewish topics to communities around the world.

Education

Rabbi Blech received a Bachelor of Arts degree from Yeshiva University, a Master of Arts degree in psychology from Columbia University, and rabbinic ordination from the Rabbi Isaac Elchanan Theological Seminary.

Milestones

Rabbi Blech is the author of twelve highly acclaimed and best selling books, with combined sales of close to half a million copies, including three as part of the highly popular Idiot's Guide series. His book, Understanding Judaism: The Basics of Deed and Creed, was chosen by the Union of Orthodox Jewish Congregations as "the single best book on Judaism in our generation"....

TIKKUN OLAM

JUDAISM, HUMANISM & TRANSCENDENCE

David **Birnbaum** & Martin S. **Cohen**

Editors

HARVARD MATRIX

(spine) TIKKUN OLAM

(spine) Birnbaum & Cohen

(spine) HARVARD

(side text) David Birnbaum | Mesorah Matrix Series

(side text) LIGHTS OF CREATION & TRANSCENDENCE

(side text) EXPLORING HIGHER DIMENSIONS

*Martin Samuel Cohen**

– born and raised in New York City, where he received
his B.A. summa cum laude from the City University of
New York and ordained as rabbi in 1978. In addition
to his ordination, Rabbi Cohen earned a Ph.D. in the
history of ancient Judaism in 1982. The recipient of post-doctoral
fellowships at the Hebrew University in 1983 and Harvard University in
1993, Rabbi Cohen has also lectured on the History of Religion at Hunter
College of the City University of New York and taught Bible and Talmud
at both the Jewish Theological Seminary of America in New York and at
the Institute for Jewish Studies attached to the University of Heidelberg in
Germany.

In 1986, Rabbi Cohen left Europe to come to Canada, where he accepted
the pulpit of the Beth Tikvah Congregation in Richmond, British Columbia.
In 1999, he left Canada to assume the pulpit of Congregation Eilat in
Mission Viejo, California, the position he left in 2002 to become the rabbi of
the Shelter Rock Jewish Center.

In addition to his work as teacher and rabbi, Rabbi Cohen is an author
and has published two scientific studies in the history of pre-kabbalistic
Jewish mysticism, four novels and four books of essays, including the
Hebrew-language Sefer Ha'ikarim Livnei Zemanenu. From 1997 to 2000,
he served as chairman of the Publications Committee of the Rabbinical
Assembly and is currently the chairman of the editorial board of the
quarterly journal, Conservative Judaism. Rabbi Cohen's edition of the
Book of Psalms, called Our Haven and Our Strength was published by the
Aviv Press in 2003. He is also the translator and editor of Shelter Rock's
prayer book, published in 2007.

An avid amateur pianist and a great lover of dogs, Rabbi Cohen is married
to Joan Freeman Cohen and the father of two sons Max, Emil and a
daughter, Lucy.

* *Shelter Rock Jewish Center online*, http://srjc.org/?page_id=32 (accessed November 8, 2012)

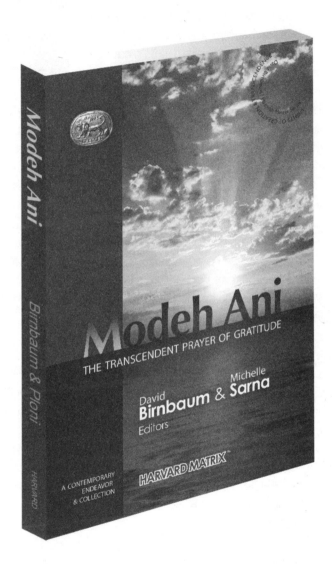

Modeh Ani

Birnbaum & Ploni

HARVARD

Modeh Ani

THE TRANSCENDENT PRAYER OF GRATITUDE

David
Birnbaum & Michelle
Sarna

Editors

A CONTEMPORARY
ENDEAVOR
& COLLECTION

HARVARD MATRIX™

Michelle Sarna*

As a member of the New York University community
for nine years, recently as an NYU Law School Tikvah
post-doctoral scholar and previously as an NYU JLIC
educator, Michelle Sarna was gratified when Shalhevet,
NYU's Orthodox student group, elected its first female
president four years ago – succeeded by three more female presidents.

Yet, beyond the college campus, the Orthodox community continues to
hold back talented and passionate women from serving their communities
in senior leadership positions that reflect their capacities. Sarna's unique
appreciation of this issue came from her experience balancing five children
with completing her Ph.D. on the transition to adulthood, serving as the
National Associate Director of the Jewish Learning Initiative on Campus
(JLIC), and coordinating the YCT Rabbinic Wives' program.

Sarna, a Gramercy resident who serves now as the director of the Edgies
Childhood Center at the Educational Alliance, was motivated to engage a
diverse group of Orthodox women leaders in meaningful conversation to
inform public policy practices. She co-facilitates the Orthodox Women's
Leadership Project, an independent initiative she founded last year
in partnership with Advancing Women Professionals and the Jewish
Community.

"Many Orthodox women are not being maximally engaged by Jewish
communal life," she says. "The caliber of the opportunities to be active
community participants and leaders are not adequately compelling and
the entire community is losing out."

The group is in the process of crafting initiatives that will advocate for
deliberate expansion of meaningful leadership opportunities for qualified
Orthodox women, which she hopes "will enrich the entire Jewish
community in the process."

---

* *The Jewish Week online*, http://www.thejewishweek.com/special_sections/36_under_36/
michelle_sarna_empowering_orthodox_women (accessed November 8, 2012)

publication: Summer / Fall 2013

to be placed on publication information mailing list,
email: HarvardMatrix@gmail.com

reprinted from *5 Towns Jewish Times*   www.SummaM.org

Prospects For Mideast Peace?
Pages 4, 5

Sholem Aleichem: A Jewish Mark Twain
Page 13

LONG ISLAND
JewishWorld

Vol. 38# 11 March 20-26, 2009 • 24 Adar - Nisam 5769

One Dollar Two Dollars Outside of Metropolitan N.Y.C.

'Cracking the Cosmic Code'

In God and Good, the second in his Summa Metaphysica series, David Birnbaum tackles life's 'Big Questions'

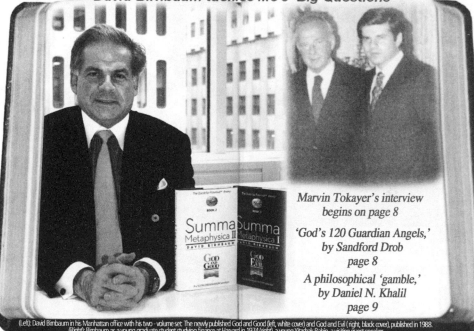

Marvin Tokayer's interview begins on page 8

'God's 120 Guardian Angels,' by Sandford Drob page 8

A philosophical 'gamble,' by Daniel N. Khalil page 9

(Left): David Birnbaum in his Manhattan office with his two - volume set: The newly published God and Good (left, white cover) and God and Evil (right, black cover), published in 1988. (Right): Birnbaum as a young graduate student studying finance at Harvard in 1974 (right), a young Yitzchak Rabin, a visiting guest speaker

HARVARD MATRIX™

MANHATTAN

Phone: 212 - 695 - 6888   Fax: 212 - 643 - 1044

available on Amazon / go to www.SummaOptions.org

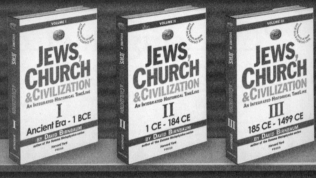

works by **David Birnbaum** Mar.1.2012

HARVARD MATRIX

Harvard Matrix is a multi-media "platform" – based out of Manhattan – which typically publishes works simultaneously in three modalities:

Hardcover for Amazon et al. [see www.AmazonX1000.com]

eBooks [see www.eReader1000.com]

Flip-books online [see www.Harvard1000.com]

Additionally, the "platform" www.HarvardMatrix.com features YouTube videos [see YouTubeX1000.com] relating to symposiums *et al. focused* on the works.

As well, the platform has other contemporary offerings including Birnbaum's Manhattan Observer column [see www.Observer1000.com]

Authors currently under the Harvard Matrix umbrella include:

Rabbi Saul Berman, Rabbi Yitzchak Blau, Dr. Judith Bleich,

*Rabbi Chaim Brovender, Rabbi Reuven P. Bulka, Prof.
Elisheva Carlebach, Rabbi Shalom Carmy, Rabbi Alfred
Cohen, Rabbi David C. Flatto, Rabbi Barry Freundel,
Rabbi Menachem Genack, Rabbi Hillel Goldberg, Rabbi
Nathaniel Helfgot, Rabbanit Chana Henkin, Rabbi Simcha
Krauss, Dr. James Kugel, Rabbi Dr. David Mescheloff,
Rabbi Aaron Rakeffet-Rothkoff, Rabbi Shlomo Riskin, Dr.
Tamar Ross, Rabbi Sol Roth, Chief Rabbi Dr. Jonathan
Sacks, Dr. Lawrence Schiffman, Dr. David Shatz, Rabbi
Shubert Spero, Dr. Suzanne Last Stone, Rabbi Joel B.
Wolowelsky, Dr. Avivah Zornberg*

Harvard Matrix endeavors to publish works, which are vibrant
and cutting-edge, if not paradigm changers.

David Birnbaum, a graduate of Harvard University, is editor-in-
chief of Harvard Matrix – as well as the author of several of the
works. In addition he is co-editor of the works in the Masorah
Matrix division series.

*

Birnbaum's iconic work God and Evil – which introduced his
new paradigm Quest for Potential$^\infty$ hypothesis, was originally
published by KTAV (Jersey City, NJ) in 1988. Four subsequent
printings followed in the 1989-2000 period. KTAV still offers
the work in its catalogue.

Harvard Matrix offers the work as Volume I of 2-volume
Summa Metaphysica.

MANHATTAN

WITH CREDIT TO
KTAV PUBLISHING

$17.00 / book

$34.00 / set

God and Good

ISBN: 978-0-9801710-0-6